Soloflight to Oz

A Wing And a Chair

Soloflight to Oz

David Sykes

A Dave Sykes Publication

Copyright: © 2011   David Sykes

First edition: Published November 2011

Published by: David Sykes
                     Park Lodge, High Road
                     Earlsheaton, Dewsbury
                     WF12 8BB

ISBN Number: 978-0-9570950-0-7

Printed by: AB Group Batley

Table of Contents

Acknowledgments

I would like to thank all the sponsors that supported me on my flight and these are
www.whiteroseaviation.co.uk White Rose Aviation - the Over Flight Clearance Specialist
www.pmaviation.co.uk P.M. Aviation - Microlight Aircraft Manufacturer in
twww.cbsbutler.com CBS Butler - Precision Human Resourcing
www.premieraviation.com Premier Aviation - Aircraft Charter for Business and Leisure
www.airsportstraining.co.uk Airsports Training - The North of England's premier Microlight Flight Training School
www.microlightstore.co.uk suppliers of all aviation goods
www.twff.eu The Wellness Foundation
www.directtile.co.uk Direct Tile - Importers and stockists of all tiles from across the world
www.dhtransport.co.uk D.H. Transporter & Sons - Specialist steal transporters & extender trailers
www.pavers.co.uk Pavers Shoes - UK's leading comfort footwear specialists
www.adaviestransportltd.com Andy Davies Transport - Nationwide distribution, same day, next day
www.the-original-stone-paving-company.co.uk The Original Stone Paving Company - Natural Stone Sets and Cobble Driveway Specialist
www.gyrocopterexperience.com Gyrocopter Experience -Gyrocopter training in the UK
www.maptrax.com.au Maptrax - Digital Maps for all of Australia
www.logoquality.co.uk
www.yorkflyingclub.co.uk
And a special thank you to www.jeppesen.com for supplying all the charts and flight guides for the flight.

I would also like to thank Brian Milton and Richard Meridith Hardy for their advice for my flight. And Thank you to **everybody** who helped me along the way on the whole trip. Also a big thank you to Dick smith in Australia for all his support and help and Rob Hibberd at www.airborne.com for looking after me in Newcastle and packing my quik up for transport back to the UK, Also www.stewertshipping.co.uk and www.vangaurdlogistics.com for bringing my Quik back to the UK.

Foreword

As we began to freefall, Dave again tried to restart the engine. His gloved finger only elicited a sad wet thumping sound from the insubstantial aircraft. Over the headset, Dave let me know that, "we'll have to wait a couple of minutes before trying again; don't want to flood it."

In some ways, microlights are safer than other fixed wing planes when the engine splutters and dies, as their similarity to hang gliders allows a relatively measured descent into a field of French cows. This fact, so reassuring when discussed in the pub, did not leave me entirely relaxed now we were 8000ft up.

After a pleasant four days hopping around northern France crammed in the back of Dave's plane, suddenly I felt the paralysing terror more usually associated with a severe stroke. We were beginning to drop quite rapidly, and I was hoping my atheism wasn't going to turn out to be a huge mistake. At that moment, over the headset I caught Dave patiently humming a song by that renowned spokesman of our times, Boy George. He appeared to be gazing at the grand Rhone chateau to our left with mild disinterest.

Quite what a morally vacuous lizard had to do with events at that time will, I suspect, remain beyond me. However, many months after the engine had exploded back into life and sent us soaring upwards, I thought frequently of Dave's detached calm. I thought of it every time there was a snide comment about his flight to Australia; every time someone looked at Dave's wheelchair and made a quick judgement of his abilities; every time we pored over some map of the subcontinent and I had secret doubts due to the sheer distances involved.

Ultimately, Dave is a ferociously determined man, and anyone who knows that also knew that he would complete his mammoth trip come what may. What follows in this book is a testament to his steadfastness, courage and ability.

Rory Martin, October 2011

From The Beginning

Born in June 1967 in a small town in west Yorkshire I was brought up with my mother and father in a place called Heckmondwike.

In the year 1993 I had a serious motorcycle accident that nearly killed me, I was on my way to work when a car turned right on me without looking and I ran straight into the side of him at speed.

I broke my back and all my ribs with two punctured lungs, a broken clavicle bone and a broken left femur bone in my leg, I also lost use to my left hand for a short while.

The hospital staff gave me a 70% chance of dying for the first 3 weeks and then that got reduced to a 50-50 chance before I finally came out of intensive care in Pinderfields Hospital 2 months later.

I still was on a ventilator for a short while after, until my lungs started repairing themselves. I got told I would never walk again while still under the drugs. My life had ended. I laid flat on my back staring at the ceiling of the hospital bed for 3 months before gradually sitting up; the first time I sat up was for 10 minutes and made me feel sick. I looked down at my legs not moving and I couldn't feel them what a mad feeling that was I didn't know if I was upset or not at the time with all the pain in the rest of my body. The physios at Pinderfields put me in the Gym and tried to teach me how to live being in a wheelchair - I tried doing it their way but couldn't, so I started doing it my way which they didn't seem to be happy with but it was my body. After a few arguments with the Nurses and physios I was let out for weekend leave to get me back into life outside hospital. At the time I was living in a flat with 6 other people but that was no good for me with steps up to my room, so I went to live with my girlfriend at the time. That didn't work so I moved out to live on my own. I then started to learn to live from a wheelchair and it is not easy. The relationship with my girlfriend ended which was a shame and all of my friends seemed to disappear. The chair must have frightened them all away! My life had been completely turned upside down now.

Life went on and I met somebody else. In 1998 I decided to do a sponsored tandem skydive for charity. So I went up to a place in the Lake District and did one from 10,000ft - it was awesome! I asked if I could do it again – it was possible but the instructor asked me if he could try out a new canopy he was thinking about buying. I agreed and we went back up to 10,000ft but on landing I broke my left leg just above the ankle. I didn't want to go to hospital in the Lake District so I drove back home to west Yorkshire and then went to hospital. There I had an operation where they inserted a titanium rod. My girlfriend told me I cannot go and do sky diving any more (or she would finish with me!), so I found microlights - that's got to be safer.

I started flying in 2000 in a nice cheap and cheerful microlight called a Pegasus Excel and soon got the buzz for going places, albeit fairly local, an hour here and an hour there.

But this wonderful little trike wasn't going to take me just that bit further, so after a trip to a microlight show at Popham in the south of England I made a decision to buy a new machine.

After a wheel about I chose a Mainair Blade 912; the factory offered to make and fit some hand controls, which made a big difference in what machine I was going to purchase.

The Blade finally arrived after going backwards and forwards to the factory to design and get the hand control system working correctly. It was now time to try system out in the sky, I had organised the chief technical officer from the BMAA, a man called Guy Gratten, to come along and do some flight testing with me.

With a new machine in front me and hand controls that were completely alien, we took off and did some manoeuvres that worked perfectly just as I thought they would do. The paperwork was processed and I now had them approved by the BMAA as a Modification.

I had seen this video of a man called Brian Milton who flew a microlight around the world and I thought that is what I want to do! Now I had the machine to do it as well. Not long after I got my Blade I went to Northern Island for a couple of days with a group from the York Flying Club (YFC) and that really got me into travelling in the microlight. So I set to with my friend Dave Seiler whom I had started flying with and organised a trip to France for a week travelling around. It wasn't long after that when I decided to have a trip to Spain crossing the Pyrenees. That was it - I now had the bug for travelling around!

In 2004 a new machine called a Pegasus Quik was brought out so I went and had a look at it; it was very nice and had a much smaller wing which would help me with the hand controls. So after a bit of thinking and should I / shouldn't I, I decided to bite the bullet and get one. I part exchanged my Blade towards it and it left me completely skint! There was no more money. However now I had the bee's knees of the flying machines, I could go anywhere now.

On the first trip I wanted to see how it did for fuel, so I went off to Northern Spain for a week with a couple of the flyers from YFC. After getting back I spent a year just flying around the UK, camping at different places. Then one night I was sat in a pub near to the airfield chatting to a guy called Mark Bussetti from Island microlights in Malta. And it came out after a beer "I will fly down to Malta to see you" and he just laughed and said "no you won't" - I said "I will". So I got a group from the YFC together and organised the trip. In 2007 four of us flew two microlights to Malta, making us the first flexwing microlights to fly from the UK to Malta.

All the time I had this dream to do what Brian Milton had done, and fly around the world.

I flew to lots of 'fly-ins' and spoke to many people about my dream and they all said I was mad but I knew that it would happen one day. I decided to get in touch with Brian Milton and speak to him about it and he said it would be possible but it would involve a lot of very hard work. So I decide to have a practice run and look at flying from York to Sydney in Australia. But I would fly this completely on my own. A solo flight from York to Sydney

First of all I had to think how much it would cost? How would I get the money to make it happen Then when would I do it and what year.

So from late 2007 to early 2008 I started looking at a route from York to Sydney, I spoke with a guy at White Rose Aviation about it and he gave me some advice. The first thing I did was to source some maps of the world. I managed to get hold a set of ONC charts from America which are what their Air Force use, however they only went part of the way there - some were out of print and would not be reprinted. Then I spoke to Brian Milton about the route and guy called Richard Meredith Hardy who had just flown the route. I was told that the maps that were not available any more didn't matter as from Greece onwards I would be using Airways Charts – which are what the air liners use. So I did a bit of research into them and found some on eBay to have a look at. I also bought an IFR flight guide for one of the airports I knew I would be going into just to have a look at the sort of thing I would have to cope with on the way.

So after a few months of sitting with my GPS and a pile of maps at a table and emailing different people I came up with the route, it was to take me through France, Italy, Greece, Cyprus, Egypt, Saudi Arabia, Qatar, UAE, Oman, Pakistan, India, Bangladesh, Myanmar, Thailand, Singapore, Malaysia, Indonesia and Finally in to Australia. That was preliminary any way.

So now that I had a very basic route sorted out, I had to cost it out, I sat and worked out a rough mileage of 12,000 miles and calculated how much fuel my Quik would need to get there, In addition I had to account for the cost of hotels and food along the way. There was a huge costing of airport landing fees to work out and handling agent's fees which would be one of the biggest costs. Then there were the Visas to sort out for the different countries and I also had to get permission to fly into the countries with my machine and some of the permissions involved diplomatic clearance as well.

But how would I get the money to do all this? I started by spending literally hours and hours searching for company addresses and the people to get in touch with at the companies. After a few months I had thousands of different names and addresses. So I sent out a promotional pack together with the costing, out by post to hundreds and hundreds of companies to see if they would be interested in sponsoring a solo flight to Australia by microlight. There were a huge number of people who would not even respond – did they think I wouldn't get there? I continued to try and attract sponsors in so many different other ways. I wondered if I was doing something wrong so I contacted some companies that specialised in getting sponsorship and promoting products and companies, but they wanted too much money – far more than I could afford to give them.

So after a nearly two years of chasing I decided to try a different way so I headed to different air shows to advertise my trip. I even flew into Farnborough International Air Show. While I was there I managed to attract some sponsors and made some amazing contacts for the trip but still did not have enough to make the trip happen. So I turned to the Media and got them involved, but still not enough was coming forward. Would I ever get the money?? Then I decided to go to local companies to give them a chance of being a sponsor and have their name on the side of the aeroplane, this seemed to be a better way and I started to attract them.

It was now into 2010 and the money was slowly coming in so I decided to set a date when I was going to leave and see if that would make a difference. And it did!! I set the date of September 2010 and people then started to come forward with offers. I was still going to different shows and being laughed at and their comments that "I must be completely bonkers and I would never make it" just went over my head... I knew I would get there and was confident about it. Even people who knew me from my local area sat laughing at me.

I remember going to a microlight show on the Isle of White and I took a bucket around to see if the guys there would chip in a bit and they did! It was really good I raised £420 although I remember one guy who just flicked a fifty pence piece at me laughing saying "yeah all right of course you're gonna get there" I smiled and said thank you – after all every penny helps.

Time was now going on into 2010 so I went to a local company with a mock up fuel tank that I had cobbled together with card board and asked them if they could make a similar tank from aluminium. The guy wanted to know what it was for, so I told him and he laughed but said he would do it for me. I wanted to know the cost but he just said we would sort it out when it was done. I left it with him for a few weeks and kept going back to see if it was done - he was taking his time but also making a nice job of it. Then I had a phone call from a friend who said that the receivers had just gone into the factory and closed it down, to warn me that if I had anything there I had better go now. I

12

jumped in my van and shot down to see them they had the seat from the Quik and my wheelchair there and the tank that was nearly finished. I managed to get my bits back and asked them about the tank. The response was "Dave if you can get it finished elsewhere take with you" so I did and asked how much for the work that had already been done on it, "nothing I don't want a penny off you, we're closing down and I'm out of a job, so nothing enjoy your trip" Wow what a nice guy so a big thanks to Tony for that.

I took the tank and a friend arranged for it to be completed. Once it was finished I had it pressure tested for leaks, then I fitted it and made the fuel pipe. The next job was to get a larger oil cooler fitted to the Quik so it would keep the oil cool in the hotter countries like Saudi and India. I priced one up from the dealers and found it to be far too expensive so I found one on eBay to save money. Then I had put the water radiator further out in the airflow also to keep the engine cool with parts from the aircraft manufacture. I also fitted some landing lights to the Quik just in case I ran out of daylight and had to land in the dark like Brian Milton did on his RTW trip.

I sourced a lot of things on eBay and eBay came in handy for example when I was looking for a life raft as I managed to get a single person raft for a very good price. While I'm talking about life rafts because I am in the wheelchair I needed to find out what it would be like if I had to ditch in the sea on my trip should the worst happen, I did some research and found a water survival course that I could attend. I got in touch with a guy from the Northumbrian Police diving and training academy up in Newcastle and they welcomed me to bring the equipment I would be wearing on the trip and try them out under controlled conditions with them.

I turned up with the immersion suit and a life jacket that I was going to wear on the trip. First I got into the immersion suit and the life jacket then I had a bit of a briefing about jumping in to the pool. After that I was carried up to a platform and I was told to deploy my life jacket, which I did, then I shifted along to the edge of the platform and jumped in. it was quite amazing really because my legs were effectively a dead weight and they floated to the surface in the immersion suit before my head did. So I was laid in the water face down though a scramble with my arms soon turned me over but my legs were still just floating me around in all directions. It really opened my eyes to what was going on in the water and how not being able to walk affected the immersion suit. The Police divers were quite surprised too. I then had to climb in to a life raft which was a right job as well because my legs just kept floating up underneath it so when I tried getting in they just got caught up in everything.

If I did have to ditch I would be really struggling to get in my life raft that is for sure. So after a chat with the divers we decided that it would be better for me not to have a full immersion suit but just a floatation jacket which would keep me warm and stop the cold water shock when I jumped in. I am so glad that I went on this course so a big thanks to the Northumbria Police divers for allowing me to join their course.

So I now had the Quik ready to go and I had a life raft I needed a PLB from somewhere and thanks to one of the YFC members I was lent one for the trip - thanks Richard Smith! Still with lots to do and time creeping up on me, I was unsure if I could make the deadline. I needed a new GPS system that would be able to take all three continents in the data base but I couldn't afford to buy the one that would have been the dogs dangly bits - well I could but it would have eaten into the funds for the trip. So I decided to stick with my handheld GPS that I'd had for ten years. Now the departure date was getting closer and I still didn't have enough money to set off! I needed to buy all the current charts and flight guides for the trip which was going to be expensive. So it was back to eBay but to sell things this time - I went through my garage and house and everything that I didn't or hadn't used for a while went onto it.

My girlfriend was shaking her head at me saying I'm completely off my rocker but she was behind me all the way with the flight and knew I would do it. That was nice to hear.

It had now got to August and still I was short on sponsorship, so I decided to postpone the flight until I had enough, I didn't want to set off and not get there - that was not an option. Everybody now knew I was serious about the trip and started to believe in me - the money started coming in from everywhere in different amounts, over Christmas 2010 people were pledging sponsor money and I forgot to mention but I had decided to do the flight and raise some money for charity along the way and the charity I chose was the Yorkshire Air Ambulance. A local Air ambulance helicopter that is kept up in the air just by donations and in fact a couple of my friends had been in it over the years so without doubt a well-deserved charity for which to raise money.

After a trip to the Aero Expo I managed to secure a sponsorship deal with **Jeppesen** who do all the aviation charts and flight guides for the aviation industry - that was a huge help, so a big thank you to **Jeppesen** for that.

It was now into March in 2011, 3 years since I had started to think about and plan my trip to Australia.

The time had come so I had now set a date for the 28th of April to set off! My girlfriend Lesley just said "get on with it now because I'm not having another year of you going on and whingeing about the flight, JUST DO IT"!

That was it I made the phone calls and I the ball rolling with applying for the permissions for the different countries / getting my Visas sorted out. But first I thought I had better go and get my passport renewed so it was over to Liverpool for that. Now I felt sick I had done it, I was going for it!! I told all my friends and they were happy for me but still thought I was mad. The flight guides and charts turned up from **Jeppesen** and I had to go through the whole box to sort out what I did and didn't need - that took forever, even with help from Lesley my girlfriend.

I was contacted by a guy from a well known TV company that wanted to do a documentary on my trip - I said "yes, no problem". We did a few days of filming while I was preparing for the flight and it seemed to be going well and I thought to myself "everything is falling in to place now".

It was now down to the last two week before I was to set off for Oz. Did I have everything? I don't know, I hope so! I had grabbed a handful of spares for the engine - I had fuel filters and spark plugs, oil filters, fuses, spare inner tubes for the wheels, I had wire for the electrics and a host of other bits and pieces. I even bought a spare hand held GPS from a friend at the flying club. And just in case I bought a brand new high powered battery for the Quik and fitted that, little did I know but it turned out to knackered. The newspapers were now getting interested and asking for interviews so I had to do all that. I set off with the intention of being a SOLO FLIGHT and that is exactly what I wanted it to be - I was going to do this trip to Australia completely on my own with no ground support and nobody flying alongside to make sure I was OK. I had also organised everything myself apart from the clearances to the various countries which was handled by Mike Grey at White Rose Aviation.

I was really getting nervous now - will all the planning come together finally? I told my family that I was going and all I got from my sister was "I don't want you to go you might not come back" that cheered me no end! All the Sponsors stickers were now getting printed. Then I received an email that the TV Company were no longer interested in filming my flight! Only a week left to go and that happened. I didn't let it get to me, so I got the camera system I had all wired up and working and thought I will make do with that. I couldn't sleep at night now, I was up every hour on the hour feeling sick but excited at the same time.

With just five days to go, I had people giving me cheques towards the trip- fantastic... thank you to everybody. I was backwards and forwards I had to go to collect my passport up from the Indian Embassy in London complete with my new visa stamped inside. I went to the bank and got a pile of American Dollars and a pile of Euros for fuel. That was it - time to start packing my bag for the trip!

With two days left to go, I went to the airfield and packed the Quik up ready to go.

This is book is story of what happened day by day.

Day 1, 28th April 2011 - Rufforth to Headcorn, England

Hello, today was a very emotional set off from Rufforth with so many people coming to wish me well and see me on my way, I had to keep going into the hangar to stop myself from bursting into tears in front of everybody.

So the time finally came for me to get into the Quik for the first time of the trip, my hands shaking and heart beating like mad all I could think was am I doing the right thing.

I said goodbye to Les my girlfriend and climbed in to the Quik, loaded my wheelchair on board and tried starting the engine. But the battery was flat.

After a quick search by some of the local flyers, a pair of jump leads arrived.

This is a good start to the trip I thought and a minute later the engine jumped into life. I taxied out past everybody who had turned up to see me off, all waving and taking photos of me.

I took off on runway 23 and headed out to the east before turning south, avoiding Doncaster Robin Hood Airport.

The first half of my flight to Kent was quite nice, a bit bumpy in places with a ground speed of around 100mph until I got to the Wash near Sutton Meadows, a small microlight airfield, where I got wet with a 1000ft cloud base and light rain.

It then rained again harder as I was crossing the river Thames.

Once over the Thames I approached an airfield called Lashenden (Headcorn) home to the Tiger Moth club in Kent and gave them a call on my radio. They instructed me to join downwind for the runway 29 - it was a 16knt cross wind.

After landing, a couple of guys called Colin Watney and Rodney Solomon came over and gave me a hand with fuel, which Colin very kindly provided for me.

I filed a flight plan for the Channel crossing to Abbeville and got myself back into the Quik, it was a bit of a struggle with the wheelchair but I'm sure that I will get the hang of it as time goes on.

I got cleared to taxi out and activated the flight plan. It was still very windy, but manageable, so I set off.

As I flew out from the coast just south of Lydd and around a danger area near Hythe the visibility was pretty bad, but I could see blue sky in the distance so I thought I would carry on. However, about half way across the channel the visibility really deteriorated and the cloud started to close in, so I climbed to 3,500ft where I could see further ahead. Then as I got closer to the French coast, that closed in so I dropped down to 500 ft to see if it was any better but it was the same, cloud right down to the sea, so I climbed back up to 2,000ft trying desperately to find a way through.

All of a sudden it was white-out, no ground, no front visibility and white above me only about 6 miles off France now, so I turned back and tried to head north and for Le Touquet, but the visibility just got worse further north and I was still out at sea.

That's it I decided, I'm off back to Headcorn and I spent about 20 minutes getting back out of the cloud heading back to the UK.

Colin Watney had seen my tracker head back so he came back to Headcorn to meet me.

I stayed overnight at Colin Watney's house (thanks, Colin) and planned to head back to Headcorn the following morning in the hope that the weather would have cleared up enough to cross into France.

Day 2, April 29th - Headcorn England to Abbeville, France

Royal Wedding day!

I had a wonderful night last thanks to Colin Watney and his wife. This morning I woke up to fog covering Headcorn until late morning, when it turned into mist.

Colin took me into the airfield late morning where we put some more fuel in the Quik after yesterday's attempt to cross the Channel, and had a look at my aircraft battery as it just didn't seem to be charging at all. I had bought a new high powered YTZ14-BS battery two weeks prior to the trip and it was knackered - so there was no option I had to find a new battery. However where do you find a new battery on the Royal Wedding day? Everywhere was closed, so I asked around the airfield and came across a guy in the Tiger Moth club who had a brand new unopened YTX9-BS, the same as supplied at the P.M factory, which he could sell me - how lucky was that?

I fitted the battery and then sat around checking Metars and ringing the ATIS at Le Touquet Airport. They kept telling me "400ft cloud base, IFR (Instrument Flight Rules), flying 1500meters visibility, mist" until it got to about 12.30 when it said "1,300ft cloud base, 3,000metres visibility'". I went in to the office to see Jamie the airfield operator to see if it was possible to file a flight plan and his reply was "Do you want have a go at it again then, Dave?".

"Yes, please" I said, and filed a flight plan for 2pm UK time.

I took off on 03 Runway into a very stiff breeze, and once I reached about 2,000ft the ground started going hazy so I stopped at that height until I got to the Channel where the horizon disappeared. I dropped down to 1,000ft where I could see the ripples in the sea to the left and right below me but in front the visibility looked about 10ft!! But wasn't. I knew that at Le Touquet the visibility was 3000 metres, so I carried on.

I was about five miles away from the French coast before it came into view. The wind then picked up to about 20-25knts and was as rough as hell and as I crossed land the wind coming up over the cliffs was really kicking me about. I Approached Abbeville overhead at 1,500 ft and it was another cross wind! I did one approach but it was far too rough and gusty and it nearly put me into the ground upside down so I had to do a go around and have another attempt at landing. After a struggle with the bar I got the Quik down safely.

I taxied in and parked in front of the ULM hangar and the flying instructor there said I had better get it inside before the storms really started - I looked behind me and the sky was getting darker.

I decided to stay there for the night as there were lots of thunder storms forecast around the area. And within the hour sure enough two major storms blew through the airfield, so I was glad I got the aircraft in the ULM hangar with Ludair (thanks, guys!).

After the storm settled down, I went down to the Hotel on the airfield to see if they had a room for me - luckily they did, so with my Quik safely in the hangar for the night, I got my bits and pieces into the room and got ready for the next day's flying, Sorting out my maps and drawing lines on them.

Then I spent the evening in the hotel restaurant watching the storms, eating and drinking beer, talking to the hotel owner.

Day 3, April 30th - Abbeville to Wanafly

Got up this morning after a few beers in the Hotel bar in Abbeville the previous evening, to lovely blue skies, hurray!!

I went up to the ULM hangar and got loaded up and set off to Dave Lord's at Wanafly, a private airfield and flying school just north of Limoges. The first hour was fine with a tail wind and scattered cloud at 1,800ft but once I got to the Rouen River, the cloud base started dropping and dropping until I was about five miles past an airfield called Bermay, where the cloud base suddenly got really low and started filling in to a complete blanket cover.

As the cloud was getting thicker I dropped down below it to see what it was like. I was met with a 100ft cloud base - *"far too low!"* - instantly I climbed back up and went back in to Bernay still with a 100ft mist but being able to see. It was far too dangerous to carry on at the moment.

While on the ground at Bernay I spoke to a couple of pilots who spoke very good English and they said it would clear shortly. After about 30 mins it started clearing so I took off once again, destination Wanafly.

The cloud base was now about 1,500ft so for the first 20 minutes it was lovely, then cloud appeared again and dropped me down to 500ft for the next 30 minutes.

After that it was beautiful blue sky all the way down to Dave's through the beautiful French country side, although I have to say it was very thermic. As I got closer to Dave's airfield I radioed in, but it wasn't until I was about five miles away that he picked up my calls.

I approached his field over some trees and dropped into his 500 metre runway, taxied up a thin taxi way right up to his front door and barns.

I was met by Amanda Lord and a couple of their friends.

After a quick beer, we put my Quik into a barn for the night out of the way, then Dave and Amanda fed and watered me and we talked about my flight ahead and what I might encounter along the way.

If the weather allowed it, my Destination the next day was to be a small glider airfield called Fayence in the south of France.

Day 4, May 1*st* – Static, Wanafly

After all the messing around at Headcorn with the new battery, I then spent all day with Dave Lord sorting out a new problem – I had to fit a new radio interface and headset. By this time it was too late to get anywhere to tie the aircraft down and find a hotel, so I decided to leave it for now and set off early in the morning to Fayence.

I would like to explain the problem; after leaving Headcorn on my second attempt over the channel I heard a weird buzzing in my headset that I had not heard before and thought nothing of it, but when I called up Dave Lord at the airfield it was very quiet and

I could hardly hear him. So yesterday Alan, Dave's mate, got his SWR meter out and we started checking my aerial and found one rough strand of co-axial screening was shorting to the main pin of the BNC connector. We fixed that, and then checked out the Icom A22 which worked fine. However it was still not all working right and remained very quiet, so we then tried a Microavionics powered interface with my Lynx headset.

It was still the same.

Buggered?

So we decided to try another headset as well, while we we're at it.

It was just the same.

Dave went flying in the SkyRanger and I gave him a call "*123.550 radio check G-CDVO*".

Dave came back saying lots of background interference.

"*Just a minute, Dave*" I said and I changed the aerial configuration from the standard one fitted.

"*Don't do anything else; don't touch it, that's perfect*" Dave Lord said.

So, with that problem sorted, I planned to be up at 7am for my next leg to the south of France.

Day 5, May 2nd - Wanafly to Fayence

I got up early, we got my Quik out of the barn and I loaded it up and said my goodbyes to Dave and Amanda. I then taxied out to his private airstrip, with Dave escorting me in his Sky ranger. I took off towards the trees and Dave flew alongside me, checking the radio all the time, for about 20 miles before he headed back.

The radio seemed to be working fine now, so I carried on heading south to Fayence.

The first three hours were lovely and smooth as it was early morning and I enjoyed taking in the sights of France, but then the thermals started and the further south I got, the more the wind got stronger..

Towards the south of France I had to climb up over the edge of the French Alps. I knew that it might get a bit rough and it did! I started climbing up to about 5,000 ft; the wind was now at about 20mph, and a headwind, not nice.

I was getting bounced all over now and the mountains were getting higher, I was now getting scared as I don't actually like heights! On a couple of occasions the thermals and wind lifted me right out of my seat, pulling the base bar around.

Then the mountains got higher still, I was now at 8,000ft ft and really getting bounced about. The views over the mountains at this height were fantastic still having snow on the tops of them just like a picture postcard.

The wind was now a good 35mph, still a head wind and really gusting, the wing was all over and I knew that it was going to be a difficult landing if the wind didn't drop.

I approached Fayence - the wind was still at 35mph and horrible! I dropped down and set the Quik up for landing straight in on finals, getting thrown all over - "focus you'll be alright" I said. I went in with the bar getting pulled all over as I concentrated but then just as I was about to touch down, a strong side gust of wind tipped the wing down nearly hitting the ground so I powered on had to go around again which I wasn't happy about because it was so rough, I just wanted to be on the ground now.

I finally landed at Fayence after doing the go-round with a 35mph wind rolling over the mountains at me having spent 5hours 30mins flying, I taxied in to a nice sheltered area behind the hangars and managed to get a bollocking for parking where gliders park.

"Not powered machines" he mumbled in French, waving his arms around frantically at me.

So I moved off and found a nice piece of grass behind some trees where I could park, that I would be able to pull straight out of in the morning. A guy then pulled up in a car and babbled something to me *"I'm English"*, I said,' then he spoke English.

I thought I was going to get another mouthful for parking in the wrong place.

In fact, he was just going home from his school next door to the airfield and came to say hello, I asked if he knew the Hotel Aurberg de le Pins in Torrettes, he did and so I asked for directions.

I had found the hotel back in England before I set off on the trip but it seemed further away from the airfield than I thought.

I put my wheelchair together and got out of the Quik then tied my aircraft down so it wouldn't blow away overnight, while doing that I spotted a couple of guys messing around with a glider so I went over to see if they spoke any English, they did and turned out to be Germans on holiday.

So after a chat and finding out the best way to get to the hotel, I set off wheeling myself there.

I only managed to get about half a mile before the couple of glider pilots pulled along side of me and offered me a lift to my hotel.

I instantly said yes and jumped in their car and they took me there.

The restaurant in the hotel was closed for a refurb so there was no food, but I did manage to get a lift about a mile down the road to a small French bar type restaurant,

It was quite funny as there were a few of local workers in, all drunk and falling around.

They even came and bought me a drink, talking to me while I just smiled as I don't speak any French at all. I had something to eat while being entertained by the locals and then later I managed to get a lift back to the hotel from a passing taxi.

At the hotel I saw the weather forecast on TV - the wind was looking a lot lighter for the next day. My plan was to file a flight plan and leave the coast just north of Nice and head straight across the water following a VFR route along the coast before heading out to sea going past Corsica to a place called Il Gabianno, just south of Pisa.

This was going to be my first really big water crossing of around 175 miles.

At this point I would like to say big thanks to Dave and Mandy at Wanafly for their fantastic hospitality and help over the previous day or so - much appreciated!

Day 6, May 3rd - Fayence, France to Il Gabbiano, Italy

I got up this morning at about 6am and rang for a taxi.

"Sorry, monsieur, no taxi until 10am".

I texted the German glider pilots that I'd met at Fayence Aerodrome who said they would pick me up at 8.45am.

They picked me up and took me to the airfield, where I found my aircraft surrounded by goats! What an amazing sight that was, so I took a couple of pics before the sheep dogs herded them away. I loaded myself and the chair up - which takes an hour to do, I hope I get quicker at it as time goes on – started the Quik and set off to Italy.

My first reporting point was at the edge of Cannes just out over the sea, and then out another 30 miles to sea before turning towards Corsica. With 175miles of water in front it is a very weird feeling to watch land disappear behind you into the distance.

It does make you think of all sorts I have to say – *"what the f**k am I doing? I must be insane on a Rotax engine!"* – but the one thing I have found out so far about long water

23

crossings is that once the land disappears and it's a bit cloudy or hazy, you have to really concentrate as there is no horizon as such. You have to look down at the water rather than what's in front of you, or you start to feel a bit dizzy!

The crossing today with a slight tail wind wasn't too bad, but it still took about two and a half hours over water. Finally I got over land and was faced with an instant 20mph cross-wind. As I arrived at the airfield at Il Gabbiano, it looked like there was nobody there so I landed and then it turned out that the Italian army were there doing parachuting exercises, all in their camouflage suites.

Therefore I couldn't see them on the ground. I waited at one end of the airfield while a group had just deployed their parachutes and then taxied back up near the hangars.

I would have carried on but there was a huge storm brewing on my intended route so decided to spend the night at Il Gabbiano. I got out, tied my aircraft down and spoke to a few of the army guys before looking for a hotel and fuel for the night.

I pushed myself down a dirt track, dodging pot holes and rocks, for about half a mile to a farm house. A guy came out all smiles (he was the spitting image of one of the brothers in the video game super Mario) and I asked if he knew of anywhere I would be able to stop close by. To my surprise they had got some accommodation that they rented out.

So thanks to Giuseppe and his brother, I managed to get a lovely room at their farm "La Ronca" and 100litres of fuel brought for me. Then later in the evening Giuseppe took me into town where I went to a local restaurant and had a couple of beers. Well, I was in Italy so pizza is must to pizza and

Day 7, Sunday May 4th - IL Gabbiano to Scalea

I got up this morning at 5.30am so I could get away nice and early at 7am. I got to my Quik at six after the push down the dirt track struggling with my maps and bags and started to pack up; at 7am Giuseppe and his brother came to wave me off but beforehand gave me a bottle of the wine that they produce on their farm. What a wonderful place they have - well recommended to go for a break by anyone.

I started up, waited for the oil to get up to temperature before lining up and taking off with virtually no wind.

What a lovely couple of hours I had heading down the coast of Italy towards Rome as it was dead smooth, with no turbulence at all. As I got closer to Rome I headed inland to go around Rome's controlled airspace but as I did the clouds started building and shaking me about. Before long they were towering above and all around and getting thicker. As the ground went higher, the cloud was coming down to meet it and so there came a point when I had to change course. I was intending to drop into a small airfield at Valamonmone to say hello to an Italian trike pilot from Facebook, but with the cloud filling in this was now impossible.

Spiralling down through the towering clouds that were starting to fill in right down to the ground, it was now raining, so I opted to head back out for the coast. I was now was past Rome but I still had to go past Naples.

So at 500ft and less with the low cloud and rain, I ended up tracking down past Naples, Mount Vesuvius and the Adelphi coast. The Island of Capri was quite something to see as I flew past. Looking at the black clouds and rain now ahead, I was taking short cuts straight across the bays quite far out to sea until it started raining very hard at which point I had to go back in closer to the coast,

At 500ft and below, the cloud and rain came down, it was now raining quite hard and there was nowhere to land if anything happened. I was now at 300ft and in rain, hugging the coast as close as I could get and I couldn't see that far in front. Eventually Scalea came into view and there was the most amazing looking anvil-topped cloud just south of it. Best get in quick before that kicks off then I said to myself.

I radioed in but there was nobody answering so I flew straight in giving blind call, I landed in the rain and now I was very wet, I taxied up to the parking apron and a guy came to meet me and asked if I was stopping over for the night?

Yes, I think I am.

I managed to get the Quik squeezed into their hangar for the night and after a few phone calls from the airport office I found a hotel called "Felix" on the sea front.

The guy who had come out to meet me offered to give me lift there and so I gathered my bag and maps and got dropped off there.

I sat in my room getting my route sorted out for the next day, before heading to the restaurant. Hopefully, if the rain stopped, I would get to Malta tomorrow..

Day 8, May 5th –Scalea, Italy to Luqa, Malta

I got up at 5am and went into the bathroom, but my wheelchair wouldn't go through the door, so the only thing I could do was to throw myself on the floor and literally crawl to the toilet, before crawling back to the bed.

That's all I need before going flying, but it had to be done.

At 6.30am and after watching heavy rain storms from the window in the hotel, I got into my chair, got my gear together and waited for the taxi to arrive. I went off to the airfield watching the towering cumulous all around Scalea.

I was hoping they would go away!

After paying my charges, checking the weather on the internet and making a few phone calls to different airports in Italy, I decided that it was time to go, even though there were big black low clouds right down to the ground in the hills around Scalea.

I wondered if it was the right thing but thought, I could always turn back if I'm not happy. After take-off I headed straight out to sea to go around a huge rain cloud that went down to the ground inland and headed south to Sicily. There was a huge storm out to sea on my right and the cloud was getting thicker and lower again! I really wasn't sure if I could get to Sicily. As I got near Lamezia, I started hugging the coast again at 300ft, the top of the king post on my Quik just rubbing in the edge of the cloud, and 'hey-ho' it started raining again! By this time I was about 10 miles from Sicily and it then stopped raining and the sky turned blue - "*thank you*".

It looks like I would get to Sicily after all..

I headed towards the Messina Straits, between the toe of Italy and Sicily, where I found huge cumulus towering over the hills inland and covering Mount Etna. So I had to stay out at sea and go through the Messina Straits. I had been warned that the wind can get quite bad going through there and at 500ft and getting thrown all over as the wind tunnelled through the straits, it was not nice! The aircraft was encountering sink in the air and at 500ft it was really making me nervous. As I passed an ocean liner on my right hand side the Quik just dropped about 100ft.

So at 400ft getting thrown about, I powered on and climbed up again to 500ft.

As I passed Mount Etna I could see smoke coming out from the top, penetrating through the cloud.

27

As far as know Etna is still very active and keeps erupting, so to see a live Volcano was quite special even though I was being bounced about. After passing Etna the wind calmed down for a while.

I was heading in to a small airfield called "Marina Di Modica" where I met Leon from Island Microlights who had flown over to escort me into Luqa in Malta.

Leon rang ATC in Malta and filed the flight plan for both of us. To get to Malta there was 55 miles of water to go. We took off from Marina with a very stiff sea breeze blowing, and then headed out over the sea to Luqa 1hour 15 minutes over the water where ATC gave clearance to land. The wind was fairly strong and cross winded but I got the Quik down safely at the International Airport in Malta without incident and parked on the north apron next to a Citation jet. The handling agents from Air Malta came in a van and took me to passport control and immigration in order to get cleared and complete the paperwork.

After that I, I returned to my Quik, got back in and then I had to get clearance to taxi across the main runway to a spot at the south side where I was to tie my Quik down near the Island Microlights Hangar, as I would be stopping here for two days. Leon Xuereb from Island Microlights took me to Andrew Cilia dad's B&B for the two days (another member of Island Microlights), and I was then taken out for a few beers and meet the other members of the microlight club.

Day 9, May 6th – Static, Malta

A day off today! I was picked up at 8.30am by Leon and we went on the ferry over to Gozo for the day. Also with us were Graziella, Leon's wife and Becky and Charles Cilia. It's really funny Charles has got a grey Parrot that talks and it barks like a dog, if you say to it, "your not a dog" it starts bobbing its head up and down saying "im a Tiger, I'm a Tiger" "give us a kiss" so funny.

We looked around the stunning island of Gozo and sampled the fine beers they had to offer, but not too many as I had to return to Luqa Airport for a press conference at 5pm. At Luqa we were met by some of the Island Microlight pilots and a TV crew (I felt like a TV star!) I did an interview with the TV and also a local newspaper Malta Today.

Soon afterwards I started feeling very tired (as it is quite hard work, this York to Sydney thing!), so I was dropped back off at the B&B for a rest.

Later that evening we met up with few of the www.islandmicrolightclub.com pilots and went to a local restaurant in St Julian's Bay for a meal.

It was good to meet up with some VERY good friends again on Malta rather than back at York where we usually meet. After the meal we went and had a few beers around different bars in the centre, before heading back to Charles's B&B at about 3am.

Day 10, May 7th - Static, Malta

I had a sleep in today. I was picked up at 10am by Leon again - what a top man he is! This time we went for a tour around the Air Museum in Luqa that holds a Spitfire, a DC3 Dakota and a Hurricane that was brought out of the sea and rebuilt by the museum, among other old aircraft and items from the past.

In the afternoon, we had been given clearance to go back into Luqa airport so that we could get the Quik loaded up with fuel ready for my departure the next day. It only took 100litres to fill, not bad really considering it holds 145 litres.

By 5pm we had finished refuelling, so we went to Leon's dad's house for a few minutes on the way back before going to an amazing barbeque. We went into some woods where there was also a campsite and there was Edgar Buttigieg and his family and a few of their friends. The chef that was doing the cooking for everybody buried a 40 gallon steel barrel in the ground, filled it with wood and set fire to this, this was the barbeque!

After a short while they put a net mesh over the burning wood and filled the drum with what looked to be most of a lamb wrapped in foil, and covered this with a rusty old sheet of steel, then covered it completely in soil and sand making it air tight. Apparently it works like a pressure cooker and cooks the meat through very quickly! I had never seen this before. It only seemed to take an hour before everything was cooked. Leon gave me a full leg of lamb to have a chew on along with a beer.

Then we just had a really good laugh talking about a whole host of different subjects.

I had a really good night - it was completely different from the norm.

We went home early so I wasn't too tired for the departure the next day.

Day 11, May 8th - Luqa, Malta to Corfu, Greece

I was picked up by Leon at 7am to go to the airport where we went through security checks before we could get to the aircraft itself. Then I had to go to flight operations and fill in a flight plan to Corfu and sort out immigration. I had decided to fly straight across to Greece rather than going back to Italy the day before as the airports I wanted to fly into seemed a bit hostile towards microlights for some reason?. . Then it was back to the Quik where I was met by a group of pilots from Island Microlights who had come to wish me well on my way to Corfu – thanks, guys!

I got myself into the aircraft again (I seem to be getting faster at this now - it only takes me just over half an hour) and then I got pushed off the grass on to the apron.

"G-CDVO request radio check and engine start."

"Engine start approved G-CDVO…"

I had a six hour flight in front of me to Corfu. I wasn't sure but thought I must be the first person to fly a flexwing microlight from Malta to Corfu. On this departure I was having an escort out with Leon in his Technam aircraft with a TV camera man inside filming for Malta TV.

We got clearance to take off on Runway 23, and then we were cleared to fly a full circuit around the island over Marsascala Bay and past the Grand Harbour at Valletta, before turning on my track to the north and leaving my escort Leon and the TV camera man at Portomaso Tower, north of Valletta.

I had a six hour flight ahead of me and ALL over water, this was to be one of the longest flights over water of the whole trip and I would be flying it at just 3000ft. The first three hours were fine, nice and smooth and not too windy but then it started getting a bit boring as all I could see was the blue sea, there was no land in sight, lovely blue sky and the water was flat calm. In fact my eyes started going funny with all the blue, it seemed to take some real concentration to not fall asleep.

Once I'd been going for four hours it was time to transfer fuel from my auxiliary tank into my main tank; I had only tried this back in the hangar in York.

I grabbed the cable that I had wired up to a fuel pump under the seat and plugged it into a cigarette lighter socket on my dash board, reached down to a fuel tap that I had put just underneath my right leg, opened it up and switched the pump on.

Nothing seemed to be happening for a few minutes but then the fuel gauge started going up, it was working a treat. Once it said full on the gauge I turned both pump and fuel tap off. That was a bit unnerving as if it didn't work I would have been ditching in the sea and swimming to Corfu!

After the fifth hour, *"Hurrah, land ahoy,"* so not long to go now.

I Gave Corfu International airport a call on the radio,

"*G-CDVO microlight, inbound 15 miles to run.*"

Excellent, as I approached Corfu there was now a stiff breeze – I was not happy after such a long flight with not that much wind, had it picked up just for me?

 As I flew in over the land getting bounced about, the runway came into sight which looked good as it sticks out right from the edge of the sea. I set the Quik for finals then

Control said, "*Where are you G-CDVO?*"

"*G-VO over the threshold trying to come down, sir*"

"*OK, no problem.*"

The heat from the ground made it difficult to come down, but eventually I got it down.

I taxied in where I was met by a group of about ten people taking photos and smiling away.

"*Hello, David, we are so pleased to have you visit us at Corfu international Airport. Anything you want we can provide for you.*"

What a nice group of people they were.

"*I need a hotel please.*"

No problem they said (aircrew rates as well!) so they took me to the airport flight operations offices to sort out the necessary paperwork and check out my passport before I returned to tie my Quik down for the night.

The only place to tie it down was on the apron itself, in between some other private aircraft, with wires fastened to the ground. It wasn't due to be too windy but just to be sure, all the ratchet straps I had were used.

I was taken to my hotel for the night which was just down the road. It was not the most wheelchair friendliest place I have stayed I have to say - there were steps into rooms from reception, but the friendly hotel staff promised to give me a hand up and down them. In the night we had very heavy rain and thunderstorms. I was wondering what my Quik will look like the next morning?   I looked at the weather on TV and folded up the maps ready for my flight the next day to Zakinthos.

Corfu International Airport

Day 12, May 9th - Corfu to Zakinthos

The Britannia Hotel close to the airport where I had stayed was not really adapted for wheelchairs in any way. As soon as I got there, there was a step in to the hotel, then another into the corridor, before another into the room. The night porter ended up giving me a lift in to the room - not ideal but when in need you just have to ask and get on with it!

I got up early and made my way up to the airport pushing myself up the road and into Arrivals to the Olympic Agents help desk so that I could sort out my day ahead, a flight from Corfu to Zakinthos International Airport. After a short wait I was met by the same guy who had met me the day before at my Quik and he took me through passport control, down to flight planning and the flight operations room.

Everybody from the Olympic team was there, including officials from the CAA for the airport, all wanting a picture of me. They believed (incorrectly it later turned out) that they hadn't had a flexwing microlight fly in to Corfu before.

High winds and thunderstorms were forecast, but I didn't have that far to go - only 150 miles.

The wonderful people at Olympic Agents had helped me out no end but it was time to go.

I climbed into the Quik and got engine-start clearance at which point it started raining (*great stuff again!*). It was hard to believe the amount of rain I'd seen in Greece!.

The rain was not bad enough to stop me going, so I taxied out, lined up, and got cleared for take-off after which I disappeared south towards Zakinthos. This was another sea-crossing, 150 miles and in the rain but never mind. I had to fly no higher than 1,000ft, because there was a military air base nearby that was active and ATC kept me at that height all the way there. After 40 minutes I wondered if it would stop raining and whether the visibility would get better.

Hurrah! Yes it did get better, not that good, but definitely better. I could now see a coast line for a change. After two hours Zakinthos came into view. I gave them a call.

It seemed very quiet, I thought I had the wrong frequency for them but I tried anyway,

"*G-CDVO Zakinthos*"

"*G-CDVO you have clearance to land, report 4 mile finals, wind 15knts.*"

Awesome! It was like having long finals from Corfu! So I went straight in.

When I landed I was met by another group of the Olympic Airways agents to sort out my aircraft parking, help me tie it down in the wind and also find me a hotel.

Once again I put the wheelchair together and climbed out of the Quik– I am starting to find this very hard now it is very tiring and drains my energy. Then we went to the flight operations office to sort out the paperwork and meet the airport staff.

It seemed to be getting to be a routine this major airport stuff, it was completely out of my comfort zone compared with back home at Rufforth.

Then it was off to the hotel - very nice it was with lovely steps into it (I still don't do steps) - but I was helped in anyway. I got into my room, and wow, yes, it was 9.30 at night. So I just had time to get something to eat before returning to the room and plan for the next day's travelling to Rhodes.

I did some typing for the blog for half an hour or so.

I was absolutely knackered. *Need a day off soon!*

Greek Islands

Day 13, May 10th - Zakinthos to Rhodes

I was wide awake at 4.30am worrying about the flight ahead as the weather was forecasting 45 knot winds on my route from Zakinthos direct to Rhodes International, a distance of 425 miles.

A representative for the handling agents – Olympic - picked me up at 8.30am so I could get my flight plan done, and then get my Quik sorted out for the flight. When we got to the airport I was met with all the staff of Olympic ground handling and the CAA for the airport. All this for little old me, that was nice.

I went in to Flight Operations to check the weather and get a flight plan sorted out, only to find crap weather forecast on route – *again!* So we had a ride over to the tower and I had a word with them. They advised me to go via a different route so that I wouldn't have go over the 9,000ft mountain on route past Tripoli.

Should I stay or should I go? I decided to go.

I re-filed the flight plan and went back to the Quik to see if it had survived the thunderstorms and heavy rain that we had the previous night. It was fine, so I got loaded up and had a photo session with my new friends.

Preparing for take-off, I remember thinking that this is going to be a very long and probably rough flight.

Air traffic gave me permission to back-track Runway 34 but I probably won't need all 2,228 metres. I just pulled around and reported "*Lined up for take-off G-CDVO*"

"*Cleared for take -off*" came back, and off I went.

For the first two hours it was OK, just a bit windy crossing over from Zakinthos to the Pelopones and tracking down the coast past Kalamata, but as I got closer to Kerkira I started getting thrown all over, seriously lifting me out of my seat and in attitudes I had never been in before. I looked at the ASI - I was doing 35mph over the sea, with an airspeed of 80mph. I was right in thinking that this was going to be a long flight! I knew that Milos Airport was closed as well so if the weather got too bad I couldn't go in there. For a while as I went around the island of Kerkira I was thinking "*this is it, game over*" - the Quik was all over the sky and I was crapping myself. Small fair weather clouds were now building so I had to skirt around them as they were producing terrible turbulence.

Eventually I managed to get a ground speed of between 40-45mph, though still getting kicked about like a cork at sea – at least this was better. I had now been in the air for four and a half hours so I thought that I had better refill my fuel tank from my big 80-litre jerry can in the back seat. I did this without any problems and carried on. Five hours merged into six hours of just sheer fright and turbulence before Rhodes finally came into view. I thought, about time, I've never been so pleased to see land, my back and arms were killing me with all the turbulence. I gave Rhodes a call on the radio – the lady ATC sounded really stressed out with all the traffic she had going into Rhodes so they had me orbiting for a few minute while a few of big jets went in.

Then it was me, "*You are number one, report two mile finals*" she said

As you would imagine I did not need too much of the 3305 metre runway so I just flew down the runway until I was about 100metres from an exit point on the runway and

35

then landed. I taxied in past all the jets – the holiday makers getting off the jets were looking at me - they must have thought I was mad.

Rhodes Airport
As I was ordered to park up at the end of the apron I followed the yellow lines to the waiting marshal who waved his bright orange table tennis bats at me. Once again I was met with another group of Olympic ground handling agents who staged a photo shoot again with me.

I am getting quite good at this smiling for the camera thing.

As the wind was still strong I asked if there was any where I could park my Quik for the night and after a bit of discussion I managed to convince them to let get it parked in the airport fire station, it was funny as the fire men had to lift it up and carry it sideways into the fire bay.

Day 15, May 12th - Cyprus after failed attempt at Egypt

After a terrific night with Demetrius and his wonderful family in their home, it was soon 6.30am the following day.

It was time to get up.

I needed to get the paperwork sorted out for my flight to Alexandria in Egypt, and Demitri said he would help and show me where to go at the airport. We arrived at Paphos International airport and went to HEMES flight operation room to sort my flight plan and fill in General Declarations (GenDecs), two copies to customs, two copies to passport control and two copies to flight operations office.

Now I was able to fill in the flight plan. This was done in the flight operations room and faxed to the tower. Right, having gone from one side of the airport to the other, it was time to go.

A very big 'thank you' to all the staff at Paphos international Airport for their very much appreciated help and support and for supplying all the fees through the airport for a very reasonable rate for me – **free!** And especially to Demetrius for his help.

I went through the security checks, putting my bags through metal detectors and then on to passport control just as if I was going on holiday except I was able to go straight to the front of the queue being aircrew. Then it was out to my Quik. The wind was picking up just in time for my departure to Alexandria - great stuff, I couldn't have timed it any better.

Engine started and a quick twiddle around with my headset to get them working in both ears, I was given clearance to taxi and follow the Follow-Me car that they had sent out for me to take me to holding point Golf before departure.

"*G-CDVO line up, cleared for departure, after take-off, turn left and climb to 7,500ft*".

I did this, taking off with a slight crosswind and headed straight out to sea towards Egypt climbing up to 7,500ft. After about 20 minutes a big storm was around me and I was flying in, out and in between the towering cumulous clouds forming, I was not happy at all it was kicking me about the sky something terrible and there was a 40 mph headwind at that altitude. Once I was clear of Paphos controlled airspace, I changed frequencies from Paphos Tower to Nicosia Flight Information, and flew out leaving the storm behind me, by now the sky was just full of scattered clouds at 7,000ft.

So I carried on weaving my way in, out and around them until it came to change over to Cairo ATC who advised me that the Mode Charlie Altitude on my transponder wasn't working. This meant that they could not identify me by number and height on their radar screens.

I would NOT be allowed into their airspace!!!!

Right, what do I do? So I gave Nicosia a call again on the radio.

"*G-CDVO returning to Paphos.*"

"*G-CDVO OK, I'll advise Paphos and Cairo.*"

Great stuff, here we go, back into the storm that I had just been through, the only trouble now was it had built up and was worse.

I headed back with a nice tailwind but I had to go in and out and drop down to about 500ft to get underneath the storm now, wet through again and with bad visibility I picked my way through it, then I gave Paphos tower a call and they cleared me straight into land with the storm getting worse.

When I landed back at Paphos it was blowing a gale. I taxied into the area where I had parked that morning. Then the big storm came in and I just sat there in the Quik holding on to the bar in the rain for a while until Steven Monkcom, an ex-pat Briton and microlight pilot living in Cyprus returned to give me a hand.

The airport manger also came and asked if I was OK.

"*No problem, sir*".

After a few calls from the airport manager I managed to secure my Quik to a secure under-cover area thanks to the Minister of Transport on the airport and the staff at Paphos International until I was able to fix my transponder problem. Steven rang an avionics expert who works for Cyprus Air in Larnaca and we arranged to meet him half way from Paphos at Limassol Airport so he could have a look at my transponder. Steve drove over and the guy arrived and said "*well I can have a look on Monday for you when I'm there and I will get the Machine to check everything out*"

I stayed with Steven Monkcom, his wife Ann and their daughter at their home for the night. I sat at their dining table with my transponder and wiring loom in bits, checking out the wiring and connections. I did not find anything wrong and it was 12.30 in the morning. We had two more encoders to try out in the morning once we pick them up from different sources around the island

I'm knackered and fed up now - it seems be nothing but problems and bad weather.

Day 16, May 13th - Repair day at Paphos, Cyprus

So 6am came and it was time to get up, I need to get this transponder fixed or my trip will be over because permissions will run out for Egypt and Saudi. So after being carried down the steps at Steven and Ann's house we departed to pick up another encoder belonging to one of Demetrius' friends. We picked that up then went to the Quik at the airport with three encoders to try out.

We went and got a security pass and tried out the three encoders. Nothing happened! It was still the same - so my transponder must be knackered. Steven rang around, as I did, but came up with nothing, no more transponders in the whole of Cyprus that could be bought!

If I don't find something soon this could be my epic trip over. *That's not going to happen!* Not after all the planning.

After going here, there and everywhere, I came to an arrangement with Steven and his friend Alan Carter. The agreement being that I would buy them a new transponder and they would sell me the Mode-S that was fitted in their Mainair Blade 912.

Mmmmm. What do I do?

This meant another £2,000 for a new transponder that I couldn't really afford, but if I didn't get one, then the trip would almost certainly be over for me.

So I had to bite the bullet and the deal was agreed with Steve and Alan. We took the transponder out of their Blade 912and headed over to the airport again, back through security to fit the new one so I could get going. All this took time, and it looked like I wasn't going to fly that day.

A phone call was made to Demetrius to see if he could find a hotel for me in Paphos for the night, and within the hour he came back and said he had found one. Not only had that, but the Mayor of Geroskipou paid for it for me!

Bonus!

We finished installing the transponder and then I got dropped off at the hotel for the night, and had a few beers relaxing and doing interviews with the local media and doing the blog.

Hopefully everything is sorted out now.

THE MIDDLE EAST – OFTEN CLOSE TO FAILING

Day 17, May 14th - Paphos to Alexandria

I was up early again - 6am - worried about the flight, because I knew that I would have to climb back up to 8,500ft to get into Egyptian airspace which would be fine except for the fact that I'm scared of heights!

I was picked up by Alan at 7.30am and we headed back to the airport again, where I went straight through to flight operations to see what papers I needed to fill in again and take around the airport to various people.

It was quite good as the staff in the airport operations room said "We'll take them for you" so I didn't need to go around the airport again.

So I went down from there and passed through passport control like you do when you're going on holiday, before being picked up by a bus on the apron and taken to my Quik.

I got my kit aboard and once again a few airport staff turned up to wish me well, which was nice. I said my goodbyes to Demetrius and Steven thanking them for all their help over the prior couple of days. I would also like to thank Hermes Airports, the director Andy Frangou, Deputy Director Aris Hadjigeorgiou, Director Assistant Georgia Michael,

Hermes operations managers and the Civil Aviation department, plus the Dedha Los microlight club. Thank you!

I lifted myself into the Quik once again and stowed my wheelchair on board ready for departure.

So it was time to go then.

I gave ground radio a call and got clearance for engine start, then cleared for taxi straight away, so I taxied out to the holding point and changed to tower frequency who said *"G-CDVO line up and cleared for take-off, Turn left after take-off and climb to 8,500ft G-CDVO"*, So I lined up as instructed and read back all of my flight plan to them with the reporting points. Then took off and turned left straight out to sea and made a slow climb to 8,500ft as I had done only a couple of days previously.

The weather was lovely and sunny with not much wind (around 15mph) and I went from Paphos Tower frequency to Nicosia Information as I left the controlled airspace around the airport at 20 miles out.

Once I got 150miles out to sea towards Egypt's FIR (Flight Information Region) I changed to Cairo Information.

BUT just before the FIR – an official reporting point – Air Traffic Control said they had lost transponder altitude again.

I needed, they said, to return to Paphos.

Not again!

I was at 8,500ft and as I turned around and started to drop down and head back to Paphos. The guy on ATC said, *"G-CDVO, this is Nicosia, we have you in view on our screens now, you can carry on to Alex if so wish"*

"Affirm, I would like to carry on."

Back up to 8,500ft where it was freezing cold - I was fed up! There were some fair-weather clouds in front bubbling up but nothing too bad, nothing to make it IFR up there. After three hours of flying through the fair weather cloud I had permission to start my descent into Alex. I found this so funny, as the "descent" was what you would do in an airliner, not a frail little microlight.

I flew in a big arc to Finals at Alexandria as instructed by Cairo ATC, as I got down to 4,000ft the cloud was filling in so I requested to drop further to 2,500ft which was approved by ATC, but it then started to get a bit crappy and windy. Soon I was battling with the bar in a 30mph crosswind rolling over the city at the airport.

As I lined up for landing on finals the Quik was at a good 40 degrees to the runway, it took some battling down and I was using up a lot of the runway at Alexandria but I managed to get down without damage having used quite a lot of the runway – for once I was glad it wasn't Rufforth at York or I would have had to go around a few times before touchdown. As I taxied in I was met by about 20 people from AN ground handling agents. I thought, I don't need all this.

I sat in the aircraft holding on to the jerking bar in the strong winds, as they made me park crosswind on the apron

The wind was now awful.

Still sat in the Quik not even being able to remove my helmet and headset because of the wind I said to one of the officials "*I need to park it in a shaded area away from the wind*".

"*You park it here in this bay*", he told me.

"*No, you don't understand, there is nothing to tie it down to on the apron here.*"

There was a lovely row of palm trees right in front of me which would have been just perfect. He was adamant.

"*No, you have to park here*".

After a few minutes of arguing, with them claiming that for safety reasons my aircraft had to park in the middle of the tarmac with no means of being tied down, I changed my argument.

"*OK, then I will park it here, and when I return to in the morning and it has blown away onto the lovely Egypt Air jet parked next to me, the airport will be responsible.*"

I pointed at one person in particular, the hot-eyed type whose last thought in the world is safety, and I said, "*I will blame you in particular*".

They still weren't moving, so – still holding on in the high wind – I said "*OK, how long for a flight plan to be processed?* " 30 minutes was the reply. "*File me a flight plan to 6th of October Airport in Cairo then. I'm out of here, and you can all bollocks.*"

46

They filed me a new flight plan, and after about an hour, I was saying to them I am running out of daylight time why is it taking so long. The ATC guy said to me, "*You won't get there before dark now.*"

I shouted back, "*I know that after you messing me about, now sir, can you cancel it?*"

We finally came to an arrangement and I moved to another parking bay, normally reserved for business jets.

I tied my aircraft up to a couple of rubber chocks. That was it!

I said, "*This is on your head pal, not mine.*"

They then sent a bus to take me 100ft to the terminal building and I told them what I thought of them, and that I wouldn't be paying for all this.

It is just not necessary!

I went through passport controls getting pushed around and with people falling over me, an amazing experience in itself here in Egypt,

And then the AN agents put me in minibus and I got taken to a nice 3-star hotel, resisting all their efforts to book me into a 5-star one – it's the commission, you know. When I got to the hotel there were about 5 steps up into it the Wi-Fi was broken, so I had no blogs to upload.

I went to the hotel reception to find somewhere to go and eat but nobody understood a word I was saying so I had a meal in the hotel that wasn't the best thing I had ever eaten and then went to bed knackered.

(Alexandria Airport has a terrible reputation for bloody-mindedness. Brian Milton went through on his 1987 microlight flight to Australia, with a fee demanded for every move he made, hands out everywhere,. The Indian adventurer, Vijay Singhania, the following year, needed every ounce of power from the Indian Ambassador to Egypt to avoid being fleeced. BM)

Day 18, May 15th - Alexandria to Cairo

I was getting picked up by AN Agents to go to the airport at 7.45am. They turned up in a mini bus again so they had lift me in too (well, if I'm paying for it).

I got to the airport, went through passport control and outside to the apron only to be stopped.

"You must wait here!"

"My aircraft is there, 100ft away"

"You must wait for bus to take you there"

Like hell I will, making me pay for a bus to take me 100ft twice.

I set off

"Come back, you can't go, you must wait for a bus"

"Bollocks, I'm not paying for a bus, get the airport manager now"

I got to my Quik within 10 seconds without a bus, and asked if there was more paper work to fill in before I go.

"No, Captain, you're OK to go".

I got into the aircraft, ready to go, and was cleared to start the engine. This was to be a trip from Alexandria Airport to 6th of October airport in Cairo, for refuelling only, as the airport was being used for military training that day. Then the plan was to head on to Luxor for two days.

I taxied out past a few of the Egypt Air jets on the apron and on to the same runway I had battled to get my Quik down on the day before. I lined up and was cleared for take-off to 8,500ft again.

Great stuff just what I didn't want.

It was only going to be a 1hr 30min flight to Cairo's airport, so not too bad. When I took off I found the wind was still rolling over the city and kicking me about, but by now I was starting to get used to that.

For the first 30 minutes it was fine. Visibility wasn't that good, very hazy-looking into the sun but also cloudy low down. The ATC guy routed me around some danger zones near Cairo before changing over to the airport's frequency. It was very nice and different because as I went over the Nile the scenery changed from the green delta to desert, an amazing sight, green to brown.

As I got closer to October 6th Airport it was just desert and even at 8,500ft I was getting thrown about in the thermals, which was unnerving, let me tell you!

"Descend and join overhead for Runway 01"

Then it really did start getting bumpy as I got lower down and joined downwind. I landed on Runway 01 and taxied in to refuel, ready to go, but there was no sign of any military aircraft around. I asked ATC what had happened. *"What Military?"* they said.

So I said.

"Can *I stop here for the night to sort out my radio?"*

"No problem" they said.

I made a quick phone call to Eddie Gould to see if it was possible to stay with him in Cairo.

"No problem, we'd love to have you".

The guy who met me on the tarmac offered to take me to Eddie's house in Cairo. The roads in Cairo are quite amazing; two lanes filled with three to four lanes of traffic - a free-for-all race to the nearest 6 inches at 70mph!

Good fun!

After what felt like a two hour drive we got to Eddie's where I met him and his pharmacist friend Achmed who gave me a hand up the stairs to his house. Then later Eddie, Ahmed and myself went out for a drink to a local restaurant where we had a couple of chicken kebabs washed down with a beer. I was tired after the days flying and Ahmed was working a night shift so we went back early at 10pm.

A visit to the Pyramids was planned for the next day!

Day 19, May 17th - Static Cairo – but see the Pyramids at Giza

I slept -in at Eddie's house until 8am, I certainly needed it! We were picked up about 9am by the mini bus from Cairo International airport where Ahmed works at flight operations, and we went to visit the famous pyramids at Giza - if you haven't seen them close up before they are amazing.

I had a few photos taken with the Pyramids and got harassed by the locals with camels wanting us to have pics with them, so I gave in and had a few taken with the camels. Afterwards we went back to the minibus where I was picked up and thrown in as the seats were just too high for me to climb into myself. Then we went to see the Sphinx before heading back towards the centre and a nice drive around Cairo in the hectic traffic as Ahmed had been working all night and needed his bed. There were no bars around the area where Eddie lives, so you have to go to hotels if you want an alcoholic drink. So Eddie and I sought out a nice hotel not far from where he lives and had a few beers at the side of a swimming pool in the afternoon sun.

Later that night we had a pizza delivered to Eddie's house and I got the maps and things ready for the next day's flight to Luxor.

I even filed the flight plan.

Spokes of Arabia

Day 20, May 18th - Cairo to Luxor

I woke up at about 4.30 with a tannoy wailing. I didn't know what it was about but felt it must have been something along the lines of "it will soon be day light, so be awake" (in fact it was the first of the five Islamic calls a day, calling the Faithful to prayer).

I was picked up at 7.30am by the AN agent Islam and we went through the Cairo traffic again (awesome) and made our way to 6th October airport. Eddie came along to see me off.

We put our bags through the x ray machine and Eddie was cleared to come out on to the apron with me. Then we went over to the Quik where the wind was now blowing a good 20 knots.

Then I thought, flight plan, as the plan I had sent the previous night had been rejected and I had to make a new one. Islam the agent went to Flight Ops and asked them how I could fly to Luxor. He was told I had to file an IFR flight plan – Instrument Flight Rules – with a minimum altitude of 8,500ft.

I said "What if it's cloudy and I can't go over the top?"

Islam shrugged his shoulders, "I don't know" he said.

I loaded the aircraft up and we moved it to a position in the wind where I could get in. Then Islam came back and I asked, "What about a VFR flight plan?"

"I'll ask" he said and wondered off, He came back from Flight ops and said "if you want to fly a VFR flight plan the minimum Altitude is 9,500ft and it will take 3 weeks to get clearance from the military"

I asked Eddie to go and find out what was happing to save me time going back and forwards. He came back and said they were willing to file an IFR at 8,500ft as I have no oxygen, but they wouldn't move on VFR, so an IFR plan was filed.

As I got in the Quik getting ready to go, the wind had really picked up. It was a bit of a struggle putting the wheelchair on the Quik with the wind but I sorted it with help from Islam and Eddie.

There was only my aircraft on the apron so I was cleared to taxi out and take off as soon as I was ready,

So I gave them a radio call and taxied out struggling with the bar and I got a call "Wind 25 knots" ATC said as I lined up.

51

And then *"Take off and climb to 8,500ft above the airfield"*.

I took off and climbed circling the Airport as instructed and it was as rough as hell all the way up to 8,000ft. I turned on my heading and got clearance from the tower to change to Cairo Radar. At this height there were stunning views overlooking Cairo I have to say, and heading away from Cairo there was nothing but desert for miles and mile and miles.

As the hours passed by it started to get rough again, lifting me out of the seat and whipping the base bar violently out of my hands. Gusting winds pushed me into some really odd positions, nose-down and going up at 1,000ft a min, then going down at the same rate with the nose up on full power. Being bounced around at this altitude was starting to make me nervous now, so I climbed until I was at 10,000 ft above the desert just to get away from violent thermals. The air was getting thinner, I was tired and yawning a lot, it was now hard work. But before long it was time to change to Luxor, where they said *"G-CDVO descend 3,000ft, on heading 180"*.

Then it was *"G-CDVO descend another 3,000ft and then descend another 2,000ft you are now on a full IFR approach into 20 runway"*. And in my doing so all the instruments on the Quik started to mist up, it must have been the change in temperature.

It was really funny as they vectored me in as if I was a 747 or something rather than a microlight.

I landed in very little wind although it was still very thermic and I could tell the difference in heat straight away compared with being so high - it was really hot now (about 90F).

As I taxied in the guy in the tower said *"Taxi to the marshals waiting.. that is a beautiful flying machine you have there"*.

"Thank you sir that's very kind of you". I said.

Once again the AN Agents were waiting to take me on the bus to the terminal, but first I needed to tie my aircraft down in its current area in the middle of nowhere on the apron. I wasn't too concerned as the there was virtually no wind and after I asked if it was due to pick up the answer was no, so then on to the bus to passport control where I had my passport stamped and entry Visa stamped. The rep was very nice and we were out of the airport in just a few minutes and at the hotel they had booked for me.

"Four- star" he said.

"No, I asked for 2 stars", I said, but then I could not be bothered arguing over it, *"Oh, forget it, just take me there."*

I was really looking forward to leaving this country the following day!

The hotel was very nice and overlooked the Nile. So I sat writing my blog as the sun was going down over the Nile and I was on my own. Les, my girlfriend should have been with me to see this on a romantic note.

Later in the evening after sorting out my charts, looking at my next leg over the Red sea to Saudi Arabia and doing my blog, I went across the road from the hotel to a local Murphy's Bar for something to eat and drink. However there was a central reservation running down the middle of the road with a kerb that must have been two ft high which made crossing the road something of a challenge!

So I flagged over a couple of locals who were sat around with horses and carts harassing people for tours around Luxor and I got them to lift me over to the other side. Then there were about 20 steps into the Murphy's Bar, so I asked one of the lads who had helped me over the road to give me a hand up in to the bar.

I kept noticing that the same lad was now hovering around the bar waiting for me to go, I tried to ignore him but it didn't work.   He continued waiting, saying *"it's ok sir, I wait for you and give you lift back down"*

And sure to his word he did he dropped me down the steps on the way out and grabbed one of his mates to give me a lift back over the kerb in the middle of the road. But he did want me have tour around Luxor with his horse and cart, so I agreed for him to come to the hotel at 9.30am the next day. ☺

Day 21, May 19th - Luxor to Jeddah in Saudi

I was picked up by the AN rep at 7.30am and taken to Luxor International Airport. I went straight to immigration to get my exit visa stamped and then we got on the bus that took me out to my Quik, which was parked all alone in the middle of the apron. There was little if no wind at all and looked like it could be a nice flight, all 493 miles of it.

After about three minutes the fuel bowser turned up and about 20 people came to help and take pics. The Quik got filled up with just 98 litres of Avgas, and I was ready for the off. Just a small matter of the flight plan so the AN rep produced an Egyptian flight plan for me that I filled in and he took it to the Tower for me.

With the Quik now loaded up once again I got myself in, I stripped the chair down and loaded that in, (getting faster at it all the time) and it was time to go. I said my farewells to everybody and I gave tower a call for engine start:

"G-CDVO request engine start and taxi"

"G-CDVO, taxi to holding point Alpha"

"Holding point alpha, G-CDVO"

Off I go to holding point Alpha.

"G-CDVO you are cleared for take-off, after take-off change to Radar frequency"

So after repeating back what he had just said, along with my entire flight plan, I lined up and took off into beautiful blue sky.

As soon I as I took off it was thermic and rough, and I climbed up nice and steady whilst taking in the amazing rock formations and valleys running through them all the way up to 9,000ft which was the level to which my flight had been cleared, There it eventually smoothed out - excellent, maybe a nice flight for a change!

The route from Luxor to Jeddah is just about a direct straight line, using the Airways Charts that you have to follow (same as the airliners) but it was still about a seven hour flight. The first hour was fine then ATC told me that there was traffic at my 3 o'clock, and asked me to make a new heading of 210 to avoid, I was looking all around for the traffic but I could not see anything.

So ATC then instructed me to go back on my original heading direct to Jeddah.

I got to the coast of Egypt and the Red sea ahead was a beautiful blue with the sun on it. I had another big water crossing of around 6 hours in front of me, so I did a quick check along the engine temperatures and made sure the fuel pump and tap were working for midair refuel.

Then I went coasting out over the Red Sea for another few hours. I have to say that sea still looks the same whether it's the Aegean or the Red sea, it's bright blue – with the exception of the English Channel which is brown!

Anyway at 9,000ft it was freezing cold with not a cloud in the sky, I had a few hours in front of me. What do you do for 7hours at 9,000ft on a flexwing? Well, you listen to the engine a lot. I had music but it put me off and couldn't concentrate.

So I turned that off, ate sandwiches, drank water and that's in between talking to the ATC. That's about it believe it or not flying a flexwing microlight on this trip keeps you busy all the time you don't have chance to relax.

After 6hours of swapping frequencies from different Egyptian ones then on to Saudi Arabian frequencies I finally got Jeddah Approach who vectored me down in stages. I think they thought I was a jet airliner with the circuit they gave me (4 miles finals) as I turned down wind I was telling ATC that I didn't need all this space especially with such a strong wind.

They wouldn't have it and continued to take me on to 4 mile finals I changed to the tower frequency, who then cleared me to land. Then they realised I was only doing 45-50mph over the ground and to make things worse my electric-trim was stuck on slowing me down, so trying to pull on a bit of speed to gain more ground speed was very hard work, and to top it all there was also a 25mph headwind once again.

Tower said to me "*can you go a bit faster please?*"

"*I'm trying my best sir, but you told me to come here*". Meanwhile there was another aircraft asking ATC what they should do, so ATC sent them out to sea about 110 miles.

Finals took me straight over Jeddah city with the wind rolling over it and made it very rough flying,

I finally landed half way down the runway and the woman in the tower was saying "*Expedite taxi, expedite taxi*". With the wind blowing me around and the trimmer stuck on, the bar was near the front strut, which meant this was very hard work. This didn't help as I use one hand on the bar to steady the wing, and one hand steering on the ground; I don't steer with my ft like other flexwing pilots, so in wind its dammed hard work. I had just cleared the runway and a 747 landed after me going straight passed this must have been the aircraft that ATC had sent out to sea.

By the time I had taxied up to Sierra taxiway the 747 was now in front of me and a 777 was following me. I kept looking back at this 777 and I noticed the pilot looking at me waving and smiling. So there I was sandwiched between two big jets, quite funny really (it turned out later that the 747 was the aircraft that had been sent out to sea 110 miles) and after 20 minutes of taxiing following orders and taxiways a *Follow-Me* car came out and took me to around to the executive apron to park up.

Jet Aviation, the main handling agents came over and asked who my agent was, and after a few phone calls to friends it was confirmed that Jet Aviation was going to be my handlers. I got myself out and into my chair while we decided the best place for me to park up for the night would be.

Then it was decided to put the Quik into the secure yard of Jet Aviation for the night. Next thing was to go and sort out customs and immigration. I went into the main office of jet aviation and I filled in the necessary forms, whilst someone took my passport away to be stamped.

After an hour my passport had not been returned. After two hours I started to ask questions.

"Do I have a problem with immigration, sir? All my paperwork's in order isn't it?"

"Yes, sir, it is".

So, what's the problem?

"Immigration want a paper copy of your flight clearances".

"I haven't got one" I said, and one of the guys at Jet Aviation popped up and said *"you don't need one we haven't had a paper copy in 25 years I don't know what's going on".*

Seven hours went by, very slowly. When it came to 12.30 at night, I said: "Forget the hotel. I'll stop here. I want to get away at 6am."

And then they said that I couldn't go to a hotel until this issue was sorted out.

They ordered me a McDonalds and I stopped in the crew quarters at jet aviation for the night. I still did not have my passport.

Day 22, May 20th - Saudi Hospitality - A Reality Check

After the night in the crew room I was awake at 4.30 am to get ready for my flight to Riyadh. I went into the Fight Ops room to see if my passport had arrived.

"No, not yet sir".

So what is the problem, I asked again.

"Still immigration, sir".

I kept going back and still nothing. I went back again at 6.30am, then at 7.30am and one more time at 10.30am.

"Can somebody please tell me what's going on?"

After a few phone calls to the British Embassy in Riyadh and a couple friends there, I got a response that it was one person in Immigration that had not been there that long and didn't understand that there were no paper copies. Even the Airport management and Flight Operations got involved. They wanted to know why I was still here. Everybody at the whole airport seemed genuinely upset by the situation with immigration. But this guy had now to get in touch with the Chief of Immigration in Riyadh but nobody was able to get hold of him.

I finally got my passport back, stamped ready to go, but it was now 3.15pm and I didn't have enough time to fly on to Riyadh.

"Now, can you get me a hotel, please?"

"Yes, no problem."

Jet Aviation kept saying *"We are really sorry about this, it hasn't happened in 25 years"*.

Don't worry I said, it's not your fault; you are all trying your best. Then they had to get clearance from immigration to take me to a hotel!

"I'll tell you what, forget it, I'll stop in the crew quarters again". I said

Then I spoke to the guy who was working the night shift and I filed my flight plan ready for the flight to Riyadh to make sure everything was fine with it.

After that I went back into the crew room. I had a pizza, coffee and a can of coke brought in as you cannot have Alcohol in Saudi. Then I did some typing to my blog and went to bed knowing that I would be departing to Riyadh the following morning. I never saw Jeddah city at all which was a real shame.

Day 23, May 21st - Jeddah to Riyadh

My alarm went off at 4.30am as I needed to get away early to avoid the thermals of the desert now that I finally had my passport back all stamped up. So flight plan filed, I was taken to my Quik where the fuel bowser was brought over to fill my aircraft tank. It took 97lts of Avgas to fill - that's not bad for the previous 7 hour 30 min flight from Luxor.

Fuelled up and ready to depart, I had a photo session with the staff at Jet Aviation. Just before I got in I decided to throw my tent away in order to make a bit more room in my Quik, as I thought I was unlikely to need it. Now the heat was amazing. I was just dripping with sweat the temperature was 43°C (109°F) and it was only 6am. I got in to the Quik with the guys at Jet lending a hand whilst just shaking their heads and smiling at me.

Then I was pushed out onto the apron where I radioed into Jeddah ground frequency and got clearance to start my engine and when ready to taxi. Normally it takes about 10-15 minutes to warm the engine in the Quik, but when I turned on the ignition, the skydat said the oil temp was already 43 degrees - amazing!

I was cleared to taxi – in fact they got me to taxi all the way from the north apron parking down Bravo taxi way to Bravo 1 holding point which was at the very end of the 14,000ft runway.

I really didn't need all that runway but that's where they told me to go.

When I got there, I had to change to Jeddah tower frequency who asked me to line up on runway 34L

"G-CDVO, you are cleared for take-off, after take-off climb to 5,000ft and at your discretion turn onto heading and change to Radar on frequency 124.00"

I lined up and took off, looking at the huge airport and climbed to 5000ft then turned and headed through the desert towards Riyadh.

The first 3 hours were absolutely stunning, flat calm conditions, visibility good for a change and as time went on the desert colours kept changing from a darker brown to a lighter brown. Not far into the journey, there were some small mountains poking out of the sand that rose up a couple of thousand ft - quite an amazing sight!

If anything went wrong with the Quik now I was truly on my own. The only thing that would be able to reach me here was a helicopter.

One of the highlights was seeing lots of camels running around in the desert and the Bedouin tents scattered around. I sat there thinking that when Brian Milton came here on his round the world trip he must have seen the same sights. How lucky I was to be one of the few pilots to fly a flexwing this far; and it was so nice and calm that I was able to enjoy it. I was even getting a bit emotional as I had been planning this trip for so long to see these sights, which were truly amazing.

There is a road that goes between Jeddah and Riyadh which stands out like a sore thumb, disappearing into the distance and with no sign of any traffic. I had been told that along the way there are fuel pumping stations and that there are also airfields for re-fuelling if need be although I couldn't see any. Apparently they look like your average service station but you could land on the road and taxi into the petrol station for fuel.

Five hours of stunning desert scenery were passing by me now, lots of Camels and sand Dunes.

As the desert started to really heat up, the thermals were kicking in and I could see small sand twisters around. I had started dodging them as much as I could, but I did end up getting thrown all over in a few that I just couldn't avoid which was just horrible. As you got close to the twisters, the air colour changed from light brown to dark brown and visibility deteriorated and it all happened really fast.

Six hours into the flight I was getting a bit bored, looking at nothing but sand, camels and sand twisters – well not really, how can anybody get bored with that? As I got closer to Riyadh the ATC changed me to Riyadh Approach and then as I got closer still across to the Tower frequency.

"*G-CDVO do you have airport in sight?*"

"*G-CDVO Erm not yet!*"

It was now very hazy with the sun. Suddenly, I could see it in the middle of the desert, it looked huge.

"*G-CDVO, affirm I now have airport in sight*"

"*G-CDVO you're number one to land on 34R*"

So I joined from the left and went past runway 34L and then turned onto to finals.

"*G-CDVO cleared to land on 34R*".

There is a 34L but that is the Royal runway and Royal Apron.

I landed without too much battling; it was just very rough with the heat of the desert throwing me around. This was something I was getting used now, along with crosswinds.

I taxied in behind a *Follow-Me* car who took me along the big maze of taxiways to the GA apron so I didn't get lost. Jet Aviation were the agents here, but I was also met by Shawkat, a good friend of Paul Chaplin, a Gyro pilot I had met in Rufforth earlier in the year. After being marshalled to a parking spot I got out of the Quik which we tied down on the apron in a parking spot between two small Lear type jets. I was not too bothered about the wind this time, but we anchored it to some rings concreted into the ground anyway.

I went to immigration which was only a short walk away to get my passport stamped, and met a guy called Dale Welham who works for the British Embassy in Riyadh, and who had helped sort out the problem I had with immigration in Jeddah.

Without a doubt this is the best flying day of the journey so far.

I was taken by Shawkat and Dale to a lovely apartment just down the road from the airport for the night. After a good wash getting the sand out of my ears and hair, I looked at the charts for the next day's flying, I was really glad that the apartment had air conditioning because it was so hot! Later Shawkat picked me up and we went to a steak house for a meal.

During the evening, Shawkat got a telephone call from a journalist who wanted to meet me. I agreed to meet with him and he came along to the steakhouse with a photographer from the *Arab News*. Later we went back to Shawkat's house for a coffee in his garden and I met his wife. Before returning to the digs, I ordered a taxi and went up for a nice sleep before my flight the next day.

Thank you, Shawkat and Dale for everything. It was much appreciated.

Day 24, May 22nd - Riyadh to Doha, Qatar

I was up at 4.30 again and a taxi took me to the airport. It was so warm 38℃ (100℉) even at 4.30 am. Wow! Once at the airport, I had to go and get my passport stamped and an exit visa put in, then onto the flight operations office to get fuel that I had ordered the previous day sorted out.

I said to the guys, *"Where's the fuel?"*

"We don't have any left, sir"

What! Yesterday I was told this would be fine. But I really needed some… after a few phone calls to the management, the reply came back *"There is no fuel, sir we have no Avgas left, and we cannot bring any onto the airport for you"*.

"Have you got any 95 octane like you said that you would supply instead?"

"No sir we have none of that left either"..

Great stuff!

After an hour of head scratching and more phone calls we came up with the solution of siphoning some 95 octane out of the airport trucks into jerry cans and filling me up that way. This was agreed, the trucks were brought over and they searched for some jerry cans.

We siphoned out of the trucks, fine, but to put the fuel in to my Quik meant holding the jerry cans over the top of the Auxiliary tank to siphon.

They came along with a conveyor belt machine that is used for loading suitcases and luggage on to aeroplanes, which they used as a platform over the top to siphon the fuel down.

It looked hilarious I couldn't stop laughing there were about 6 men involved in refuelling my little Quik, parked up next all these million dollar jets.

It took 100 litres to fill. Once that was done I went in to pay all my navigation, landing fees and handling agent fees.

The cheeky buggers charged me the same price for the fuel drained out of the trucks that I would have paid for Avgas! It was then time to file the flight plan, so after finding out the best way to go with ATC it was filed.

This was quite a complicated route as I had to get a clearance to overfly Bahrain's airspace as well in to Doha Qatar. So I filed it for 5,000 ft which was the lowest altitude I was allowed to fly at to Doha. Then I finally got back out to my Quik and got loaded up ready to go, with my charts all prepared and all the frequencies I would need for this flight ready on my map boards. Then into the Quik again I went with my wheelchair. By now it was really heating up, 43°C and sweat was ju st dripping off me.

This day I would be flying in my t-shirt, no jackets or anything. My jackets were now packed up where my tent had been stowed in the Quik

I finally gave ATC Ground a call on the radio for engine start and taxi. Once again the engine oil temperature was already at 43°C before I'd even started the engine! I was given clearance to taxi out the short distance to the holding point Bravo and change to the Tower frequency

"G-CDVO at holding bravo 1"

"G-CDVO, line up 34R"

I lined up and put my trimmer on, or at least, I tried to. Nothing again, the trimmer had bust again, but at least this time it was stuck off.

I was cleared to take off, and turn on to the heading to my first reporting point on the flight plan called ETBAS which 20 miles out, at my discretion after take-off.

I knew I was in trouble, fully loaded with fuel, 43°C, no trim and a Quik wing - this was going to take some getting off the ground!

I put on full power and I was right, it seemed to take forever to get off the ground, plus the climb rate was very much reduced. On top of this, it was already rough with the heat as I climbed to 5,000ft, getting thrown all over. I tried to get the trimmer working flicking the switch on and off, sticking my fingers underneath the dash board messing with the wiring – but still nothing - this was going to be dammed hard work! In the thermals, trimmed off, with a passenger on board the Quik is awful and with the fuel taking the place of the passenger it was just the same – it was better when it was trimmed to take off. I was pushing the bar out to slow it down, dammed hard work and getting thrown all over in the heat

After an hour of being battered around the sky, the visibility started to deteriorate with the sand in the desert blowing around. I began to dodge the sand twisters that were whipping up everywhere. I could hear interference on the radio and then lost contact with ATC altogether.

Now it was just sand all around. There were no roads to follow, absolutely nothing, the visibility quickly started going really dark brown and getting really rough. I began looking for somewhere to put down, because this was not getting good. I turned back around to have a look behind me to see if I could go back but it had closed in behind with a big sandstorm. Shit! All I could do was carry on, looking for a road or some kind shelter to put down on. Still at 5,000ft the ground disappeared, when I couldn't see the ground below, I dropped lower but when I was at 1,000ft (according to my Altimeter, sat nav and transponder) there was still no ground in sight at all so I climbed back up in case I flew into something that I didn't know like power lines or a mast.

By now it all looked the same. The sky was brown above and in front. I now had absolutely no visibility in front, to the left, right or below. It just got worse. And now I was getting covered in sand. The sand covered my visor and windscreen so much that I couldn't see forward. I lifted the helmet visor and got sand blasted in my face. I was really scared now. I had absolutely nowhere to go. It was obvious I could not go down because of the risk of crashing into the desert.

The only thing to do was to climb and climb, but I had no artificial horizon.

What do you do? I thought this is game over.

Keep calm Dave, you're not going to die just keep calm and I will pull though this!

I climbed up with zero visibility.

But there was a very slight difference in the sky's colour above. All I could do was fly looking either way up at my wing to where the wires go in half way down the leading edges. I kept looking from side to side, keeping them level, measured again the two different colours of the sky above and the sand storm - I was now deep in a terrible storm.

There were two hours of flying like that, with no proper radio contact. Crapping 'em, I was! Eventually I thought I would try giving a call out to any airliners on the frequency, to relay a message for me letting Dhahran know that I was fine (!). An American guy flying a Canadian airliner relayed a message through for me. As it happened, ATC in Dhahran had been trying to call me and were worried for me as they knew about the sandstorm. Another two hours later, and after getting really disorientated a couple of times I managed to get in contact with Dhahran and they found me on their radar screens. They told me to climb, so I did until it started brightening up. I was now at 6,000 ft but I still couldn't see the ground. As I got closer to Bahrain I watched the sand storm disappear behind me, and the ground came back into view.

Talk about crapping 'em!

As I went out past Bahrain and with the sandstorm well behind me, I noticed the ground speed really pick up until I was heading to Doha at 125mph. Then I couldn't believe it the transponder went off again.

After messing around, turning it on and off, they finally got me back on their radar before changing me over to Doha Airport frequency.

I was instructed to join downwind at 1,000ft then report turning finals. As I came down I was so glad the trimmer wasn't working, so I could keep speed on as I came in with the now strong wind.

It was a very busy airport, Qatar jets were queuing for take-off down the taxiway, waiting for me to land. After landing I spotted the Follow-Me car that was waiting for me and it was still blowing an absolute gale. Where I was told to park seemed worse! I was holding on to the bar now, trying to stop the Quik getting blown away and I spotted a hangar door which was open.

"*I want to put my Quik in there out of the wind*"

"*You can't do that, that's the Royal hangar!*"

Oh ok what about the hangar next to it then..

"*You can't put it in there neither that's Qatar Executives Hangar*"

'*Can you ask them if I can please mate, I'm knackered*' I said

He made a phone call and the response was yes, bring it over. I was covered from head to foot in sand, and so was the Quik, and whatever their objections I managed to get it in out of the wind.

That has got to be one of the worst flying days to date, really scary.

I just sat there in the Quik for a few minutes in peace, before starting all over again and getting the wheelchair together,

I was picked up by the usual bus that all main airports seem to send and was taken over to Passport Control and Immigration to get my passport and Entry Visa stamp. Then it was off to a very nice 5 star hotel for the night. I was so glad that day was over.

That's a day I will never forget as long as I live!

Day 25, May 23rd - Doha to Abu Dhabi (Part One)

I thought I would get up a bit later this morning, as was only a 193-mile hop over the water today to Abu Dhabi. I went to the airport and was met in the Departure Lounge by Tom Chatfield, Head of the Technical Dept. at Qatar Exec Airlines, and also Sigrid, Head of PR for Qatar. We had a coffee and a chat before I had to go back through Passport Control to get my passport stamped with my Exit Visa before filing my flight plan for Abu Dhabi.

I was picked up by a bus once again and then taken to the Qatar Exec Hangar, next to the Royal Hangar. I had a chat about my Quik with the staff at Qatar Exec and had a few photos taken, then I loaded up and got into my aircraft with them intrigued how my wheelchair pulled to pieces and went on to my Quik. This was done inside the huge hangar and they then pushed me outside into the wind.

I said my farewells and gave the Tower a call.

"G-CDVO ready for engine start and taxi"

"Erm, G-CDVO, call me back in ten minutes as we extremely busy at the moment and have 10 aircraft waiting to depart"

"No problem, G-VO"

I sat and watched 10 Qatari jets take off. What a busy place it is.

Then I gave them a call: *"G-CDVO ready for engine start-up"*

"Approved, G-CDVO"

"G-CDVO, request taxi to Papa for intersection departure"

"G-CDVO approved taxi Papa. Holding Short"

"G-VO Papa Hold Short"

"G-CDVO after the 767 lands and departs Charley line up runway 34"

"G-VO lined up 34"

"G-VO cleared for take-off, wind 320 degrees, 14knts, climb to1500ft, turn right straight away"

I took off and turned right straight over the top of the airport, and flew over the new Doha airport they are building. This is huge and it looks amazing. Apparently it is costing more than $200 billion.

"G-CDVO Doha"

"G-CDVO"

"G-VO we have lost you on radar, can you recycle your transponder"

"Recycling transponder G-CDVO"

Not again, no, no, no. I am really sick of this now.

"Doha, G-CDVO, do you have me yet?"

"G-CDVO, negative. Be advised Abu Dhabi will not accept you without a serviceable transponder"

I turned my transponder on and off, on and off. It wasn't working at all now. Then the call was made to me

"G-CDVO, return to Doha".

'G-CDVO RETURNING TO DOHA'

It looked like I had been sold a dodgy transponder. I was not happy at all, this trip was just eating up funds that should not be happening. Because they couldn't see me on radar now, I flew back in at 500ft, landed, and taxied back to the Qatar Exec Hangar. They came out to see what was wrong and I asked

"Would you mind if I put it back in your hangar until I sort the problem out?"

"No, be our guest no problem..."

After lots of phone calls from Qatar Executive to see what I could do with the broken transponder, I soon realized that nothing would be happening with it that day. So I had to get the bus sent back around to pick me up and take me back to Passport and Immigration to get my entry Visa stamped once again and then take me back to a hotel. The bus turned up and I went back through the Terminal and Passport Control to an awaiting taxi that took me back to the hotel.

Better luck tomorrow.

Day 26, May 24th - Static in Doha

I went to the airport to get my transponder sorted out, with the help of the staff at Qatar Executive, Tom Chatfield and Michael Lindgren. And the top man who was assigned to me for as much help as I needed Qatar Avionics expert Srinivas Reddy.

We spent all day testing out the transponder and the wiring, only to come to the conclusion that the unit had a software problem. Where can I get another transponder here in Doha? The phone was abused for a few hours and one of the staff went across the airport to try get something sorted out at an aviation club. But absolutely nothing!

I said *"Stuff it, I have had enough of this, I'm going have one sent over from the UK and at least I know it will work"*. I would just have to get all the flight clearances re-applied for by White Rose Aviation, and sit it out for a couple of days until DHL could it there. So then it was back on the bus and back to Passport Control to have my passport stamped once again.

For security reasons, the only way I could get to my aircraft in order to do repairs was to sign out through Passport Control and get the bus out to the hangar.

Later that evening I was very kindly invited out for an evening with Tom, his wife and son. *"Yes, I would love to, Tom thank you very much."*

Tom collected me from the hotel at 5pm and we went into the local area, along with three of the Bombardier technical support team from around the world who were here to support aircraft at Qatar Exec. We then went to a local Qatari bread shop in a Bazaar with an original clay oven where Tom's wife and son met us, before heading off to an Iraqi restaurant for some well recommended kebabs and a good feeding. Later it was a lift back then to my hotel for some alcoholic refreshments, as I drowned my sorrows thinking would I ever get to Sydney?

Day 27, May 25th - Static in Doha

There was not much to say about this day. I went to the Airport, got signed in went to the hangar and decided to rewired my broken headset with Srinivas, the avionics expert, I had to drill a hole in the side of the headset then put another wire over the top headband between both sides.

Once that was done I made a quick phone call to L.X Avionics back in the UK who was sending me a new transponder out to see if it was on its way.

This had been sent by DHL on an urgent delivery. Later I got the bus back to the Terminal where I had my passport stamped and was presented with a $2000 bill for landing fees and navigation fees and they also tried charging me for parking my Quik in the Qatar Exec Hangar.

So I told the management at Qatar Exec and they went mad

"Don't worry Dave we'll get that lot sorted out for you, nobody charges for parking in our hangar either."

After that, I went back to the hotel to catch up on the Blog and sulk again.

Doha Airport

Day 28, May 26th - Still static in Doha

Day 28, May 26th - Still static in Doha

I checked the internet to track the delivery my new transponder with DHL. ACE stuff! It was now in Qatar but more importantly it was at the airport. I went down to reception in the hotel and asked for a taxi so I could go to the Airport and get the Quik sorted out.

"Taxi please, to the airport"

"No problem Captain David"

When I got to the Airport it was really busy, so I met a guy from a ground handling agents who managed to get me rushed through and fast-tracked back through customs, where I got my exit visa stamped again, then the bus arrived and took me once again to the Qatar Exec Hangar. I went straight into the offices to see where my transponder was, *"It's not here yet Dave"* was the reply. There was a problem with import duties. Tim said, don't worry, I'll have it here before 12pm.

Oh! Thought it might have turned up before that....but anyway.

They wanted to charge me import duty on the transponder. We said, hang on a minute, you can't charge that because the part is coming airside. It is not strictly entering the country. Also, it is being fitted to a UK-registered aircraft which is also airside, and will be returning to the UK. Tim told them all this and the part was released. He went over to pick it up for me.

"Hurray, it's now arrived"

I opened it up the package and there was no 15 pin wiring plug with it!

"Oh well, never mind, I'll use the old one."

I took the 15-pin plug off the old transponder to fit it and to my amazement; one of the pins was knackered! What was I going do now?

I'm was not sending back to the UK and waiting another few days.

"Srinivas, do you have a spare 15 pin plug anywhere?"

He just sat there and laughed. *"No, Dave, we don't use them. We use 9-pin and 25-pin only. You won't get a 15-pin plug anywhere today"*.

No, no, no, not another problem!

"Right, Srinivas, do you have a one-eighth drill bit and a small connector for just one pin?"

He said *"Yes, why?"*

I am going to drill out the one damaged pin; he laughed shaking his head at me you have no chance he said.

That was it I set about it like a micro surgeon and managed to drill out the damaged pin on the 15-pin plug and inserted a new one with a new wire. It really was like doing micro surgery. I fitted it, Srinivas got some fancy box of gizmos, we linked it up to the Quik and tested it out - the transponder was working perfectly. Hurrah! So a big thanks to L.X Avionics back in the UK for sending that out so quickly.

The only trouble was, it was now 5.30pm and there was no way I could get to Abu Dhabi today. But at least I was fuelled up and transponder fitted and working for tomorrow.

Back to the hotel then and get ready for the flight Abu Dhabi. First, back on the bus to Passport Control to get my visa cancelled again, by now the passport staff were asking questions about why I was going in and out and not flying anywhere.

But I managed to convince them that it was the last time I would most certainly be leaving the country to the UAE tomorrow. I had a beer or two and something to eat in the hotel bar and then went to bed early.

Day 29, May 27th - Doha to Abu Dhabi

I got up really early at 4am so I could get away on time; I had been there too long! The hotel taxi took me to the airport and I went straight through Passport Control, had my visa stamped and then I filed my flight plan to Abu Dhabi El Bateen OMAD airport. I got on the bus which took me to the Qatar Exec hangar for the last time.

I loaded up my Quik, ready for the off, fuelled-up, new transponder fitted and working and headset repaired. It was quite windy outside. I got into the Quik inside the hangar and the agent pushed me outside.

"G-CDVO request engine start please"

"G-VO engine start approved"

I started up. Once again, the engine oil temp was already at 43degrees.

"G-VO request taxi"

"G-VO taxi Papa, Hotel to Hotel1"

"G-VO request taxi to Papa for an intersection take off"

"Erm! G-CDVO approved, hold short Papa"

I was waiting for further instruction when a big Qatar jet airliner went past me. I had my wing tied to the front strut, slightly down and into wind, because it was easier to taxi that way in a strong wind. I watched in horror as the airliner turned its back to me, four big jet engines facing me. In a mad panic, I frantically undid the bar from the front strut. I had just got it when the blast from the jets hit me, and started to pin the wing down to the ground.

Then ATC said "G-CDVO Line up, 34"

I went straight out of the jet blast and onto the runway as fast I could. I thought "you prat" - well actually what I said was a bit stronger than that!

That could have been it, blown away like that Citroen 2CV on Top Gear with Jeremy Clarkson.

Anyway I was cleared for take-off and to turn right onto my heading, straight over the brand new Doha airport that was being built next door and then out to sea. This leg would be just 193 miles, but over water all the way to Abu Dhabi

ATC were very good on this flight, checking that everything was OK which made me feel a lot happier compared with what had been happening over the last few days.

I was flying along happily at 3,000ft, and I came across the oil rigs of the Middle East scattered everywhere over the Arabian Gulf, some were so big that they had three helipads and were linked together by bridges. There were huge sand banks with runways built in them from one end to the other. I started relaxing now the transponder was working and the headset was fine as well.

My back ache wasn't that bad today and my bum wasn't as numb has it had been. This was truly a hands-off flight. I was even able to take my sandwiches out and bottles of water from my in-flight meal without worrying about them going through the propeller, which is quite an art in a Quik doing 75 mph.

The coast line of Abu Dhabi came into view and looked amazing, with high rise buildings all along the sea front with the beautiful blue sea glistening.

ATC just seemed to be more relaxed and more helpful and as I changed over to Abu Dhabi Approach they were friendly and said "good afternoon G-CDVO are you having a nice flight, please continue on your approach and report joining downwind left hand circuit"

So I reported joining downwind which meant me flying over the city.

I flew straight over the city at just 1,500ft, looking down at the streets and towering buildings below that seemed within touching distance. In the UK this just wouldn't be allowed!

At the end of the runway was a huge white Mosque, its domes standing out like a sore thumb, apparently this was called Sheikh-Zayed Mosque. I turned onto the base leg just looking at the Mosque thinking how much that it must have cost to build it was so big.

I called finals to land. The guy in the Tower said *"You are cleared to land G-CDVO wind 15knts"* so just another windy landing again.

Once down I taxied in to an awaiting marshal waiving his table tennis bats at me and then the duty Airport Manager and another official for ABAC (United Arab CAA) came to welcome me to El Bateen Airport and Abu Dhabi. After a brief chat with them, Dave Lynch a friend of mine who had moved out here from York a couple of years ago was allowed to come on to the Apron to see me. We talked for a while longer. Then I asked if it was possible to put my Quik in a hangar out of the sun and wind, he said *"I will ask but the only hangars available belong to the military"*. Then his phone rang to let us know the military had allowed me to put my Quik in one of their hangars.

I put my helmet back on and taxied down the apron past a few military helicopters to a hangar where another marshal was waving his arms at me. I taxied straight in to the hangar and turned around so I was facing the doors. I parked next to what looked like an old Boeing Stearman biplane, but wasn't. A bus came to collect me and take me to Arrivals to get my passport stamped and Entry Visa stamp put in. El Bateen Airport is reserved for private jets and the military now that they have a new airport. The airport building is something else – the inside is covered in gold and marble, with huge chandeliers all over. While I was waiting for my passport to come back we were taken in to the Presidential Suite for a look around – usually reserved for prime ministers and Royals - and now myself and Dave Lynch had been added to the list!

Cups of coffee were brought to us - anybody would have thought that we were royalty! It was very nice of them they were so nice and helpful. Apparently Hillary Clinton had been in the same room only the week before. My passport came back so I went to get my bags and put them through the security x-ray machine. To my amazement, the headset that I had repaired twice got tangled up in the rollers on the way out! I couldn't believe it. You couldn't write a script about things going wrong like this.

"Don't yank on the wire like that or you will break them, hang on!"

It was well and truly jammed in!

We had to dismantle the end of the x-ray machine to get the headset wire out, and yes it was damaged, but by how much? Dave Lynch offered to go back down to the Quik and test it out for me. I was just sat there shaking my head thinking *"this could only happen to me!"* Dave came back from the hangar all smiles *"its OK Dave it still works"* well thank God for that.

Right, can we go please before something else goes wrong?

We went outside to where Dave had parked, underneath a canopy covered in marble and gold again and in front of a huge marble fountain, it was really classy.

Then we had a nice drive through Abu Dhabi up to Dubai where Dave had kindly booked a hotel for me. But before going there we went sight-seeing. When in Dubai you have to go and have look at the tallest building in the world the Burj Khaliffa, and the only 7-star hotel in the world the Burj Al Arab. Dubai is an amazing place, with towering skyscrapers and hotels some of which had 100 floors!. They were awesome. The famous Palm is nice but not what you would expect when you drive on it. Really it was a lot like a housing development with a massive hotel perched at the end. We then went to Dave's house to collect his wife Hailey and daughter, before we had food and a beer watching the fountain display at the Burj Khaliffa the world's tallest building as darkness fell. By the time that finished it was decided that it would be waste of money going to stop in the hotel so I ended up stopping at Dave and Hailey's house. So a big *'thank you'* to Dave Lynch and Hailey for putting up with me.

73

Abu Dhabi

Day 30, May 28th - Abu Dhabi – Muscat (or not, as the case may be)

After a wonderful night out in Dubai with Dave Lynch and Hailey and their daughter Sophie, I got up at 7am with everything in hand. Dave drove the one hour from Dubai to El Bateen Airport in Abu Dhabi, and we managed to get him a pass through Passport Control which allowed him to come airside and help me get loaded up before departure.

While we were waiting in the Presidential Suite in the Airport, I asked about agent fees and landing fees. Was there any chance of scrubbing them as I was doing the flight for a charity? After a few phone calls to the agent's bosses, it was agreed to scrub the agent's fees but the airport charges still stood. That was that, so time to go to the Quik. I had my visa stamped and cleared with Immigration and then the bus turned up and took us to hangar 27.

"Ok guys, can I get fuelled-up now then please?"

"Yes, sir, would you like Avgas or 95 Mogas".

"95 Mogas would be great, thank you very much".

And off they went to get it sorted for me.

After a while I said *"where is the fuel? I have to get off."*

"Soon, sir, soon".

Then they came back and said *"Sorry, sir, we have no 95 Mogas".*

"OK then, get me Avgas".

"Sorry sir, no Avgas, only Jet A1".

"You have had me sat here for nearly three hours, telling me that you have 95 Mogas and Avgas 100LL. Now you say you have neither! My flight plan is now due and I have no fuel. I need fuel; this was ordered a long time ago."

"Sorry sir, we don't have any" then the agent said *"The only way to get the fuel you want is to go to the petrol station and fill some jerry cans".*

"OK, let's do that, can we?"

"We don't have any jerry cans, sir".

So after a lot of searching around the airport, a cleaner turned up with a few plastic cans.

"Excellent, let's go".

Dave Lynch and an airport official from the agency went off to the petrol station while I sat around programming my GPS and looking at my clock. They came back with 80 litres of 95 octane fuel costing 183 AEDs (£30), but then the security guard wouldn't let them through on to airport!

"You can't bring fuel onto the airport," he said, *"and your friend can't come airside either."*

"You have just sent us to the garage for fuel. What are you all playing at?"

A guy turned up with a trailer saying *"You can only buy Avgas from here".*

Now I am really mad. Get me the Manager of this Airport now! The Manager turned up.

"What problem, what problem? You can have Avgas here, not 95 brought onto the Airport".

"First you told me that I can have 95 Mogas fuel or Avgas 100LL, then you said you have none, so we went to the garage with your staff, and now I can't bring the fuel onto the airport. Then the Avgas trailer turns up. Does anybody know what's going on here? It is now too late to fly to Muscat. All my permissions have expired and will need applying for again. This is due to your incompetent staff. I have 80 litres of fuel sat outside in a car that could explode due to the heat and I want it inside here in my aircraft. Come and look at my engine."

On the strut near the tank filler cap there is a sticker that says, recommended fuel 95+ octane.

"I want that in, not Avgas now."

Eventually he backed down and said *"I will have to get the fire department to come and cover the fuelling".*

"I had better not be charged for it".

"No charge, no charge".

Ten minutes later the big airport fire tender turned up with seven fire-fighters who were more interested in my Quik than fire regulations. They got the biggest fuel pump I had ever seen out and tried putting it in my fuel tank filler, but it was too big then two of them went off and couldn't find an electric socket to plug it into.

It was like watching a comedy program.

"Why can't you just pour it to the tank?" it won't take that long and it won't need all 7 of you to do that?"

They agreed, but then said they needed to go and find a funnel and two of them wandered off while I sat there fuming at the carry on. Eventually I couldn't wait for them anymore so I cut up a water bottle to use as a funnel and got 3 of them to start filling my Quik up, they poured in 80 litres of 95 Mogas.

Finally Job done, so then it was back through Customs to get my visa stamp cancelled and back out to Dave Lynch who was still hanging around for me. Amazing to be in a country that produces so much petrol, yet it then took me seven hours to get 80 litres from them.

I was getting sick of everything going wrong. I had bruises all over my arms and they were aching all the time and my back was killing me! I could only hope that it would be tomorrow. So I had another night at Dave Lynch's house in Dubai.

Duty Manager El Bateen airport Abu Dhabi

Day 31, May 29th - Abu Dhabi to Muscat (Nearly Abandoned the Flight)

I was up really early at 4am. I wanted to beat the thermals, because I had 10,000ft of mountains to cross going into Muscat, and Dave had to go somewhere as well. We got to the Airport for about 6am, fuelled-up , ready to go, and flight plan in hand...but no handling agent yet.

The security guard on the main desk made a phone call and after a short wait the agent arrived, all smiles - this looked to be promising - and said "Passport, and I will get immigration for you". Excellent!

At this rate I should be away for 7am.

Immigration turned up and stamped my passport.

"Can I go to my aircraft now?"

"No sir, my boss needs to see you first".

"OK, fine, can you go get him please".

He makes a phone call and tells me the boss will be here in five minutes.

I wait and I wait and I keep saying *"Where is your boss? I have to go!"*

"Just wait, Captain he will be here shortly".

I am brooding, I have to go, and I have 10,000ft of mountains to go over before it gets too dangerous. After an hour of asking there was still nothing happening and I was getting really mad. It got to 9am and I had to say, *"Will you lot please let me out of here as you are now putting my life in danger because of the mountains I have to cross".*

I started to force my way out to the apron to my Quik but was stopped by security.

"You cannot go, Captain".

"Well get your f###ng boss down here now then!"

I was thinking, you are all seriously putting life in danger you don't understand the mountains will kill if I'm not away from here soon.

At 9.30am his boss, manager of the Airport, turns up all smiles, and says *"Has everything been OK for you captain? We have scrubbed all the charges and handling fees for you at our Airport and may I say how privileged we are to have you here. Also I would like to invite you to attend our Air Show in January next year, all expenses paid to get you here and fly, Captain".*

Well, what do you say to that? I was not to know how close this decision to go later in the day, came to killing me. I said, thank you and was very pleasant with him.

"Can I go now, please?"

"Of course captain, can I have a picture with you".

So the bus came and I went out to the hangar and got in my Quik in record time cursing and swearing under my breath, had a photo session with everybody and then finally set off. The wind had changed direction from when I had landed previously, so I took off directly towards the great Mosque and out over Abu Dhabi. As I climbed out over Abu Dhabi the views were fantastic.

The temperature was now 38°C (100°F) and getting wa rmer. I remember thinking; this is going to be one rocky ride to Muscat.

I flew out of Abu Dhabi air space and was transferred on Abu Radar. They kept me safe around the International Airport which was only a few miles away and the flying was fine for a while, rough, but nothing too frightening. Then I came across some small mountains. It was windy and thermic and cloud was building over the tops of them, I looked and thought if I go for it now over the top, with the cloud being so low I would get trapped in the valleys, so I decided to run along the ridge of one of the mountains before daring to turn and cross them.

I turned in at 6,500ft, just underneath the cloud that was building, and it happened – Bang! Bang! Bang! - all over the sky, as I had feared. As the mountains rose up in front of me so did the clouds, the air now rough was shaking not just the aircraft around, but me as well. I started to think about my own sanity in being there. What was I doing? I must be absolutely crackers. Why couldn't I just have stuck to a nice 15-minute trip to Breighton now and again!

I could see big Cumulous building on my track, getting dark and it looked to be getting worse.

After about an hour of being severely beaten around the sky, with the bar being pulled out of my hands, it started to rain. These were not normal rain drops like we have in England, but very big and painful rain. I was only flying in my t-shirt as it was so hot. I managed to fly through that OK, and headed towards the 10,000ft mountains which I had to cross to get to Muscat. More cloud was building all around, now with CuNims (Cumulous nimbus or thunderstorms) and I could hear the electrical interference over the radio.

I was at 8,000ft and not at all happy. If I been here three hours earlier like I wanted this might not be happening.

But I am here, so deal with it!

After twenty more minutes of being battered around the sky I just couldn't handle it any more. *"That's it, I'm putting down, I don't care, I don't want to die"*.

With tears in my eyes like a baby I started looking for somewhere to land. This was not easy given the terrain I was flying over. I could see a small town in the distance so headed to that and flew around it looking for somewhere safe to land. I found a road that looked ok but then saw that it had lampposts all along the side of it, so that was no good. I found another one that might be big enough but this was a dirt road. I flew over it to see what it was like and then came down lower to have a closer look but as I got down to about 100ft I saw there wasn't a chance of me getting down without crashing as the turbulence was far too rough. I felt I was close to being inverted.

So I powered back on before hitting the ground and climbed back up.

Now the waterworks really wanted to have a good go.

I was saying to myself, stop this, you'll be fine, just don't do anything stupid and remember what you were taught when learning to fly.

Then I heard my call sign get called by an airliner Muscat who relayed a message to me to say the weather was 6km visibility. OK, I reasoned, I will climb back up and have another look. No, it doesn't look like it from here – it was still black and raining in front. So I decided to make a detour further south, but that meant going higher. So I climbed to 9,500ft and feeling quite sick now with what could actually happen to me in these mountains I went for it.

It was like being in a washing machine on fast spin. All of a sudden I got hit in the face with high winds. I was going up at 2,000ft/min with no power, and the bar into my chest getting pulled towards the CuNims. Shouting at them "NO YOU'RE NOT HAVING ME". There was nothing for it but to put the Quik into a spiral dive at 45-60 degrees and try get down that way. I managed to lose 500 ft, all the time telling myself, I can't cope with this anymore, crap weather all the time, everything breaking on me.

When I get to Muscat I'm throwing in the towel and going home.

I'd had enough!

I finally got through the mountains with the diversion south and gave Muscat a call on the radio. They sounded pleased to hear my voice as I was late arriving and they were worried for my well-being.

I was routed out to sea for a few minutes of orbiting before they gave me clearance to land. I taxied in behind a Follow-Me car, absolutely drained of energy, still a bit wet, to the waiting marshals and around twenty to thirty of the staff at Oman Oil and Oman Air. There were lots of them all clapping and taking photos, they gave me flowers and said anything I needed would be mine, and what a privilege it was for them to have me fly in. They even filled my fuel tanks with Avgas for free. After the photos with Oman Oil on the apron I was whisked through Immigration like a film star (it had never been so fast) to meet the boss of Oman Air where I had a few photos taken with him and other Oman Air staff.

Then I went outside, with all the people in the airport looking and pointing at me. I really did feel quite special at that point.

Outside I met Ian Ord who had sorted all this out for me – Cheers, Ian - who took me to a very nice hotel that Oman Air had very kindly also offered to pay for! At 7pm Ian and his wife came to the hotel for a meal with me and brought along Chris Sowerby and a French guy whose I completely forgot! We had a really good night. Later after Ian had gone home, I went down into a Philippine bar with Chris and had a few beers watching karaoke and laughing at how bad some of the singers were!

All the horrible events of that day's flight were washed away and I was ready for tomorrow. A big thank you to everybody at Oman Air and Oman Oils for everything - you made my day! And also a big thanks to Ian for organising it all for me and Chris for the night of entertainment. It was much appreciated.

I was now ready to carry on!

Oman Oil staff

Day 32, May 30th - Muscat to Gwadar

The previous evening had revitalised me to continue with my trip.

I must carry on now!

I was up at 5.30am and Ian picked me up around 7.30am. We went back to Muscat International where staff from Oman Air had a parking place waiting for me at Arrivals. I jumped into a chair with a number of on-lookers and was presented with another bunch of lovely flowers by a very beautiful lady from Oman Air. I was then fast-tracked through the network of Customs and paperwork to my Quik.

Fantastic! I was through in 10 minutes.

At my aircraft I was surrounded by the staff of Oman Air and Oman Oil. A few more pics and I was ready to go.

So I did a super fast strip of my wheelchair and packed it on to my Quik before making a call on the radio to Oman Ground.

"G-CDVO requesting engine start please".

"Engine start approved G-VO"

After just a few minutes while I waited for the oil to get up to temperature, I gave them another call.

"Request taxi, G-CDVO"

"G-VO taxi Runway 24"

A Follow-Me car then escorted me to Holding Point 4 for Runway 24.

While I was sat waiting for a jet to come into land, a Boeing 637 taxied right up behind me and waited (I have the pictures).

I was cleared to line-up and take off. Once off the ground, I was to change to Muscat Approach on 121.20.

The first hour was wonderful, 85 miles out to sea in the smoothest of air hardly touching the bar as I flew across the mouth of the Persian Gulf, heading for Gwadar in eastern Pakistan, close to the border with Iran.

Looking at nothing but blue sea in all directions and thinking how nice and peaceful it was.

Then ATC called: "*G-CDVO Muscat?*"

"*G-CDVO, Muscat*"

"*G-CDVO, Iran have changed their minds. Your flight plan is now void, you cannot carry on, you must turn back to Oman or you will be intercepted and shot down.'*

Oooooough!

I didn't actually fancy been shot down - though it would make a good news story.

I asked the ATC if they had a telephone to hand. Yes was his reply.

So I said to him "*Please would you give Tehran a ring and ask them which way I can go so I don't get shot down*".

"*G-CDVO OK, stand-by, I will get back to you*"

After about 10 minutes I reached a reporting point just short of a hundred miles out to sea and gave ATC a call back.

"*G-CDVO, have you had a reply from Tehran yet?*"

"*Yes G-VO, sorry sir yes, if you detour to ALPOR reporting point, they will accept you and you will not be intercepted.*"

Pheeeeeew!

That bit of quick thinking saved me getting shot down; I'll change my nappy later.

From then on it was a lovely flight right until I reached the Pakistan coast, about 10 miles east of the Iranian border.

I gave Gwadar Tower a call, nothing at all - have I got the right frequency?

So I tried again and again, then they came back to me and they gave me some vectors to come to the airport on, but it looked very murky over land. Then as I got closer, the wind started picking up. I came over land looking at the dusty runway cut into the desert. I joined down-wind to land and all of a sudden that was it, I couldn't believe it, I was in a sandstorm again! As I turned onto base, it was lifting me out of the seat and bouncing me all over however I could still see at the moment so I carried on and I turned for finals to land.

I got this over the radio:

"G-CDVO, clear to land, wind 25knts gusting 38knts".

Why me? What have I done to this world?

I was now on finals and the runway just disappeared out of my view with the sandstorm, I could see nothing but sand now, with the sand hitting me in the face and blasting my arms.

I trimmed the Quik off – yes, it was working for a change –then I fought my way through the sand and high winds, whilst holding the bar and keeping the Quik straight. All the way down it was a right handful, but I finally got down to the ground, although I'll never know whether it was luck or management.

Just after landing and as I was trying to taxi in this high wind, some kind of twister hit me. I was now holding on to the base bar for dear life. It was crazy wind pulling at the wing trying to tear it from the aircraft. Then the wind took me sideways right off the taxi way and put me into a ditch, the front wheel sinking and the back wheel lifting off the ground literally trying its best to turn me upside down in the trike.

I couldn't do anything except hold on.

The wing went down to the ground and the base-bar pinned me in my seat crushing on my ribs.

That was it, I couldn't move.

I was going over, I could feel it lifting and going over.......

I quickly turned the magnetos off, struggling as I was sat there waiting for the inevitable and the engine stopped. I managed to look at the control tower through the sand twister and call them on the Radio.

"G-CDVO I cannot move I am pinned in to my aircraft can you send help out please"

Within minutes the fire engine crew and awaiting staff appeared running from the dust and sand.

"Hold onto the wing or I'm going to get blown away!"

About twenty staff grabbed hold of the Quik and pushed me out of the ditch and then holding on to it where they could, they wing-walked me to the Control Tower out of the main wind to try shelter me, The boss came down from the Tower and after a quick chat it was agreed that it would be safer if I put the Quik into the Fire Department for the night. They pulled out the fire tender and to my amazement a group of staff and police physically picked up my Quik - with me in it - and carried it sideways into a parking bay under cover.

Some of the guys pulled the wheels from my wheelchair off the Quik while I put the body of it together.

I climbed out with a big audience filming me on their iPhones, while I tried to sweep as much of the sand off me and my Quik as I could. I was absolutely covered in the stuff and as quickly as possible I pulled the trike cover from underneath and covered the Quik up over the engine.

I had a look at the front wheel where I had gone in to the ditch and everything was fine with no damage sustained. Once we had made sure the Quik was safe and secure for the night I was thrown into the airport ambulance which took me to Arrivals in the Terminal Building.

The sandstorm was now whipping around quite violently and the Control Tower and Fire Station kept going in and out of view through the sand blowing around.

I watched the officials walking about chatting and looking at me.

"What's happening? Are there some papers I need to sign, is everything OK?"

"No sir, everything is Ok, we are just waiting for the police to come and check your passport, then we will take you to the hotel."

That sounded fine! I sat there sweeping sand off me (like a small snow drift on my lap) and scraping the sand out of my ears - so I sat and waited patiently.

A few more people came out to see the fool that had just landed in the high wind and sand. They were all smiling and pointing at me. In the UK everybody would just take the mickey and call you mad. Then one said

"Captain Dave, we are so privileged to have you here."

They genuinely meant it!

The Police turned up and gave me a bit of an interrogation but nothing too serious. Then he removed a rubber stamp from a carrier bag and stamped my passport and said there you go..

He didn't look the happiest person I had ever met I have to say.

I had a few papers more to fill in with my agent who had just driven (250 miles!) from Karachi to meet me. Then he said, OK, let's go!

Well! Everybody was so helpful. This was outstanding.

(This was Gwadar, the place that Brian Milton called 'the armpit of the world' when he flew through on his flight to Australia in 1987, and the Indian microlight pilot Vijay Singhania was charged $11/litre on his 1988 flight. Mind you, Osama Bin Laden has been through since.)

I went outside with seven of the agent's staff to get into my car to the hotel and I was met by about twenty security people all with guns, telling me that's my transport.

I climbed into the car they were pointing at and once I was in, the driver put up some glass shields to black the windows out. This was a bit strange, even though it was sunny.

Three guys got in with me and told me the glass shields were for my security and safety. They said there was some unrest in the area with it been so close to the Iran border and they didn't like foreigners - Brits.

We set off from the Airport then stopped about 5 minutes down the road where a 4x4 pick-up full of Security guards pulled in front. Sat in the back of the 4x4 were four armed guards with machine guns. I looked at the guys in the back of my car and they said: "*it's for your safety, captain.*"

It was unreal, the sort of thing you see on TV.

We were speeding through the streets like I was important and they were not going to stop for anyone.

Then we turned up a small back street, no tarmac, just rocks.

I thought, sh##, where are we going now?

We pulled up outside the back door of the hotel and waited as there was another truck with armed guards to come. They made way so I could get out of the car under cover before taking me into the hotel under armed escort.

You couldn't have dreamt this up. You only see it on TV. It doesn't happen to you.

I got taken to the room where I would be staying for the night and was told not to open the door to anybody as it wasn't safe. They told me that they would be just upstairs and would ring me if they were coming. Later the phone rang, it was one of the security guys who said he would be bringing me some food shortly and would knock three times.

Sure enough there were three knocks on the door, so I let him in. There was an armed guard stood right outside my door. I had some food and refreshments before being left alone, knowing that I should be safe with an armed guard outside my room all night.

Gwadar tower

Day 33, May 31st - Gwadar to Karachi, Pakistan

After little sleep, not due to the guard outside but because the hotel ran on generators, and twice during the night it ran out of fuel causing the A/C to go off.

I got up and the same thing happened as when I had arrived the previous evening.

I had to wait in the hotel room until the other armed guards arrived, before going back out to the same car as the previous day.

This time when I came out of the hotel there were a few Pakistani locals who were stood in front of the line of armed guards looking and chanting something at me.

I was whisked into the same car with the blacked-out windows and armed convoy through the locals and back to Gwadar International Airport. It was all a bit surreal really! Then I went back to see what my Quik looked like after the previous day.

We arrived at the Airport at around 8am

We had to wait for the airport staff to arrive; but in the meantime a fuel bowser arrived with an armed Army car (complete with cannon on the back) to escort it into the complex.

The wind had calmed a bit, it was only 20 knots now.

I went through Customs and then my bags were thoroughly checked which I can understand. I wouldn't want to take anything through like my mucky knickers.

But strangely, they let them go through. Once through that I went to the Fire Station to see how my aircraft was. It was completely covered in sand and dust, same as yesterday.

I brushed off what I could and even managed to get some oil spray to put on my air filters. Then the wonderful staff picked my Quik up and carried it outside of the Fire Station for me.

In front of a large audience I got into the Quik and put the wheelchair away ready to go and the agents came over and said *"we will see you later as we are your agents in Karachi"*

The guys were going to spend the next 18hours driving to meet me there - amazing!

So now I was all ready to go and still brushing the sand from myself and the dashboard of the Quik. I gave the Tower a call.

"G-CDVO - request engine start."

"Yes, no problem, engine start is approved, taxi to runway 24 down the right hand side, line up and wait."

So I started up. The vibration shook a lot of sand off the wing and it fluttered down over me covering me once again. I thought it will blow away when I take off no doubt. I let the engine warm up then I taxied out in the very windy and dusty airport.

"G-CDVO - lined up."

So I lined up holding on to the bar with a gorilla like grip.

"Cleared for take-off G-CDVO, wind 25knts, after take-off turn down the coast and change to Karachi Radar"

I took off towards the sea and headed out to the coast. As I turned south there was a small formation of rocks about 1,000ft tall right on the coast, so I made my way around them looking up at them and getting the wind rotor blowing over the top of them.

89

The sand around the coast was very pale and the rocks just looked like something that should be on the moon.

An hour passed by just following the coast line with very flat pale desert as far as the eye could see. Then the visibility started to deteriorate and it was getting cloudy so I went back closer to the land. After a while I could see that the ground was rising up into mountains then the air got rough once again, I was also going in and out of cloud. My flight plan took me all the way down the coast to Karachi - what a very beautiful landscape Pakistan has - before I was to turn out to sea before heading direct into Karachi airport *(The first man to make such a flight, Ross Smith in 1919, said it was the bleakest landscape in the world - BM)*.

About an hour before I turned direct to Karachi, the visibility deteriorated again, with mist and low cloud and I was bounced all over the sky. With no horizon I was working really hard to stay a VFR flight, the guy at ATC kept on saying: *"Are you maintaining 3,000ft or climbing?"*

"G-VO, I'm trying to maintain 3,000ft but it's very difficult with the low cloud"

So they changed my route and vectored me back to the coast and said: *"G-CDVO, follow the coast at 3,000ft until instructed otherwise"*

"G-CDVO, sorry, sir, but the cloud is at 2,000ft and I am VFR"

"G-VO no problem, just choose your own safe altitude"

"G-VO, it's looking like 1,800ft"

"G-VO approved advice of any change please"

I followed the coast and went over the top of a ship-scrapping beach. It looks like the ships just drive themselves up onto the beach, before being cut up for scrap. What a sight that was!

"G-CDVO do you have airport in sight"

"G-CDVO negative no airport in sight yet"

Then the ATC Controller instructed me to turn left and sent me straight over the top of Karachi city at 1,800ft. I got bounced from pillar to post, it was so rough and my ground speed was over 100mph so I knew it was windy.

Then he came back to me with

"G-CDVO report finals."

90

"G-CDVO, finals."

"G-CDVO, wind 27 knots, clear to land."

Here we go again. That's just less than 32 mph so this was going to be a very scary landing... I got it down luckily it wasn't gusting so it wasn't as bad as I thought it would be! Or am I just getting used to the high winds now?

Holding on to the bar again I taxied in but it was really slow as I was struggling to hold the wing on the ground.

I had one arm locked over the bar pulling it in to my chest and the other arm over the bar doing the steering, I could feel the bolts in the base bar pushing in to my skin now. I was sure there would be blood there when I stopped.

A marshal was waving his hands, indicating this way to him, I got to him and turned side on to the wind and he was telling me NO line up your aircraft this way.

No, I have to put my wing tip down to the wind so I can get out. I can't park into wind.

About 40 police surrounded me. I thought, s##t, all I did was land in a strong wind and put my wing down the wrong way, surely it's not worth sending so many out to arrest me ☺. As it turned out, I had parked right next to the airport security police.

I spotted a huge hangar with its doors open so I shouted: *"I have to get out of this wind or I will blow away! That hangar looks good, can I put in there sir?".*

"No, sir, not without permission from the Tower which will take 15-20 minutes or so".

After a bit of verbal discussion they came back and said it was not possible, neither would it be safe in there. So I won my aircraft a space under the canopy of the Airport Police which is where I parked for the night. I got out and between myself, a couple of the police and agents we manhandled my Quik under the canopy and tied it up as best we could. I then was picked up by a minibus and literally thrown in, legs everywhere in complete spasm. I got to the Terminal Building where I just told the staff to throw me back into my wheelchair and they don't have to worry about hurting me.

Legs everywhere they threw me back in my chair and I had a fast track through customs going past everybody who was queuing which saved a lot of time.

The airport was packed with people.

I went and filled in the necessary paperwork with the agent, they do seem to want an awful lot of paper work here I have to say, three copies of everything to everybody in the airport. After all that I was taken to the Ramada Karachi Hotel. I signed in and then went to my room to check out my cuts and bruises, before looking at my charts and flight plan for the next day. I had something to eat in the restaurant and spent the rest of the night tapping away on the computer getting my blog up to date.

Day 34, June 1st - Karachi to Ahmedabad

Happy birthday to me, happy birthday to me!.

Yaaawwwnnnn!

Wow, 4.30am, was it that time already?

Here we go again! It's funny because everybody said to me before I set off, you are going to have an amazing holiday. That's a joke! It's like a job.

I got up at 4.40am to go to the toilet before lying back on to the bed for 10 minutes trying to give my bum a rest before the long day ahead where I would be sat down. I do that just about every day. It isn't easy being in a wheelchair and that's just going to the toilet.

I was picked up by my agent and went to the Airport for 6am for an early getaway. Passport sorted and then back to Immigration again. It gets a bit tiresome I'll tell you, but if that's what I have to do to get to Sydney so be it. It seems that every time you want to fly they say, "*OK let's have three hours of paperwork first then.*"

After an hour or so of going backwards and forwards around the Airport, I finally got to my Quik. I started loading my bags and computer on board ready to go, saying "W*here's my fuel?*"

"*It is coming sir.*"

I have heard that so many times on this trip!

It is now 9am and I'm getting a bit annoyed as I had been here 3 hours now. It was ordered ages ago, where was my fuel?

"*Please, captain, it is coming*"

After another hour of badgering, they finally turned up in a little sooty van, with three big tins of premium petrol from the petrol station, then got a funnel out of the van with a piece of linen as a fuel filter across it and started pouring it in to my big tank, all 100litres of it.

Right, can I go now?

"Yes, Captain."

With the Quik now loaded up and full of fuel it was time for me to get in and put the chair away, so I said my goodbyes and gave ATC a call.

"G-CDVO - request engine start and check flight plan to Ahmedabad please"

"G-CDVO – stand-by".

After several calls and no response I took my helmet off and asked one of the guys to ring the tower and see what was going on, had my radio gone off again?

He rang them and said *"no problem Captain five them a radio call again"*

So with my helmet back on, I gave them another call only to hear *"G-CDVO - flight plan NOT approved".*

I pulled the mic back in the helmet and asked the handling agent why it wasn't approved.

"Captain, it is only 1,000ft cloud base"

"Why the f##k didn't you tell me it wasn't approved before I got into my Quik, you prat?"

After a while sat thinking and being really annoyed, I called again. Once again it was not approved for me to go; I had now already been up for six hours and was still on the ground. Then I thought of something else to try

"G-CDVO - requesting a special VFR flight plan, please"

*"G-VO, standby"…*then …*"G-VO, special VFR approved, engine start approved'."*

Brilliant – it was time to go at last.

"G-CDVO Taxi out, Papa to A1,"

"G-CDVO would like intersection, take off from Delta, please".

"G-VO Approved, taxi out to Delta line up runway 34R, wind 20knts, after take-off turn left and climb to 3,000ft. Squawk 3067". (Squawking is air-speak for setting a four-figure number on the transponder)

Still blowing a gale, I made my way out to the runway and lined up; I put in the squawk code before I took off so I didn't have to do it in the sky.

I took off and it was really murky with the cloud base at 1,000ft like they had said, however it was still flyable. About five miles out of Karachi I managed to reach 1,900ft before hitting cloud, and the weather remained like that an hour or so. However I was heading for a bleak area called the Rann of Kutch on the border with India.

The map indicated land, but there must have been a lot of recent rain because there was water everywhere, it was like flying over the English Channel really as it was dark and muddy brown and very misty. This eventually cleared and turned into desert which was pure white in colour (salt perhaps?) which made it very difficult to see the ground.

With the low white cloud and mist, it seemed as if the ground had melted into the sky. As I flew further toward India it started heating up but was still a bit misty and the Visor on my helmet started to get darker so I gave it a wipe.

It was sand in the air that was coming at me now, so I had to fly with my visor up just to see where I was going and the wind screen was covered in wet sand as well. I had to fight my way through the sand coming at me from all directions; I was now covered in wet sand all down my front and all over the Quik and it was all sticky and horrible.

Having survived that, I then spent another hour dodging big twisters in the desert. These twisters went through the desert just like you would see them on the TV towering up into the sky and ripping through anything in their paths causing widespread destruction. Unfortunately I couldn't take any pictures of them because I was too busy holding on to the bar and trying to keep my distance..

Finally the Airfield at Ahmedabad came into sight. The Airfield was closed for repairs, but I had a special permit to land on it. I gave Ahmedabad Tower a call on the radio and they gave me permission to fly straight over the city and join downwind in as tight a circuit as I needed.

So taking full advantage of that and with no 4 mile finals to adhere to, I turned finals right over the numbers of the runway.

I taxied in with a stiff wind again and was met by a barrage of on-lookers. Then a small airport truck with my fuel turned up, followed by a fork lift truck.

I had ordered a barrel of 200lt of Avgas. The barrel went up on the forklift and was brought right over the top of the engine so that the fuel would just drain down into my tanks through a pipe and funnel.

It was really annoying to have to buy 200lt of Avgas but that was the smallest amount I could buy. While the refuelling was going on I spotted a hangar with the doors open and people walking around so I asked again like I had been doing.

"I want to put my Quik in there for the night", I pointed to the hangar."

"Let me find out for you Sir as that is a private hangar"

They came back after a few calls and said OK but only if I can be there early in the morning? No problem. I taxied over and put the aircraft into the hangar out of the way. Lots of people watched me melt in the heat, dripping buckets of sweat while I put my chair together. When I got out and in the chair I looked at my Quik, it was covered in sand and dust again. It had a sandy yellow wing and yellow stripes all over the front of all the tubes - my poor Quik. I was taken to the Terminal Building to sort out all the Customs crap again and the inevitable paperwork. Once all that was done, I asked if there was a hotel close by I could get, so after a phone call we found one so it was out to find a taxi. Then the handling agent turned up in a car and offered to take there.

I signed in and went up to my room. Shortly afterwards there was a knock on my door and when I opened it a guy stood there smiling holding a birthday cake with a candle and my name on it and said complements of the hotel owner Dave! I couldn't believe it, I am half way around the world, nobody knows me and I have a birthday cake. Just brilliant ☺

So I indulged in the cake and there was another knock on the door and this time he had a birthday present all wrapped up so I opened it to find a very nice pen and key ring from the hotel staff.

So thanks to the Comfort Inn for all that.

Happy birthday to me, Happy birthday to me!

I went down for a meal in the restaurant before going back up to my room for the night, to relax and complete my flight plan and routing for the next day.

This was going to be a long one, at 630 miles, to Raipur, south east of Nagpur.

Day 35, June 2nd - Ahmedabad to Raipur

After the high charges at Ahmedabad Airport I decided that only another two stops should happen here in India as I needed to get through this country as fast as I could. So I left out Bhopal from my original route.

At 6.30am my driver took me to the Airport Gate 1 where I was due to meet the handling agent, however he started taking me to Gate 2,

'Gate 1, I said!"

"Yes, Captain."

So he went to the Terminal. He took me to Door 1, Gate 2. That's a good start to the day.

I rang the agent who came over to the other terminal to meet me about 10 minutes later, and handed me his bill.

"You pay now!"

"No, sir, you get me flying before 9.00am, I pay you then."

"OK, no problem." This statement is used a lot in Indi!.

I looked at the bill and it was so high that I didn't have enough money to pay him.

I said to the agent that I needed to find an ATM machine if he wanted me to pay this bill.

Luckily there was one just around the corner so it was back out of the Terminal to find it. I was hoping that the machine didn't eat my card.

It was fine but I had to use it five times to get enough cash out!

Two hours later I was still in the Terminal waiting for the handling agent to get my paperwork sorted out. I was not happy as the flight ahead was going to be a very long one.

I eventually get through to my aircraft. It's now 9.30am

"I told you I have a long flight in front of me!"

I got loaded up and pushed out of the hangar and on to the apron then gave ATC a call.

"G-CDVO – Stand by."

The Agent came over and said they were getting all the jets out as the airport was closing at 10.30am for repairs. I didn't care about that, I had been here for a long time and could have been away a long time ago, all I cared about now was daylight at the other end.

"You can fly in the dark, no!"

"No, I can't!"

After badgering ATC, they let me go and take off in between the Jets. I finally left at 10.30am just as the airport closed otherwise I would have been there for another day.

It was bumpy right from the take-off as the temperature was already 38degrees.

I faced a really nice eight hours of being bounced about thanks to the agents at the airport messing around. I could hardly wait!

The first four hours were OK, changing between different controllers and talking to Airliners to relay messages when I lost radio contact. Apparently the route that I was flying was to take me over a Lion or Tiger reserve on the way. That should be interesting.

As I got deeper into India, radio contact was getting lost quite a lot, and even the transponder didn't seem to be sending as many pulses.

My arms were aching like hell with all the crap weather I had encountered over the previous few days and were covered in bruises now as well, so getting bounced around again really didn't help. It was so tiring.

The countryside in India was really barren and I was constantly looking out for some wild life that might be wandering around in the middle of nowhere.

As I got near to Nagpur I had lost radio contact with everybody – none of the frequencies that I had seemed to be working. No one could pick me up. What do you do? I tried the emergency frequency 121.5 kHz, anybody help me to get in contact with Nagpur but nothing! It is a good job I was not in trouble or needing medical help.

My route was taking me straight over the top of the main runway at Nagpur, but with no radio contact I couldn't follow the route. I made a decision to go around their control zone, and risk landing in the dark at Raipur.

At least if they have me on Radar, they can see what I'm doing.

It turns out I could not have gone over Nagpur anyway, because it was covered in huge thunder storm clouds and lots of rain.

As I made my way around the north-east of the controlled zone, the rain came in. I pulled the bar in so I didn't get trapped in the rain; I judged it just right, then I spotted the lion sanctuary which was a big restricted zone. So just in case the engine stopped I kept away from it.

Can you imagine it if the engine stops and I land only to get eaten by Lions? Not good!

In front more rain storms were coming at me with fairly low black cloud and very poor visibility; I thought I would dodge around them but not this time! Rain surrounded me but not only that, I was in my t-shirt with no gloves and the rain drops were quite hard. I huddled forward behind the screen with my hands together to try keeping them from getting too cold, but this was no good.

My jacket was tucked under the dash board down by my legs and gloves were in dashboard space behind the screen.

I wonder? Let's have a go; I'm now wet and cold.

I pulled my Coat out and managed to fight my way into it. That was really difficult with wet arms. The Quik was all over the sky but after a struggle trying to keep level flight, I managed to get the jacket on. Then the gloves and, of course, two fingers always go down one finger hole! I was now dryish. It was really raining by now and I was watching the daylight disappearing behind me. I needed to get some speed on or it would be dark.

I trimmed off (yeah, the trimmer isn't stuck on) and off I went.

I pulled the bar in and went for it.

As I got within 45 miles of Raipur, the tower managed to pick me up. Excellent!

"G-CDVO - Raipur".

"G-CDVO- How long left to run to Raipur"

'G-CDVO I have 20 minutes to go"

"G-CDVO - Report runway in sight".

I could only see the airport because the landing lights on the runway were lit up.

All the street lights started coming on now.

"G-VO runway in sight now"

"G-VO - turn left, we have a 737 on long finals".

G-VO - I'll just orbit here if that's OK by you, sir"

"G-CDVO that's fine, thank you"

The jet landed and ATC said

"G-CDVO - report joining left base you are number one."

"G-VO - left base."

"G-CDVO - report finals. The landing lights are on for you. Put your lights on, please, so we can see you"

So I did and what a fantastic sight it was, coming into an international airport in a flexwing just as its dropping dark with all the landing lights on.

Annoyingly, my camera battery died as I was approaching finals!

I landed and was sent to the furthest point on the apron to park up for the night. I got out of the Quik under the headlights of the sooty van (Honda Acty) that was bringing my fuel.

The three guys got the drums out and a hose pipe and didn't have a clue how to siphon from them so I'm trying to explain to them that the drum needed to be higher than the tank it's going into.

Not easy when they didn't speak any English but I managed eventually so there we were, re-fuelling from three big plastic drums, a 100 litres of premium petrol through a hosepipe in the dark.

I made my way by wheelchair to Arrivals, asking why I had to park so far out on the apron and who would be responsible if anything happened to my Quik if the storms came through like they were forecast?

I had just got into the Terminal when the biggest rain storm came through. With torrential rain and high winds this was real monsoon rain..

I hoped that my Quik would be OK. *"It's on your head for me parking there if it's not OK";* I said pointing at the agent.

Off the agent trotted to sort out the paperwork for me, leaving me sat in Arrivals.

99

After an hour he was still not back. The guards at the airport are saying to me *"Go, Go, we close"*.

After two hours of brushing the guards away from me and the agent going backwards and forwards he finally says *"You need a 5-star hotel."*

"No, all this should have been sorted out long ago. I need hotel with internet and food".

He rang a taxi which took forever to come. The airport was completely in darkness now as it had closed. Then we went off to the "Hotel" that he had arranged for me!

We arrived there, with six steps to get in, then another six steps to the lift.

He says – lovely man – *"You walk."*

"Sorry, pal, I do love sitting down in this wheelchair, so if you don't mind I'm not going to get out and walk for you. You will have to carry me up."

On the second floor the agent came into my room and I filled in the flight plan for the next day. While I was doing that with the agent the hotel owner asked what I would like to eat so I ordered a curry and the agent finally left.

It was now 11.35pm…… It had been a long day.

The curry arrived. I think we must be spoilt back in England. The chicken looked like it had just been picked up from the side of the road and stamped on before putting it in a pot for me with legs sticking out!

Should I eat it? Yes, it was different but interesting. A quick type on the blog and it was 1am so time for bed.

Day 36 June 3rd - Raipur to Calcutta

Gosh, so tired after yesterday's ordeal, but life goes on.

The alarm goes off at 4.30am…

The agent was coming for me at 6am, so a quick trip to the toilet to get rid of the curry, then I had to get my chart folded up and ready, because this was a 530-mile trip.

At 6am the agent arrived along with the hotel staff. I was carried down all the steps once again and down the big kerbs to the awaiting taxi and we set off to the airport.

We travelled through the deserted streets and shanty town areas of Ahmedabad. People were just sleeping at the side of the road or on the back of horse and carts; it was a really sad sight to see how poor it was.

When we arrived at the Airport it was busy and the agent said to me *"Where's your boarding card?"*

"You're sorting this out! That's what I'm paying you for".

He asked me to wait and I spent the next two hours in Departures, with him going backwards and forwards but with nothing actually happening.

I said, *"Do you know what you are doing?"*

More time went by. Now I am starting to get annoyed. The day was heating up and storms were forecast.

"Will you get this sorted out? I have to get off"

"Captain, you pay"

"No. You do job, I pay"

Actually, I am getting a bit bored of saying this.

By 9.30am I had had enough. *"Go to ATC and tell them I want see them".*

"But, Captain".

I roared at him *"Go get ATC!"*

Off he trotted, and shortly afterwards the main controller arrived. "Hello, Captain".

I told him I needed to get going because thunderstorms were forecast, I had been here since 6.30am and was no further forward.

"Captain, this agent is useless, sir, he doesn't have a clue what he is doing, you should have been out of here by 7.30 am, no later."

"Can you sort it out for me?"

"Of course, Captain, and it's a real honour to meet you."

Next II went straight to Passport Control where they didn't believe I was a Captain and had a good laugh. Finally I got to my Quik in the heat of the day. It was now 10.30am and the agent was saying I needed to pay parking and airport charges.

"Will you just get out of my face before I do something that I won't regret?"

"Captain, give me $100 for parking."

"I have told you get out of my face and away from me"

So I climbed into my Quik and started putting my wheelchair on the Quik while this guy was still going on at me.

I said *"you have messed me around from the moment I got here so you can wait for me now so shut up"*

Then his phone rang and he came across and gave me a handful of money, babbling something under his breath. ATC had told him to give me all my money back because he had been so bad, and they didn't want it reflecting on the Airport's reputation.

ATC gave me clearance straight away and I was cleared to take off within 5 minutes (fantastic). On the other hand it was nearly midday and things were heating up. It was as rough as hell and I had a five-hour flight in front of me.

I left Raipur's air space and was passed on to Calcutta Radar but over the radio I could already hear electrical interference from storms.

Ohhhh, no!

Sure enough, all around there were huge cumulous building, and it was getting very rough. Two hours into the flight it was starting to become *'very challenging'*. I was not certain at any time which was the best way to push or pull the bar.

This went on for a very long time, up and down and getting bounced around.

I was getting closer to an Airport called Jamshedpur, but before I could get there I had to get through some mountains. The storms were closing in from all directions, the ground started rising and at the same time the storms started closing in around me. I was at 5,000ft going through the mountains, and when I say it was rough, that is the biggest understatement I have ever made. It was pulling the base bar out so violently I didn't think the Quik was going to hold together, and I certainly didn't think it was capable of coping with the kind of stresses I was getting. One minute I was going up at 2,000ft a minute, with the bar into my chest, the wing pointing at the ground with no power and then going down towards the mountains at the same rate, with the bar out and on full power. I was really scared now, there was nowhere to go and the visibility started to really deteriorate as well.

I couldn't turn back because I was well and truly trapped in the mountains in the storms, I tried heading further north to get away from the bigger mountains but the wind and rain just got worse.

So I headed back into the big mountains with the rain really coming down now, low cloud and squally winds.

I didn't think I could get through. I thought I might have had to try putting it down on one of the mountain roads I could see but that would have been a life or death decision to make.

The winds were really bad now battering me around and I was getting very worried. The biggest gust took my right wing up and my left wing was literally 90 degrees to the ground and the Quik just dropped out of the sky towards the mountains. I managed to get control of that before hitting the ground, and then another gust of wind straight afterwards pushed the base bar into my stomach. It was like being punched, it lifted me out of my seat and my helmet hit the nose pole. Holding on for dear life now, the visor on my helmet then blew open and nearly got ripped off I absolutely crapped myself.

All I could think was, "This is that little shit's fault for having me get away so late."

Eventually I got through the mountains and I was in a flat calm.

Like it normally is... the calm after the storm!

But not for long! I continued on towards Calcutta, but ten miles past Jamshedpur the whole sky lit up like a Christmas tree with thunder and lightning.

That's it.

I have had enough.

I'm not having that.

Back into Jamshedpur for the night.

I gave them a call on the radio and told them I was coming in.

"*Jamshedpur G-CDVO*"

"*G-CDVO pass your message*"

"*G-CDVO in bound to yourself Jamshedpur request runway in use and landing instruction*"

"*G-CDVO Runway in use is..... You are cleared to land*"

I turned around and headed straight in to land with lightening flashing all around now. I landed and what a wonderful reception! I was met by the local flying club who put my Quik in their hangar and found me a hotel for the night. Then they drove me down to it in the airport truck! Thanks guys, very much appreciated. It was the best reception I had received in India so far.

I had organised a night out with them so that they could show me around Jamshedpur but they didn't turn up to meet me.

So I went to the bar to have a few beers to calm down. All I want is a nice flat calm flight at some point instead of crap weather all the time, the type you get in the UK in the winter.

Day 37, June 4th - Jamshedpur to Calcutta to Dhaka

I had a couple of real kebabs last night in the hotel (hmmm, lovely), I didn't even suffer – anyway, you didn't want to know that!

Two guys came to collect me from the hotel in the airport vehicle (a rickety old 4x4), and took me to the Airport. I got there for 7.30am and the guys there were so helpful, I had my Quik out, prepared, me in it and my flight plan filed all before 8am.

Sorted! I had just a two hour flight to Calcutta where I had instructed the agents there to be ready with my paperwork, Avgas and Customs because I wanted a fast turnaround to get straight off to Dhaka, Bangladesh. I was cleared to take off from Jamshedpur as soon as one of their aircraft had landed back from a trip to Calcutta.

I took off – I couldn't see a thing with the haze but it soon cleared a bit. This was going to be one of my shortest hops of the whole trip. There was only moderate turbulence at 8am - still 40°C (104°F) but after yesterday's flig ht it was very manageable. Before I knew it I had done 100 miles and was in contact with Calcutta Approach getting vectored in from 50 miles out.

"G-CDVO",

"G-CDVO, Calcutta Approach",

"G-CDVO, turn heading 060".

So I looked at the Pilot 111 GPS and it looked like he was giving me short finals (4 miles). Then he said "G-CDVO turn right heading 090".

"ILS approach G-CDVO",

"G-CDVO negative on an ILS approach, VFR please",

"G-CDVO VFR approach, report runway in sight".

After 5 minutes he calls "do *you have runway in sight?*".

"G-CDVO Negative, runway not in sight yet".

"G-CDVO ETA to land",

"G-VO, 010 sir",

"G-VO Confirm 10 minutes",

"Confirm 10mins",

"G-VO you should have runway in sight now?"

"G-VO, it is very hazy sir",

"OK G-VO".

"Runway In sight G-VO",

"G-CDVO cleared to land runway 19L".

As I landed on runway 19L, a jet was just taking off on 19R. This was another very big Airport with two runways, one to land on and another to take off on. As I taxied down to the other runway I got clearance to carry on and cross the runway to the Terminal, but thought I would just wait a short while until the wake disappeared. The jet disappeared into the distance and I crossed runway 19R. Half way across I still got hit by the blast from its jet! Amazing, I couldn't even see the jet that had produced it.

I taxied in past all the jets parked up at the main terminal and down past a jet waiting for me to taxi past him to be met by the handling agents. First thing they said "*Pay sir now*". No you get my flight plan approved customs and Avgas within the hour like agreed last night and I will pay you then and not sooner.

"*Ok Captain*"; and to my pleasure that was the way it was, fuelled up, Customs and Immigration came to see me at the Quik, and my flight plan was stamped and approved. I didn't even have to get out of the Quik.

I paid my dues for the landing fees, handling agent for sorting my paperwork out and the fuel – it was expensive again but it was to be my last flight in India.

In India you get a clearance from the Air Defence before every flight which has to be stamped and cleared on your flight plan plus my flight clearance number to enter the country and land. That all went through very smoothly but the cloud was now building all around the airport and getting dark like it could rain and thunder.

So I wanted to get away from it ASAP.

I gave ATC a call and they gave me clearance to taxi out to the runway. It was nice because as I started to taxi out word had got around the airport that I was there and there were people from other airline companies everywhere waving at me and stood along the apron all clapping and taking photos

I lined up, and was cleared for take-off, with a very stiff breeze and the weather crapping out behind me. This was to be a flight of 2 hours 30 mins to Dhaka Bangladesh

The flight was OK! I still got bounced all over the sky but at least I now could see where I was going.

I would have liked to have had a night there in Calcutta to see what it was like but my permissions for the countries head of me would be expiring and it would have been a hassle getting them updated. Never mind!

After two hours of talking away to Air Traffic Control and their extremely busy airspace and also going over in to Bangladeshi airspace, I was finally passed on to Dhaka Tower which was just as busy.

I think it was the busiest time of day for landing at Dhaka.

"G-CDVO Tower'

"G-CDVO we have you on radar continue approach and report runway in sight"

"G-CDVO, will report runway in sight.".

"G-VO runway in sight",

"G-VO JOIN downwind for runway 26",

"G-VO downwind".

Then he asked me to extend my downwind as he had one on long finals.

So I did and watched while what looked like a 747 went in to land.

It was also quite interesting because as I flew down wind there was lots of what looked like small mud huts everywhere - it looked like a small town of them.

"G-CDVO report finals",

"G-CDVO report finals" - that was it I was looking directly at the numbers to my right, so wing over and get it in,

"G-CDVO finals".

"G-VO Cleared to land".

I landed and taxied in via Charlie taxiway to the waiting marshal waving his arms around at me, parked up and instantly I got surrounded by about 100 people all getting right underneath and touching the Quik. It took a couple armed guards and another official chap to get them all away from me.

Then I asked if there was any chance of cover for my Quik for the night.

A few calls were made before I jumped out of the Quik.

I was then told to follow a van that was driving around the airport and was taken to a huge hangar where I could put the Quik inside. I parked up ready to get out but it was worse there as even more people turned up.

I got out of the Quik watching everybody around me making sure nothing was going to go missing. With the Quik in the hangar, I was just getting prepared to go when one man changed his mind, claiming that the hangar that could house two Airbus A-340s had no room for me! I must go to the flying club which was 2 kilometres down the runway.

They wanted me to get back in to the aircraft, and put everything in including my chair back inside and taxi.

"Sorry, you brought me here; you can take my chair in the van for me."

"But captain…"

I told them I'm not messing around putting that lot back in my Quik when you have the van and you are coming with me.

So they agreed and threw my wheelchair and all my gear into the van and I made a quick call to Dhaka ground frequency to request engine start and taxi to relocate.

I taxied from one end of the airport to the other - I could have taken off and flown it there it was that far – and got to where they wanted me to be and parked it up behind some old scrap aircraft from a flying club and a hangar..

I got out and tied it up using concrete blocks.

Then I went into the flying school to introduce myself and let them know it was my Quik tied up outside.

The guys in the van then took me back down to the Terminal Building, where I went in through the back tradesman's entrance and then up to the Immigration and Passport offices where I completed the formality of the paperwork and the agent said *"You stop and sleep in airport and save lots of money and Visa".*

"No I want a hotel".

"OK, you have hotel then".

We were now in Arrivals which was where he had wanted me to stay and where everybody was trying to get to me and get to my bags.

He realised, *"Not safe for you here, Bad people around"*

"Yes I know I can see Thank you".

Don't get me wrong, the guys at Dhaka were really helpful and were just trying to save me money. However I needed a hotel. I didn't fancy sleeping with one eye open watching my bags all night. We went to a desk and managed to get a room at aircrew rate at a very nice hotel which also had a bar and live music!

A fairly decent day's flying for a change.

Day 38, June 5th - Dhaka to Mandalay part 1

I was really tired. I hadn't slept much the previous night, maybe two to three hours. I had terrible gut ache, I was feeling a bit home sick and missing Les as well. I was now into my sixth week away.

I was meeting lots of genuinely very friendly people along the way but it was still fairly lonely. My laptop was my best friend and my two finger typing was getting faster every day.

Less of me mooning around…I had a 510 mile hop today down to Chittagong along the coast before I was to turn inland and climb to cross the 10,000ft mountains to Mandalay. However thunderstorms were forecast so it was either going to be frighteningly turbulent, very wet, or both!

I had arranged to meet the agents at the airport at 6.30am to go through the flight-plan and general declarations (GenDecs) as well as the Air Defence clearance.

I was sat around again, waiting, getting agitated, when the agents came to take me to the Quik. I went outside and was picked up in an old Hiace van, of which the front tyre had about as much tread as my forehead!

Still it worked! The staff just threw me onto the front seat. I now had bruises all over from being thrown about like a rag doll.

The three and a half cylinder engine worked well and took me down to my Quik.

I had a fantastic audience to give me a hand into the aircraft and push it around. The sun was red hot once again and the sweat was just running off me. The heat in these countries was quite incredible; I don't know how they managed.

By now the sky was turning dark and horrible. I asked for a weather report and was shown the flying club's pc to use.

It was now 11am and none of the flying club were flying!

That had to say something.

Anyway I climbed into the Quik and as I was sat there, I just looked up and it was black.

I leant forward in my Quik put my head against the front strut, absolutely shattered and feeling a bit sick. I had maybe 80 people surrounding me so I couldn't breathe. They got moved away but still it was black.

I'm no hero.

I don't have to scare myself and risk my life.

That's it. I'm not going today. It's too dangerous.

The chief flying instructor came over, all smiles, and shook my hand.

"*Please come and have a tea with me. You have made the right decision, the sky is too unstable, and we aren't flying in our Cirrus never mind a hang glider*".

I just sat there in my Quik for a few moments, chilling, before jumping out and sorting things out.

The flying club owner moved three of their Cessna's out of their hangar and made room for my aircraft.

Everybody just couldn't do enough for me.

FANTASTIC. Thanks very much guys if you're reading this.

After tying it down in the hangar, I went back to the hotel and went to bed. I was out cold from mid afternoon until later that evening. I must have needed it.

The body had been recharged a bit now for the day ahead.

We would see what the weather brings.

Day 39, June 6th - Dhaka to Mandalay (Part 2)

After my rest the previous day I felt much better and was ready to take on the world yet again - "Bring it on!".

I booked out of the hotel - it was a very nice one. It even had ladies offering things for $5 but I had to decline. I need all my energy.

I got to the airport for 6.15am and told the handling agents to get on with the ADC clearance (Air Defence) straight away, along with Immigration. Then I was out to my Quik. A storm had just gone through and everything was flooded! Great stuff! And we were doing so well.

The guys at the Aero Club pulled the Quik out and I asked if they had any fuel. *"Sorry, we only have enough Avgas for ourselves - but we do have Mogas if it is any use?"*

"Fill her up, its better".

They had just 40 litres but this was better than none. I climbed into the Quik in the sun, which was baking hot by now and I was wet through with sweat. A big crowd had gathered to watch me set off. I gave ATC a call and I got clearance to taxi.

"G-CDVO taxi Golf, Sierra to Charlie".

Off I went following the yellow lines (trust me if you don't follow them you can soon get lost in these big airports). I got to Charlie and the ATC said *"can you pull up a bit closer to aircraft in front please G-CDVO".*

"G-VO negative, he has two big fans that will blow me away"

The aircraft took off and I was given clearance to line up for take-off straight away.

"G-CDVO climb out straight to 3,000ft and maintain".

As soon as I got to 2,000ft I was in cloud, so I settled for 1,900ft.

"G-CDVO request 2,000ft to remain VFR",

"Approved G-VO".

It was a good job that he did approve the height, as straight after that I could see rain everywhere. It started closing in around until I was in it. It was very hard rain, and I couldn't go right - it was harder there - and to the left it felt as bad.

I tucked my hands in to the middle of the base bar and got very wet,

It was raining so hard on me that I couldn't see though my visor, as it seemed to have rained on the inside as well. I could not see through the windscreen and the water was also starting to fill my pod up.

I was flying with the visor pulled up, getting wet in the face, and I was also worried about my propeller. Would it be OK? I had seen what water jets do to steel!

And would I be OK for that matter?

Luckily, the rain cleared up for a short while, and as it did, two Bangladeshi Air force jets passed by just a short distance away. These were probably the same two jets that took off from Dhaka just before me (I forgot to mention that!).

I was still at 1,900ft and ATC told me to stop at that height all the way, don't go up or down, and maintain 1,900ft.

"Not a problem, sir"

It must be the military making sure they knew where I was. I was in and out of cloud, and going around the bigger ones, but still at 1,900ft as instructed.

But then…all I could see was a wall of rain in front.

I can't get through that!

The coast looked clear so I made my way out to it.

It started raining again and the visibility was really bad now. I was struggling to see the ground and so I dropped to just 1,000ft. I told ATC where I was and why, and they were fine. I was out of the way of the military down there. I headed out to sea where it did clear up a bit.

Inland the whole country was covered in cloud and rain, so I carried on out to sea. It looked clear ahead, but as I got close to Chittagong there were massive cloud formations, storms and rain completely covering the 10,000ft of mountains I needed to cross to get to Mandalay.

Was it going to clear before I got there?

I had just gone past Chittagong and the sky was black with cloud down to the ground.

Mandalay wasn't happening today. I gave Chittagong a call.

"*G-CDVO Chittagong*".

"*G-CDVO inbound to yourselves, request landing information*".

"*G-CDVO hold down wind for runway 27 while we check your ADC*".

There I am orbiting while a big storm is coming right at me only a few miles away and they are saying they need to check if my permits are in order. They were more bothered about paperwork than me!

The guy in the Tower said "*G-CDVO you are not permitted to land here your ADC does not allow you*"

"*G-CDVO I have to land, I cannot carry on*"

"*G-CDVO YOU MUST NOT LAND YOU ARE NOT PERMITTED*"

"*G-CDVO check my flight plan, Chittagong is down as my alternate airfield*"

Shortly the storm was over me and I was getting wet and bounced around.

"*G-CDVO you are cleared to land*"

So I continued downwind and reported finals.

"*G-CDVO FINALS*'

It was nice just to have a 15 knot wind for a change, instead of the 25 knot ones I had been living with on the way down.

I landed and taxied in to the waiting marshal. As always, I was surrounded by around 40 people, and how friendly they all were.

"Hello Captain, we welcome you to Chittagong, how may we help you?"

"I need my flight plan closing".

"Don't worry Captain we have already taken care of it for you".

"Is there any where I can park out of the storms for the night?"

"Only anchor point in the ground, sir, if that's any good. We don't have anywhere to put anything under cover."

I was taken to a point on the apron between the jet boarding tunnels where there were some big rings concreted to the ground.

"Excellent, that will do."

By now the storm had moved in and it was raining and blowing my Quik about fairly violently. I made a quick exit from it, and jumped into my wheelchair then with a bit of help I had the Quik tied to the ground before it really started blowing and raining. I was taken to Immigration which took only ten minutes to sort out which was nice and speedy. I asked the same guy if he knew a good hotel for me to stop in.

"Yes sir, get a cab to the Peninsular Hotel".

After Immigration had finished with me I went out to the front of the airport door and was instantly surrounded by men trying to grab me and take my bags from me.

"Get off me".

"But sir you need help".

"No I don't get lost"

"I need a taxi to the Peninsula hotel"

One lad says *"I'm a taxi"* - I thought no you're not, (that's my joke).

"How much to Hotel Peninsular?"

"$20"

Ok you will do.

I got thrown in to the taxi van, and all the other men around are saying demanding, *"But you give me money"*.

"What for?"

"Because I help you get taxi".

"No, you didn't. Get lost".

A security guard said *"You give him money, he has earned it"*.

I threw him a dollar and he moaned.

I said *"you're not getting anything else, this taxi driver is earning his money - you're just trying to rob me"*,

The guard just said *"Go you are causing trouble here, and got his gun out"*

"How am I causing trouble when they are trying to take my things?"

The guard waiving his gun around at me and is saying to the taxi driver *"Go"*

The hotel was a good 30 minutes drive, so his $20 was well earned.

Chittagong, I have to say, isn't one the richest cities in the world, and there were a lot of poor people around in slums. But Chittagong was an amazing place. The beaches to the west are covered in old cargo ships that get scrapped. They drive them aground then just cut them up. It's an amazing view from above.

I finally got to the hotel after a 30 min drive and then I had to get out of the taxi van in the basement car park of the hotel to stop being harassed again by the locals. I went to the hotel restaurant and its small bar but I couldn't see anything on the menu that stuck out for me to eat.

Then I went to the bar and there was a man eating what looked like a chicken stir-fry and vegetables so I grabbed the bar tender and said I wanted one of them. She replied by saying that it was not standard food from the menu.

So I smiled at her nicely and gave her the puppy dog eyes.

And I had one brought for me ☺ and then went to bed.

It would remain to be seen if I would get to Mandalay the next day.

Chittagong airport

BURMESE DAYS

Day 40, June 7th - Chittagong to Yangon

I woke up really early and looking out over Chittagong the sky did not look good, but I needed to go, so it was down to reception.

"Is my taxi here?"

"Sorry captain, it's not!"

They ordered me a local taxi. It was an old battered Toyota but it worked, and I was taken through the streets of Chittagong in between all the Rickshaws trying to kill

116

themselves by pulling out in front of *everybody*. Cairo wasn't a patch on Chittagong when it came to traffic mayhem. I had never seen so many rickshaws before.

I arrived at Chittagong International glad that the old Toyota had made it so far as there were noises coming from all over it and I had thought one of the wheels was dropping off.

I got out of the taxi with everybody looking at me; it was as though they had never seen anybody in a wheelchair before. I went through security and got straight through quickly - I now had four gold captain bars on my polo shirt which seemed to make a big difference strangely enough. I am not just a guy passing through an airport now I am a captain and with that they seem to give you a bit of respect and authority!

I asked for ATC and Flight Operations and was sent straight to the Control Tower via the main apron. They invited in to the Tower and the main man in charge came down to see me and my flight- plan was filled-in, stamped and approved in 10 minutes! Then it was off to Immigration to get my Passport stamped and I was ready to go.

One hour from start to finish!

After that was sorted out I went back to the Control Tower and requested my bill for the airport charges!

I couldn't believe it.

They charged me for parking all night on the main apron, for airport landing fees, handling fees and navigation fees. I had been charged an average of $1,000 for all that at different airports but Chittagong charged me a whole $13 for everything. It just shows who was vastly over charging and robbing people!

I even managed to get Avgas at a very reasonable price. I got my phone out and rang the tower.

"Hello, has G-CDVO got an ADC number yet?"

"G-CDVO, ADC No. is 150".

That was it, I was cleared to go, and so with a few onlookers - around 40 - I climbed into the Quik ready to go.

By now time was getting on. Would I get to Yangon before it got dark?

"G-CDVO request engine start and information",

"G-VO, taxi out, cleared for take-off to 3,000ft".

117

I have to say it had never been as easy as it was at Chittagong. The last time it was this straightforward was when I was taking off from Rufforth on the 28th April. Seriously it was so easy and quick.

The route I would be following would take me down the coast for a few hundred miles before turning left and climbing over some seriously high mountains to Yangon (Rangoon).

I got clearance to taxi out to the runway and line up but while I was lined up on the runway ready for take-off, it started to rain heavily. I was not going back in now so I took off straight into the rain. Then the rain came down even harder, which I could cope with, and then it rained harder still which was sort of OK - I wasn't happy but it wasn't hard enough to make me turn back. I was 2hours into the flight and it was still raining - would it stop at all today?

Two hours flying in heavy rain – it I had been back at home I just wouldn't have done it, in fact I wouldn't have even pulled the aircraft out of the hangar, let alone fly in it!

I headed down the coast towards a reporting point, another Airfield called Sittwe. It was quite bad, I was at 2,000ft and still in the rain but the further south I was getting the worse it got and then suddenly the weather really turned bad. I was now in torrential rain, I couldn't see anything, forward left or right. I had to lift my visor up so that I could see a bit better (if you imagine driving your car at 80mph in the rain with your windscreen wipers turned off that was what it was like) and not only that, but the wind came up throwing me around, and 'holy moley' then it really started.

I got pushed down to about 1,000ft above ground level with the cloud and I still could not see in front or behind and it had got to the point where the rain was now hurting me.

The ground then just about disappeared below me – I was clinging on for dear life now! The winds took hold of me, and shook me all over the sky. Now I was not able to see the ground at all, it was a complete white-out with torrential rain at the same time. I pulled the bar into my chest and looked at the VSI. I was going down at 1,500ft min at 95mph but I didn't know if I was going down straight or in a spiral dive or anything because the wind was hitting me from all directions.

Suddenly the ground appeared faintly and I was only about 500ft above it. As I battled to take control, I could see that I was not going straight down but at about a 45degree angle to the ground. I managed to level out and have a look at the GPS. I was now doing only 43mph ground speed and I had the bar in to my chest with an indicated air speed was 90mph! That was a 47mph head wind in hard driving rain.

I looked down at the chart as by now it was obvious that I wouldn't reach Yangon that day. If I were to reach the alternative on the flight-plan, an airfield called Thandwe, that would have to do. As I went past an airport called Kyaukpu there was a wall of rain and by now it was obvious that I was not even going to get to Thandwe, and that I must go back and land at Kyaukpu. I gave them a call on the radio

Trying my best to pronounce the name right, I got clearance to come straight-in to land any direction I wanted.

There didn't look to be a lot at this airfield but I didn't care, needs must, and I didn't intend dying trying to get to my intended airport! I landed on what looked like a lake across the runway, there was that much water on it, and I taxied up to the Control Tower and what looked like a very small Reception come Terminal Building.

I parked up where a great many military and police men were waiting and looking at me.

I didn't know if this was good or bad, but as soon as I started getting my chair out they all came over and what friendly people they were!

I got out of the Quik and went over to the Tower to explain. A guy came down saying "*You should have gone to Yangon, why here?*"

I pointed up at the sky and said "*Weather, storms too bad*". He said "*You made a good choice, really bad weather, push your aircraft here.*" At that my Quik was pushed through the walkway gates up a gravel path and put underneath the control tower out of the wind. It started monsoon raining – this is quite amazing to see but when you're in it flying, it's so awful it hurts! After formalities were sorted out with Immigration and I had rung Yangon Control to explain, they said there were no issues with them.

"*No problem, captain*". I looked at my phone. No signal!

I said "*Internet?*", "*No, sorry*".

A guy from the tower came down and said "*We are very privileged to have you stop here, do you stay for the night now?*" Yes!

I was thrown into a people carrier and taken to the hotel they had sorted out for me. It was called the Vananthi, a small family owned place, but just travelling there you could tell that this country wasn't like any other country. Everybody just took their time, no rush, just wandering around like nothing mattered. I arrived at the hotel and the staff were falling all over themselves trying to help me. All I could say was "*No, not a problem, I'm OK, don't worry*"

I asked about my phone signal and was told that in Myanmar there were no GSM phones so mine would not work in the country at all, so it was rendered useless!

It seemed that they were just very friendly people in Myanmar and wanted to help in any way they could. This was a really nice place, so laid back and easy looking around that I would actually come here again to visit. Strangely enough it was nice not having any internet or phone calls to make (Les would be surprised). There was a TV in the room I was in so I could see the weather but that kept going off with the monsoon rain. The hotel owner, Mr Piece, brought me a bottle of beer and then had a meal sent over for me of prawns with rice. I sat with my meal and a Myanmar beer watching the rain outside just pounding down and flooding passed my room.

If the rain stopped, then I would hopefully reach Yangon the next day.

Day 41, June 8th - Static in Kyaukpyu

I was awake most of the night with the rain which had not stopped at all since the prior day. It pounded down all night and was still at it at 6am. If it didn't stop soon, then my trip to Yangon wouldn't happen that day. I got up and was offered breakfast by Mr Piece's daughter. "No thanks, I'm fine".

Mr Piece took me to the airport in his Shogun 4x4. I was met by Immigration and the Police and a lot of people from the surrounding area had come to have a look. The rain wasn't stopping. I had a weather report from the Tower and they checked other airports on the way to Yangon. "Sorry Captain but today is very bad weather, we were expecting a flight in from Yangon and that turned back".

I sat there waiting, hoping that it would clear up. It got to midday, cleared up and stopped raining, so I asked the Tower about the weather. They spoke to Yangon Airport who confirmed that the rain was still on my track and I would not get anywhere near Yangon today.

Tied up under control tower Kyaukpyu

OK then, so that was it, today's flying cancelled, because I needed four hours to get to Yangon and it would be dark at 6.30pm. Mr Piece brought me some lunch and I had a photo session with the locals and then it started raining again just as heavy as before.

My poor Quik just sat there outside under the edge of the control tower absolutely wet through but at least it was out of the wind that was tearing through the airport.

I asked Mr Piece if it would be OK for me to stop at his hotel for another night? He said, *"no problem we would love to have you again"*. A quick check over the Quik to make sure it was still secure then I was thrown into a truck and returned to the Varanthi hotel for another night.

It rained so much; I had never seen anything like it before this was definitely extreme weather. However on a good and lighter note, it had now washed away all the Saudi desert sand that I had collected from my Quik.

Day 42, June 9th

It had been raining all night again non-stop.

Would I ever leave Myanmar?

I went over to the Airport in the morning to see if the weather was due to lift at all, it was still raining hard, and there had now been two solid days of rain.

I think my Quik was clean enough!

I really needed to get out of Myanmar now. Firstly my flight clearance for Myanmar was just a 72 hour clearance to fly through and secondly because my money had just about run out and I had discovered that there were no such things as ATMs here or banks where I could withdraw cash from. In addition there was some embargo on credit cards, so it was a cash-only economy. What do you do in a foreign country with no way of leaving because of the weather and no way of obtaining any cash?

I spoke to Mr Piece. "*Don't worry about money; you can stop at my hotel as long as you need to, no need to pay*".

What a fantastic man!

Where in England would you get that? But nevertheless, I still needed to leave Myanmar.

Later while I was talking to Mr Piece and some of the locals at the Airport, there was a break in the weather. It had stopped raining, quick check what it's like in Yangon.

Clear, 6km visibility, wind 4knts.

It was time to go. I loaded up the Quik really fast and jumped in, there were a couple of young lads who had been helping me in and out of the trucks they gave me a hand putting the wheelchair on the Quik in super fast time I got pushed back out up the path on to the apron gave tower a call and because it was just a local airport I got cleared for my engine start for take-off straight away, and I finally left. Although it had said 6km visibility in Yangon, but this was not the case here 160 miles north east.

As soon as I took off I went straight into the cloud, the cloud base was 400ft.

I was not flying 250miles at that height - that would be suicidal, so I returned to Kyaukpyu. Another two hours passed by so I had a second attempt and the cloud base had lifted and was about 1,900ft this time, but still the mountains I needed to get over were 6,500ft high.

I headed south to see if I could find a way through, but it started raining again and the cloud was the same 1,900ft.

Skirting in and out of the cloud at 1,500ft in the mountains that are 6,500ft is not good, nor is flying down the valleys looking back and thinking, I hope this doesn't close in behind me. This wasn't going to happen today neither it was just impossible

So it was back to Kyaukpyu Airport and then back to the Vananthi Hotel for another night.

Day 43, June 10th

I got up early, but it was raining and raining and raining! There was not a lot to say about that day. It rained all day without stopping, so I caught up with the blog and watched TV.

In the evening Mr Piece knocked on my door and he was there with the minister of the local area who had come and wanted to say hello to me. So we chatted for a short while before the evening meal was brought out for me.

Only thing I learned today was how to pronounce Kyaukpyu and it is *chepshu*. Hopefully I would be able to continue on my journey the next day!

Day 44, June 11th - Kyaukpyu to Yangon

it was still raining at Mr Piece's hotel the Varanathi, but I got up anyway at 6.30am hoping and with fingers crossed that it would clear up. I had breakfast brought in for me - prawns with rice; I didn't eat much of it before I was taken to the airport by the staff at the Varanathi. Just before I left the hotel I said goodbye to the Minister of the area who I had met the night before and Mr Piece who were having some kind of meeting with all the local officials from the military. They both wished me well and hoped that I could get going today with the weather. The rain stopped finally!

That was it – the covers were pulled off the Quik and I mopped out all the water that had collected in the pod and seat. The Tower said that the weather was clearing all the time and so by 9am I was ready to go. So I climbed in the Quik the two young lads that had been giving me a hand were there again and helped me with my wheelchair.

I was pushed out onto the apron and got clearance to start the engine but when I tried starting the Quik, it just wouldn't have it. I tried and tried until the battery on the Quik went flat.

Just brilliant where on earth was I going to be able to charge my battery here in Myanmar?

I called over a couple of the Military and Police who stood around watching and tried to explain that I needed a pair of jump leads and a battery on a truck to get it started.

They both babbled something in Burmese and then shouted something at a couple of lads. Then they looked back at me and using their hands signed out that something would arrive in five minutes.

Sure enough, within five minutes two young lads turned up on a motor cycle carrying a car battery with some old wire.

So we cobbled the wire together and I poked about under the dash board connecting it to my battery. Then I got everybody to stand back while I tried starting it again. After a few minutes it finally started up coughing and spluttering like mad.

It must have been all the water that had got into the engine over the previous few days, I pulled the wires off from under the dash and threw them to the side, then moved forward so the battery could be taken away.

Finally I was ready for the off - destination Yangon. I took off in very little wind. It was fairly clear for the first five miles or so, after which there was the odd rain shower around me. I was only at 2,000ft as that Is what ATC had wanted me to fly at here in Myanmar. This made a really nice change. You can see a lot more things lower down and it makes it a more interesting and better flight. All along the coast of Myanmar there were lots of the traditional wood houses raised up on stilts with bamboo type roofs, fantastic to see and photograph. It beats looking at terracotta houses in the UK. Kyaukpyu is on a small island off the west coast of Myanmar, and as I flew over it and headed out over towards the mainland the weather started to change again.

There were still 245 miles to go to Yangon. Big storms were brewing over the mainland, but I could still dodge around them, and they were coming in from the sea also. Now the wind had turned so I had a 25mph head wind. I had a look at the map on my knees because if the weather continued to deteriorate I would have to go in to an airport called Thandwe. It's quite good because all along this coast the different airports use the same frequency for their control towers, similar to 129.825 and safety com in the UK, except their range is only about 40 miles or so. As you go past one airport, you get past on, so every airport knows you are about to enter into their airspace.

Thandwe Airport must have been concerned, because they were trying to raise me from about 50 miles away. I gave them a call back and they advised me that it was raining at Thandwe with 2km visibility but as I got closer it seemed to have cleared up so I carried on past, towards Yangon. Only 20 minutes after passing the Airport it became obvious that I would not reach Yangon and that I would have to go and land at Thandwe, Also because of the time now, I would not be able to have another attempt at Yangon today. I would have to try to find a hotel for the night.

There were trees everywhere now, and if I had an engine failure it would be hard to get it down safely. I gave Thandwe a call. *"Thandwe G-CDVO, microlight inbound due to bad weather."*

"G-CDVO confirm inbound to Thandwe."

"G-CDVO confirm inbound Thandwe."

"G-CDVO cleared to land 02, wind 15knts"

I landed on Runway 02 and taxied right up to the control tower which was situated right at the side of the apron and was met by a few locals and Immigration. They were very friendly again. This seems to be one of the friendliest countries I've been to so far on my trip. Right, what to do now?

I had very little money and I needed fuel and a hotel. Then a European face came over, all smiles.

"I have just heard that an Englishman has flown in, in a microlight and I didn't believe them so I have come to have a look" he said.

We got talking. His name was Pascal Gerken, from Belgium.

I told him my predicament and he said "*I have a friend that will be able to help*" and called him over, a man called Zaw Min Yu, a photographer from Yangon.

After a few phone calls to his friends in the area I had got a room sorted out for the night at a place called the Bayview Beach Resort. Not only that but when he found out I was in a wheelchair he organised some fuel to be brought for me. And also paid for it.

What an extremely helpful and friendly man, THANKS ZAW MIN YU.

I got out of my Quik and tied it up for the night, and then it was pushed to the side of the tower and just in front of a building to keep out of the wind. Soon afterwards a minibus from the Bayview Beach Resort arrived to pick me up and took me to the hotel, and a very nice place on the beach it was too.

Day 45, June 12th – Thandwe...A Failed Attempt!

I woke at 4.30 am and what a surprise, it was still raining. I will never complain about rain in England again! I was off to the Airport at 8.30 am, it was still raining, but one had to think positive

Stop raining and give me a break!

And it did! The kind staff at the Bayview had brought me to the Airport and had not charged me for the night in the hotel, which was very kind of them.

The weather brightened up, I spoke with the tower to see what the weather was like further down the coast and in Yangon, and they told me scattered cloud at Yangon at 6,000ft so I was cleared to leave any time. Fantastic let's just hope it is clear.

I got loaded up and said my goodbyes hoping I wouldn't be returning. The weather did look brighter, cloud scattered at 2,000ft, and it's the SCATTERED that makes a big difference in the mountains. You can go around scattered clouds.

I started following the route that they wanted me to follow, but Yangon was 160 miles away and I didn't think that I would be able to stick to it exactly with the mountains to cross. Once I was 65 miles into the trip, the cloud started getting thicker and lower and the mountains were rising until they both met. There was cloud down to the ground on the peaks of the mountains, but not in the valleys.

So I tried going down the valleys again to see if I could break through to Yangon and into the higher cloud. Not a chance!. Not only that, but it was getting very dark along the coast and rainy, and more cloud was coming in fast.

I was an hour into the flight again and not getting any further trying every way possible to get through the mountains.

That's it, I decided - back to Thandwe.

So it was bar in to my chest hoping that I could get back before I was closed-in by the monsoon rain in the mountains. As I headed back I gave Thandwe a call on the radio.

"G-CDVO, inbound returning due to bad weather in the mountains again."

"G-CDVO, no problem".

I was 20 miles out and I got a call back from Thandwe.

"G-CDVO, weather heavy rain, 500ft cloud base, visibility less than 1 mile, what are your intentions?"

There I was with nothing but trees everywhere, rain moving in, coming from all directions and the only place that I could land was Thandwe Airport, and now that had monsoon rain.

Brilliant! Why me?

"G-CDVO, my intention is to come inbound to Thandwe."

"G-VO, Runway 02 in use, report finals."

"G-VO report finals".

That was it. I managed to get out to the coast in really heavy rain, skimming the tree tops to get there, at about 300ft. The visibility was now down to 500metres ahead, so I finally got to just under a mile away from Thandwe and I reported finals for 02 and landed downwind in what I can only say was a lake with about 2inches of water completely covering the runway and apron.

I was completely wet through to the bone. I taxied in and got my trike cover out and covered myself over with it and put it over the dash board to protect all the instruments and I just sat there for a while. The Control Tower guys brought me over a bottle of Myanmar lager under umbrellas, smiling.

"You're not going anywhere today, captain."

I had the beer just dripping wet and laughing at how mad it all was before climbing out in to my soaking wet wheelchair and wet cushion. However being so wet my left leg slipped and I kicked the hydraulic brake cylinder on my hand brake, rupturing the pipe.

Fantastic, no brakes now!

I asked around for tools, they all shook their heads then one lad who happened to be the Immigration Officer said something to a young lad and a minute or two later a lad turned up on his Honda step-through motorbike with his tool roll. I cut the ruptured brake and shortened the pipe and reattached it.

Now I had to bleed them. Brakes on a Quik are hard enough to bleed at home, never mind being in Myanmar about 100 metres away from the beach with very limited tools and no brake fluid. After 3 hours of tapping on the master cylinder and twisting the air bubbles to the top and out of the system, I finally got the brakes back, which was a big relief. And it did not stop raining all the time I was doing this. I had never been so wet.

I eventually covered the Quik up and put it back at the side of the control tower in about three inches of water. The staff at the Bay View holiday resort came back in their minibus and picked me up and I went back to the resort. What a nice place, right on the beach.

But I had one small problem now I was out of money and I needed more fuel to get to Yangon after my flight today... What was I going to do?

I told the manager my predicament and he said wait here and I will speak to the hotel owner.

After about 30 minutes he came back and said if I wanted I could borrow some money from them and pay my hotel room when I got to a bank in the UK.

That was fantastic they just can't do enough for you. So I went back to the room to dry off and have a beer.

Sat in the rain just after landing at Thandwe

Day 46, June 13th

What can I say? I was really fed up today.

RAIN, RAIN, RAIN, RAIN and more RAIN.

The range of mountains that I needed to get over were the Arakan Yoma range, which run from north Myanmar all the way to the south on the west coast by the Bay of Bengal Sea. Getting over them just seemed to be impossible at the moment.

If it rained this much in the UK I bet there would still be a hosepipe ban!

I decided I was going to get drunk on the local Myanmar beer and hope that tomorrow came around quickly and that the rain went away.

Day 47, June 14th

I lay in bed at the Bayview Holiday Resort watching the monsoon rain bouncing against the windows and the palm trees trying to uproot themselves. The BBC World Weather had just been on and said that the rain would be here for the next few days. Still I had to have a go at getting to Yangon anyway. After all the BBC weather in the UK is usually wrong anyway! However every time it looks promising, it pours down again. I had been tapping away on the computer catching up with my blog while waiting for it to clear up enough to set off.

I now had the Quik tied up at the side of the control tower in front of a building with the Airport Fire Engine parked in front of it to shield the wind a bit, and it was tied up to that as well. I decided I might go for a look around at the local area after checking the Quik out to see if everything is ok, like my brakes!

All my bruises from flying had now gone.

I spoke with the manager today and he asked me if I wanted to go and see a famous Buddha who was visiting the village tomorrow, so I agreed to it.

I just look like a prune now with all the water, as if I'd been in a bath for two days. It rained so hard all day today that I didn't get to look around, and sat in the hotel again and watched TV. Talk about numbing the brain!

Day 48, June 15th

It hadn't stopped raining all night and this time it was so hard that the generators that the hotel runs on went off along with the TV and internet. I had been awake most of the night; it was only 8am, black outside and torrential still. So I got up and had a look outside, it was wild

I went out to the Reception to see what time we would be and so returned at 10.30am to be thrown in to the min bus with Eyat and a couple of the staff from the Beach View before we went off down the muddy roads of Thandwe to a small village in the middle of nowhere to meet the Buddhist 'healing nun'. All the houses here were on stilts to avoid the floods and water lying underneath them.

We reached to this small temple where there were people everywhere so we pulled up as close as we could to get me out and in to my wheelchair without sitting in 4ft of flood water. At the side of the temple there was a long outdoor gazebo with people feasting in it.

When we pulled up everybody looked, because I had to be lifted out into my chair, and then we made our way through the gazebo with everybody watching. I was met by a guy who said I had to take my shoes and socks off to see the Buddha, which I did. Then I was carried up a flight of steps to a hall where everybody sat on the floor with their legs crossed listening to the Buddha talking and doing some spiritual healing to different people.

I was asked to go to the front but my chair was not allowed. The guys I was with literally picked me up out of my wheelchair and carried me to the front of this full room and sat me on the floor in front of the Buddha.

She smiled and a spiritual healing was performed on my legs along with me drinking some holy water.

All a bit strange, but you never know.

I might be walking to my Quik later.

After about ten minutes she said, "OK, stand up" in Mandarin.

The guys helped me up and stood me up.

Yes, I could stand up!

After 17 years!

Oops!

No, I couldn't so, back down on the floor.

My legs had just had a muscle spasm and gone all rigid

It didn't work. Not today but maybe it might have to take a bit of time to work?

I would try again tomorrow.

Everybody was very positive about it working.

I decided I would give it a couple of days and think positive!

I was carried back out of the room and down stairs before being thrown back in my chair, given a quick push back through the crowds of onlookers and people waiting to be seen by the Buddha. I put my shoes and socks back on and got thrown back in the van just before another downpour.

The Healing Buddha

I went back to hotel for a while; the rain was still coming down and would not stop. I got bored of being in my room so I had a wander down the road from the hotel; the roads are really bad with pot holes everywhere.

It was flooded here, there and everywhere.

I was lifted out of the hotel down the steps and started going to explore when a young lad ran out of the hotel with an umbrella and gave me an escort.

I found a wonderful restaurant called Htay Htay's Kitchen Restaurant, a rickety wooden building with a bamboo roof.

I had the best curry so far on my travels, a prawn curry.

A few Myanmar beers to wash it down and then it was back to the hotel still in the torrential rain.

Please, weather, give me a window for tomorrow.

Day 49, June 16th

Not much to say apart from rain, rain and more rain!

By now I was so fed up that I even got a price for a truck to take me and the Quik to Yangon by road just to get past all these mountains and rain. It would cost $500 and about 18-24 hours driving.

But what should I do?

Should I spend a shed-load of money in hotels waiting for a break in the weather, or should I take the road? If I take the road, the flight won't be classed as flying from York to Sydney that was the only problem.

I had been down on the ground now for the best part of two weeks in Myanmar and I was getting really itchy feet (so to speak) to get going again. I didn't think that my brain cells would handle been stuck here in the rain much longer, and neither would my wallet! In addition, I had been the only guest at the Beach View Hotel for the last few days as well. The local aeroplane that flies into Thandwe had been cancelled for days, also due to weather.

The next time I'm in the pub talking about flying and I say "*I know - I've got a good idea, why don't I fly to Australia?*", somebody please slap me and tell me to stop being a prat! Just go to Breighton for a bacon butty - Breighton is 15 minutes flight away from Rufforth, where I fly from.

Now the mosquitoes were having a field day with me, the little bastards.

The holy water still hadn't worked. I'm still not walking. I can't understand it. They promised I would be walking in the next day or so.

I know why!

It must be contaminated with rain water!

Better luck next time?

I might go searching for a haircut Burmese style. I haven't had a hair cut since I set off. I usually have one every week back home.

Day 50, June 17th

I hadn't got my hair cut yet, and believe it or not, it was still raining. There was thunder and lightning last night so I had very little sleep once again. It's funny, I had this dream to fly around the world, but after chasing sponsors and not getting anywhere with them and the realising the enormous cost that it would involve, that was quickly a no-go.

Australia – now that had to be a good old flight. It had been 81 years since Amy Johnson flew solo to Darwin - why not celebrate that? Now I was on my way to Oz.

I didn't think it was going to be easy by any means, but day in, day out I had had something in my way trying to stop me getting there. To start with the electrical problems, then the weather, and arguing with people was just getting to be a chore.

I was now here in Myanmar where everybody was friendly and helpful, which seemed to just take away all the problems, as if it was not important anymore.

Even the paperwork hadn't been too hard work, like I was expecting. Sure there was a lot of it and it took forever to sort out, but if that's the way it had to be, so be it.

It makes me think, did I take off at the wrong time of year?

I don't know.

In England I had fog and mist over the Channel, rain in France and Italy, then 47°C (116°F) of heat going across deserts in the Middle East through to Bangladesh. I got told that if I made it through India before the end of June I would be fine.

On a better note I had now covered 9,854 statute miles so far, in just over 153 hours of flying.

Then I looked out of the window once again, and yes, it's still raining!

It's now after 2pm so no flying today again

Day 51, June 18th

I woke up early.

I had a good feeling about today, so I booked out of the hotel and was taken to the airport for 9.30am. It was still raining but not too bad.

"*Pull my Quik out for me, please*" I said to the staff.

They moved the Fire Engine out of the way and brought my Quik onto the apron for me. It looked like a drowned rat! I pulled the cover off very slowly as the area was known for wild Cobra snakes and I didn't fancy meeting one face to face! I looked inside the pod nice and slowly, the drain hole that I had drilled was working a treat, so there wasn't a drop of water inside, but all the bugs had come inside for the few days and were having a right old time. There were loads of them jumping out at me and after a good ten minutes chasing them out and checking in my gloves for them, I gave the Quik the once-over and loaded up, ready to go.

It was still raining, but it was more like drizzle and I was quite happy to go and fly in drizzle. I clambered back in the Quik, stripped the wheelchair down and put it back on the Quik. I gave the Tower a call and they gave me clearance to go whenever I was ready - they just had to give Yangon a telephone call to let them know that I was on my way and to expect me.

So in the drizzle I took off and started heading down the coast. I planned to head a lot further south this time to see if I could get to Yangon this way, but an hour into the flight the drizzle had turned to rain and had started to get heavier and heavier until I was down to just 400ft over the sea, with a 20mph headwind and torrential rain full-on in my face. The cloud over the mountains was down to the ground again. I couldn't see anything or any way of getting through again, looking back and all around it was really crapping out again.

As I got wetter and wetter and it was getting darker, I said, that's it, I can't carry on.

Back to Thandwe!

I turned back, but the storms were now building in front of me for my return. Into Thandwe, here we go again, bar-in to chest, 95mph showing on ASI and let's get back before I am really trapped out here.

I gave Thandwe a call:

"*G-CDVO, Confirm you are returning*",

"G-CDVO, Confirm returning to Thandwe".

"G-CDVO be advised that heavy rain and a storm approaching from the west",

"G-CDVO."

I was now 400ft above the coast, out at sea passing all the fishing boats in rain, doing just over 115mph, trying to get back in before the biggest black storm I could see hit me.

I could hear interference on the radio from the storm, crackling and squealing.

I called Thandwe but no response!

Called them again, still nothing! The combination of the storm causing interference on the radio and my low altitude meant they couldn't hear me.

I was now flying around the small coves along the coast, in and out of cloud and at only 300ft I really was not happy. I was so low now that it looked like I would have to fly around the fishing boats!

Only about 2 miles away from Thandwe I finally got a response: *"G CDVO, come straight in, you are cleared to land, report finals."*

"G-CDVO, straight in, report finals".

That was it.

Who was going to get to the airport first, me or the storm?

With a mile left to run, I could just see the runway disappearing into heavy rain.

Thandwe runway starts about 100ft away from the beach, heading direct inland, so on finals you are out at sea lining up to land. I came up the coast past the airport building and just turned in, right over the numbers, I touched down with a 20mph tail wind.

It was really mad because as I got down the storm was chasing me down the runway. I turned around and taxied back to a parking area with the storm right on top of me now.

Pulling at the wing and blowing me around absolutely throwing it down I struggled with the Quik but I managed to get back at the side of the tower to shelter from the storm as much as possible, and sat there waiting for a break.

The staff from the hotel came back and the tower staff came down, all with big smiles and umbrellas.

"Do you want to go back to hotel, Captain David, sir"?

"No, thanks, I am going to let this storm pass and have another go at Yangon".

Thirty minutes went by and it became lovely and calm.

The storm passed into the mountains and the sun was even threatening to come out. I gave Tower a radio call and I got no response! I tried again but still no response. I checked the connections on my radio and in all the panic trying to keep the radio dry on the way back in I had put it under the dash board.

But then as I pulled it out from underneath I had pulled the BNC connector from the aerial out and it broke contact inside. An instant repair was needed.

A pair of pliers was brought for me by one of the airport staff and I chopped the cable and refitted the connector again. I gave the tower a call to see if it was fixed.

"G-CDVO, I can hear you perfectly".

I asked the Tower if I was cleared to have another attempt and they gave me the weather *"G-CDVO the weather at Yangon is still clear and sunny"*

I started up and took off again, destination Yangon. I was going to get there!

Twenty minutes after take-off and heading back down the coast I just knew I was not going to get there that day. The cloud was right down to 100ft again and the rain was back.

I accepted defeat for another day and had to retreat back to Thandwe.

Cloud and rain right down to the ground flying down the coast to Pathein

Upon landing all the hotel staff came back, smiling again.

I threw my map boards out and said *"That's me done I just cannot get there, let's pack it up back at the side of the tower and go back to your wonderful hotel for another night."*

I got back to the hotel had a beer then went down the flooded road to T'Hay T'Hays and got drunk.

Dead simple…

While I was sat in the restaurant watching the world get washed away with the rain, about 10 to 15 buffalo came past the on the road being herded by a young lad with a big stick shouting. That's something you don't see every day.

Deadly silence, only the generator from the restaurant chugging away in the back ground for the lighting and the rain.

This village is very different from what I am used to back in the UK.

It really makes you think on how lucky we are in the UK to have power in the brick built houses with heating and lights at the flick of a switch.

Not like here in this village in the jungles of Myanmar, with candles, generators and bamboo buildings.

So I'm not going to moan again how badly done to I am flying to Oz.

I will try again to get to Yangon tomorrow.

Day 52, June 19th

4.30am. It was raining.

Well, that does make a change!

At 8.30am I got up and it was still raining. I went to reception and said "*Take me to the airport please*".

They all looked around, a bit puzzled and said OK.

About 20 minutes later the heavens opened again, and that was it, no flying again by the look of that.

"Erm, can you just hold on a few more minutes with the transport to the airport while it clears up a bit more for me?"

I had some toast and jam - that's all the hotel had left in the kitchen for me - and I sat there eating it as it rained harder.

Wind and rain for nearly 3 weeks outside my room at the Bay View Holiday Resort

Just great stuff this was. All my friends are back in the UK probably enjoying themselves flying and I'm here in the jungle at a beach resort on my own, 9,000 miles away in monsoon rain. I sat watching the small lizards running around and the workers in the hotel laying some new floor tiles for the next season.

I was just thinking... when's it all going to end?

The day passed by again all too quickly, with the rain just not letting up at all and then it was all too late to get to Yangon in the time available, so flying was cancelled again.

I looked at the maps to see how far and how far I had come so far and how far I had left to go to get to Sydney. Compared to what I had already done. It's not that far now really just a few thousand miles left.

I had really bad guts that day, I didn't dare venture very far from the toilet. I think that the fish I had last night wasn't the freshest in the world, it was a king prawn that the Hotel manager had given to Htay Htay for me to have.

140

I didn't go to Htay Htay's tonight.

I didn't fancy racing my way to the toilet tomorrow so after a look in the fridge the hotel came up with Spaghetti with a spicy sauce for me and I just sat in the restaurant. A couple of men had stayed at the hotel the previous night who were also trying to get to Yangon. I had discovered that because of the floods, they had to go and use a couple of kayaks to get through the village and 5ft of water to get to a bus that would take them there by road. That would take them 24 hours.

June 19, exchange of letters between Dave, RMH, Mike Gray and me:Hello, Mike, Brian and Richard

Thanks for the advice. I have seen the big mountains from Rangoon to Bangkok and there is a route around them with 1 or 2 airfields to go in if the weather is crap (which it is). As you say, all the help and advice is very much appreciated as you have been here before.

I have 145lts fuel capacity and the way its been averaging 12 ltrs an hour, so when I fill up with Avgas at Rangoon I will have about 11 hrs flying.

(I flew from Riyadh to Qatar then to Abu Dhabi without a refuel)

I should be out of Myanmar soon. I can get down the coast to Pantien (VYPN) then up through straight to Yangon.

Kind Regards
Dave Sykes
www.soloflightglobal.com

From: Richard Meredith-Hardy [mailto:r.mh@flymicro.com]
Sent: 19 June 2011 13:05
To: brianmilton1@aol.com; White Rose Aviation
Subject: RE: monsoons

Brian

Even if he could get the clearance, if he stays west of the mountains it's a hell of a long way with bugger all to the first possible diversion, 300 Nm from Rangoon to Miek, VYME and there's still quite a lot of Burma after that, and remember, the fuel is crap. At least the route towards Bangkok has some possible diversions, Rangoon to Hpa-An VYPA is 83 Nm and from there to Mae Sot VTPM just over the border in Thailand is only 50 Nm. The bulk of the mountains are actually after that, but at least he would be back in territory with good fuel, comms & met.

I hope my friends in Thailand will solve any problems with outrageous fees.

Richard

From: brianmilton1@aol.com [mailto:brianmilton1@aol.com]
Sent: 19 June 2011 12:22

142

To: r.mh@flymicro.com; ops@whiteroseaviation.co.uk
Subject: Re: monsoons

Dear Chaps,

To add to RMH's suggestion, why go over the mountains to Bangkok when you can go straight down the coast, heading for - but not landing at - Phuket? Is Bangkok really necessary, measured against survival?

RMH's warning of the $1,000 demanded as landing fees at Phuket should put every future traveller off landing there, but there are alternatives, I am sure.

Best wishes,

Brian

-----Original Message-----
From: Richard Meredith-Hardy <r.mh@flymicro.com>
To: 'White Rose Aviation' <ops@whiteroseaviation.co.uk>
Cc: brianmilton1@aol.com
Sent: Sun, Jun 19, 2011 11:03 am
Subject: monsoons

Mike – perhaps fwd this to Dave if possible?

==

Hi Dave

Looks like you're having a really torrid time of it there in the rain… And yes, those mountains are horribly rugged.

I expect you know already, but if you can get about 90 Nm south down the coast from Thandwe to Chaung Thar (a little bit south of the Rangoon parallel) then there's two roads across the mountains. By the looks of it on Google Earth, the northern road doesn't go above about 400 ft and the southern one about 200 ft, so everything is much lower compared to where you are now.

Doesn't look like there's anywhere to go on the coast, but once over the mountains you have Pathein, VYPN as a possible diversion.

I've been in touch with a few people in Thailand, Malaysia and Indonesia who are watching your progress and should be reasonably helpful when you eventually get there. In your current predicament you probably didn't want to know this, but I'm afraid the mountains between Burma and Thailand are worse than the ones you're trying to get over now...

Good luck, and be safe, I know what it's like when you can barely see the ground at 200ft in rain like that, and it ain't good, especially in mountains. It will stop in the end...

Regards

Richard M-H

Day 53, June 20th - Thandwe to Yangon

It was now Monday 20th June, I thought that I would have been well on my way to Australia by now - I only thought it would take me 8 weeks.

I was sure today was the day! A local woman had said to me the other day that the weather would be fine today, due to it being some days after the full moon. Let's see, shall we?

I work up at 4.30am and it was still raining!

As it got to about 8am it started to stop raining.

So down to reception and I asked them.

"*Take me to the Airport, please*"

By 9.30am, it had completely stopped raining, so I threw all my bags and charts into the minibus and got thrown into it as well. I had a good feeling about today for some reason even the staff came to the airport to wave me off.

They had even bought some fuel to fill my tanks up with. Then we set off to Thandwe Airport.

We got out of the minibus and I had a photo session with them all, Then a guy from the tower came down and said to me: "*At the moment the Airport is closed due to runway repairs, we only have 3,000 metres of usable tarmac will it be long enough for you?*"

I smiled at him and said: "*I will have a go but I'm sure that 3,000 metres will be plenty long enough for me*"

"*OK, sir if you're sure*" he said back to me.

It was time to start getting the Quik out ready to go. I made my way through the mud and flooded water to where my Quik was parked up, I untied it from the Fire Truck and took off the covers nice and slowly again.

I looked in the trike in case there were any snakes or big bugs lurking around within and then the Fire Engine was moved out of the way for me.

There was now an onslaught of onlookers arriving at the airport to see me off on my way. The hotel staff and Immigration Officials pushed my Quik out of the mud and onto a dryish part of the apron.

Then I got in and stowed my wheelchair on board ready for the off, helmet on and maps at the ready, I grabbed my gloves and a cockroach type creature shot out of one of them and ran straight up my arm and over my shoulder. Waving around trying to find where it had gone, the onlookers were stood laughing at me. Then I spoke to the Tower:

"G-CDVO, the weather at Yangon is clear, 6knt wind, scattered cloud at 6,000ft. the same as the other day, the weather at Pathein is scattered cloud at 1,500ft visibility, 2-3miles. Do you want to go?"

Pathein was an Airfield that I would be passing on the coast before turning to Yangon.

"G-CDVO, thank you for that, and yes I would like to go".

"G-VO give me 5 minutes, please"

While he was sorting the paperwork out with Yangon I sat in the Quik and had some more photos taken with my new friends at the Airport and from the Bay View Beach Resort.

The weather was still holding off for me. This could definitely be the day!

"G-CDVO, request engine start."

"G-VO engine start approved, taxi to 02 and line up when ready"

I taxied out and lined up. I had enough room with 3,000metres of runway with a truck some 2,400 metres away doing repairs and so I took off and headed down the coast to Pathein Airport.

I could see inland was filling in well with thunderstorms and very low cloud, but where I was the cloud was at 1,500ft and scattered.

I flew in and out of them for about 45 minutes. Then the cloud opened up to about a 3,000ft cloud base. Still following the coastline I looked inland to see if I could get over to Yangon, but there was not a chance yet - the cloud inland was still black and down to the ground.

I was now about 40 miles from Pathein the cloud had got lower, and inland it was now getting very wet with big storms building everywhere.

I decided to cut the corner off near Panthein Airport and I picked my way through the clouds and rain. The ground was now getting lower, it was less mountainous and with floods everywhere it was just like a lake.

About 30 miles to run to Yangon and on my right hand side a huge black storm was heading my way with a wall of rain.

To my left a big bank of rain was also closing in, the cloud base at 2,000ft.

There was nowhere to land and sit out the crap weather, there were floods everywhere - the Irrawaddy River must have breached its banks. I was now beyond the point of return so no going back to Thandwe.

The flooded Irrawaddy River

Oh well, bar in to chest and let's get through this gap in between the storms then.

I started getting thrown about and getting very wet. I dropped down to 1,000ft getting really wet but at least I could see where I was going.

I managed to get through the gap in between them before it all closed in behind me. When I looked back and there was nothing but a wall of heavy rain.

I had made it!

But over the radio I could hear other aircraft asking ATC diversion routes because of bad weather.

I got in touch with Yangon.

"G-CDVO Yangon"

"G-CDVO squawk 6244"

"G-CDVO Squawking 6244"

"G-CDVO We have you on radar continue your approach"

After about 20 miles the weather started to brighten up. Yangon radar came back to me

"G-CDVO, report 5 miles to run and airport in sight."

"G-CDVO, 5 miles to run now and I have Airport in sight!"

"G-VO - join right hand, down-wind and report finals for 21."

That was it and it didn't seem busy at all.

I called finals and was cleared to land. I was so glad to have made here after having been in the jungle for so long and with so many failed attempts to get over the mountains. I taxied in passed lots of big jets and was taken to a parking spot in between two big commercial jets out of the main part of the apron where I was met by a big crowd of onlookers and airport staff.

A guy came over with a clipboard, wearing a luminous jacket and looking very official.

"Hello, are you my handling agent?" I said as he introduced himself.

"No, captain, this is a government-run airport and you don't need a handling agent"

"Can I park up somewhere for the night then? And I need a hotel"

Just one moment he said and he gave me his mobile phone: *"Talk - phone call for you"*

"Hello?"

"Hello, mate, my name's Scott I'm from the British Embassy in Yangon. Is everything OK?"

"Hello, Scott, everything is fine. I just need to tie my Quik down and find a hotel. Can you help?"

"Dave, don't worry about a thing. You can stop with me at the Embassy residence. I'll send my driver out for you."

Well, it's certainly not an everyday occurrence that you get to stop at an official house of residence!

"Erm! OK give me about 30 minutes and I will be in Arrivals then."

I clambered out of the Quik with everybody watching in amazement at how the chair goes together then I got my Quik tied down to some concrete blocks that were dragged over for me.

Then I was taken in to an office in the Airport to explain why I was over two weeks late in getting to Yangon.

I was told that my transit clearance and Visa had now expired.

So there was an hour of paperwork and them saying I now needed a business visa to get out of the Airport.

I paid $40 they issued me a business Visa and I got out to Arrivals to be met by the driver from the British Embassy.

"Hello, Dave. I am to take you to Scott's house."

Let's go!

I was taken away in a Mitsubishi Shogun to this big white house behind high walls and lots of razor wire with spikes all along the top.

After an hour or so in this big house alone the front door opened.

"Hello, mate, I'm Scott, and you are most welcome to stop here with me, Michelle and my daughter"

"Thanks, mate, I just have to probably wait for my Thailand Permit updating."

"No worries. Do you want a beer?"

Oooooohhh.

Let me think about that for a second!

We had a few beers talking about all that had happened over the last few weeks. and then Scott's wife Michelle and daughter came home and I met them.

I was truly relaxed now after that flight that had been really testing to my nerves.

I just have to hope my Thailand permit won't take too long to update now.

Day 54, June 21st

I awoke in the British Embassy house to rain, something I was getting used to out here in Myanmar. Now I just needed my permit for Thailand to be updated so I could get going again - my next stop was Bangkok but on this route there were also some 8,000ft mountains to get over! I just had to hope that the rain would stop for when my permit comes through.

Scott and his family thoroughly looked after me. In the morning they just left me in their house as they went to work.

How trusting is that?

I spent all day on the computer, emailing and doing blogs and all manner of things just to get the flight on to the next stage.

Scott and Michelle came home from work and asked if I would like to go to the local bar for a beer?

OK, if I really must!

We went to a local hotel for some Myanmar beer and met some of Scott's friends. While I was there at the bar I told Scott about Yangon Airport charging me for parking, and about all the landing and navigation charges for the whole country.

They wanted $85 for every landing plus another $65 every flight for navigation charges. Not only that, they wanted to charge me $15 a day parking for every day that I was in the country. So the bill was going to be over $900

Scott said, *"Leave it with me. I'll have a word with the Embassy tomorrow and see if we can do anything for you."*

That would be a big bonus as I still now have Burmese money!

Day 55, June 22nd

I sat around at the Embassy residence for most of the day, waiting for my Thailand permit, but nothing arrived until about 5pm Myanmar time.

Hurray it had arrived. I was now permitted to continue on Friday 24th June to Bangkok. I was also answering one or two phone calls from the Embassy regarding my costs in Myanmar with the Airport authorities and playing silly games on the computer.

Just before tea time I got an email saying that the Myanmar Aviation Authorities had decided to scrub ALL charges while flying in Myanmar for me, so a big thank you for all involved at the British Embassy in getting that sorted out for me. Also a very big thank you to the Myanmar Authorities for waiving the Fees. It was such a big help given all the time I had spent on the ground here.

I went to the pub again with Scott to celebrate and met some more of his mates. One of them turned out to be a pilot who flew a twin Otter around Myanmar for a job. While we were talking, he was giving me some warnings about the Mountains in Myanmar and how turbulent they can be and warning me to be very careful. I said I had been finding out how bad they can be over the last week or so, being in them, but that I would remember that, thank you.

There was one hell of a light show going on outside with storms and noise.

All I could think was, would my Quik be OK!

Then the Otter pilot said "*so you're the pilot of the Ultralight on the apron then?*"

Yes, I was.

"*You must be mad, and by the way your Quik is still there. I was having a look around it today, I wish you well on your trip, Dave*".

It made me feel better knowing that the Quik was still OK.

We had several more beers watching the electrical storm outside before retreating back to HQ.

Just one more day before, weather permitting, I could head to Bangkok.

Day 56, June 23rd

What can I say? I got up at 7.30am talked to Scott and Michelle for a short while, before they went to work.

That morning I had a newspaper interview with a journalist from the *Myanmar Times* at the Residence.

He turned up about 10.30am and asked a few questions before leaving.

Early in the afternoon a British Embassy driver had been arranged to collect me and give me a guided tour of Yangon, taking in all the sites, especially the big Buddha temples and the golden city covered in solid gold (not gold leaf). That was some sight, I'll tell you.

I was even taken to have a look around the old British Embassy grounds that were closed down years ago. Not many people get to see that these days as it is under guard.

Then we went off to have a look around the different areas of Yangon from the slum areas on to the docks where there were hundreds of workers all in a line unloading ships on to trucks.

Yangon was quite an amazing place really!

Motor cycles were banned from the city centre so it was not complete mayhem.

We called at a small market which was a bit different with people selling absolutely anything, there was a woman squatted on the side of the road with a big wok type bowl piled high with prawns, although covering the prawns were a mass of flies buzzing around. It was terrible.

After a good couple of hours we headed back to the house, I was now nursing a hangover from the night before and didn't feel very well at all!

As 6pm came, I asked whether anybody fancied going out for a drink that evening before I left the following day?

Sorry, Dave, I'm fine but I will get some beer in for you if you want Scott said.

And on that comment I thought it would probably be better to stay in and have a couple of drinks in house before going to bed fairly early in order to psych myself up for tomorrow's flight to Bangkok assuming the weather played ball.

A gold Pagoda in Yangon

Day 57, June 24th

I was up early because I would be leaving at 7.30am with Scott to go to the Domestic Airport so he could get an airside pass for the International Airport.

We pulled up at Departures in the Domestic part of the Airport and Scott went in to get his pass.

Then we went to International Departures and met the security guy that had dealt with me when I landed 4 days previously. We went in to the airport and with my bags on a trolley and 60litres of fuel in 3 jerry cans; we made our way to security.

So believe it or not, I went through the metal detectors and had my baggage x-rayed with 60 litres of fuel and took it right through the middle of the airport.

Imagine doing that at Manchester airport; where you can't even take a bottle of washing up liquid through never mind 60 litres of fuel!

So anyway I spent a while going backwards and forwards getting paperwork sorted before finally going out and fuelling up the Quik ready to go.

I got fuelled up with the help of the airport staff who by now were multiplying.

In fact by now there were around 60 people watching me and the wind was starting to pick up as well.

I heard the Tower say over a hand held radio that the wind was 20knts now!!..

Great stuff back into the wind again and it looked like it was going to be a head wind as well.

I turned the Quik side on into wind so I could get in, once that way I climbed in and put the wheelchair away. My legs were having a right time today having spasms and being a right pain. All these people were just looking and wondering what was wrong with me!

Then we had a photo session with Scott and everybody who was standing around – this all seemed a bit mad because they hadn't wanted cameras to be used as I landed, and now the reverse seemed true as they were all taking pictures of me. With the photos taken, I then gave the Tower a call and was cleared to start straight away.

Some of my fans from Yangon

I asked for taxi and this is what they said.

"G-CDVO Taxi Alpha to holding Bravo"

"G-CDVO taxi alpha to Holding Bravo"

So I waved to everybody and set off taxing. When I was on taxi way Alpha and the tower said,

"G-CDVO where are you now"

"G-CDVO on taxi way Alpha"

'G-CDVO STOP WHERE YOU ARE NOW'

So I did, and wondered what I had done – I was looking around ... had I gone the wrong way??

It didn't look like it, and there weren't any aircraft coming towards me, so I thought I would just wait here then. Maybe they'll send a Follow-Me car.

I looked all down the taxiway and there were now lots of people coming out to watch in between all the big jets to see what was happening.

Then the Tower said *"G-CDVO cleared for take-off on taxi way Alpha, wind 20knts not above 2,000ft on 235 heading please"*

I just laughed and went for it, it made a change not having to taxi for miles to the runway.

I took off with all these big jets at my left hand side, so it had to be done - as soon as I was off the ground I flew down the taxi way at about 100ft, I passed everybody waving and then pushed the bar out to climb up passed the tower ☺

I climbed to 2,000ft on the 235 heading which took me out of the way of the flight path of the airport.

The visibility was pretty poor, only about 3 miles, if that and I had a 25knt headwind as well. This was going to be a long flight!

As I got out past the Yangon River and out to the Anderman Sea the visibility was really bad so I had to drop down to about 1,000ft to get a better horizon with the sea.

I just sat there for the best part of three hours, dodging around the odd scud cloud and rain shower.

I lost radio contact with Yangon for a while but a passenger airliner gave me a call asking my position for them and then said *"Also G-CDVO have a nice journey to Australia and good luck"*

That was nice!

Further down towards my turning point at a place called Dawei, I was tracking the coast and I could feel the rotor rolling off the 10,000ft mountains at my side – it was very rough.

At this point I thought I don't think I will be able get over the mountains to Bangkok but I'll have a go.

I flew closer to the land and past a huge bay with a beautiful beach but it was just getting too rough for me, so I headed back out to sea.

I got closer to an airfield called Dawei where I went inland and it was quite rough still there but very flat land now.

I called overhead Dawei and continued in to the mountains towards Bangkok. I was only about 10 miles past Dawei and the cloud got worse, eventually going down to the ground with a 25knt wind kicking me about.

It was now obvious I wasn't going to get to Bangkok yet..

It was far too dangerous!

So I went back and landed at Dawei airport.

All 4,520 metres of it, Dawei Tower said "*wind calm*"

But as I went in it was actually a full 90degree to the runway and 25knt crosswind – these crosswind landings were getting quite regular now!

I taxied in to be met by Immigration and the staff from the Tower.

After an explanation of why I had landed at Dawei, all with their notebooks out taking my details, they were all fine and happy to have me there. They asked if I would be staying over?

I said no, not yet, I'm going to see if the weather clears a bit first.

"*No problem Captain, just call Tower when you want to leave.*"

After about 30mins it cleared a bit so I gave them a call and I left for another attempt on Bangkok, but about 8 miles out the cloud was down to the ground still, I ended up flying down the valleys getting bounced all over, I was thinking "*what are you doing Dave go back you won't get there*"

So there was no way was I going to get to Bangkok like that all 162 miles of it!

I turned around and had to fly back down a couple of valleys on the way back because the cloud and rain were building around.

So I retreated back to Dawei for the night.

As soon as I landed, the Immigration Officers came to see me, and asked for my passport, then it was a phone call via the control tower to Bangkok to tell them I wouldn't be there today. I was hoping that Thailand would be as understanding as Myanmar.

There were only one or two of them that could speak in broken English which was good enough to get by with.

After a couple of suggestions where I could park they sorted a place where I could go with the Quik for the night and tie it down. Then one of the main guys there found a hotel for me.

Spot on again – they were very friendly people I certainly can't fault Myanmar in any way.

I got taken to the hotel down the rough cobbled roads in a 4x4 pickup and was given a room on the ground floor (room only, no bathroom or toilet)

The hotel was called Pale Elkari. It had a small restaurant at the side and internet in a back room that I had to ask to use and it was not running at supersonic speed.

Bangkok tomorrow weather permitting!

I went next door to try out the restaurant before heading to bed.

Day 58, June 25th

I was up most of the night with noise coming from the Reception which was right next to my room, but I didn't mind.

Also there was some kind of bug running around my room on the lino floor, it sounded like it was wearing Doc martin boots!! I didn't dare to move in bed as it really sounded a big beast and the power in the room had gone off so I couldn't see what it was?? I didn't know if this was due to a power cut or generators?

I was up early to go to the Airport so I went to sort out my room bill and get a lift up there somehow.

The lady on reception said to me the room is free of charge sir and the owner is going to take you to the Airport shortly herself.

Wow what a bonus that was! Free hotel and restaurant.

 A big thank you to the PALE EIKARI HOTEL in Dawei for that, it was much appreciated as I had just about run out of money.

158

I was taken up to the Airport in a small car that looked like it should been in a museum and was met by lots of the locals who had heard that I'd flown in and came to see me, amazing.

The weather was a bit showery but it looked ok…

So I got kitted out and ready to go. By now lots and lots of the locals were watching me from behind a fence, and the Airport staff came down to see me as well. They were fantastic, helping with anything they could.

"Just give us a call to the Tower when you want to start your engine"

Easy as that!!!…

So I clambered into my Quik after taking the covers of again really slowly and carefully and prepared to go.

Then I gave the Tower a call

"G-CDVO DAWEI, permission to start engine"

'G-CDVO engine start approved, when ready taxi out to runway 16'

After getting my oil temperature up to 50° (it was already at 38°), I taxied out and lined up on runway 16 and before I had chance to tell them they cleared me for take-off.

"G-CDVO cleared for take-off 16, wind calm"

So laid back and easy going they were.

So I took off in the calm wind!!

I got to 50ft and holy hell let go with the bar, all of a sudden I had a 30mph wind hitting me from the side!

Left, right, left, right, up, down, left and right, I was pushing and pulling the bar just to keep level! I thought that the wind was supposed to be calm?

I set off towards Bangkok, but after last night having talked to one of the locals at the Airport, I was now going to follow a river through the mountains to Bangkok although not direct it was looking like the lowest point through the mountains..

"G-CDVO report 5miles out of Dawei"

So I did and started to follow the river through the mountains, the mountains start low at 2,000ft just out of Dawei and climb to 9,000ft.

As I got into the range at 3,000f,t it was getting very turbulent with the wind rolling over the very steep mountains, in fact some were just about vertical.

I was only about 20 minutes into the flight and I could see the cloud building.

The hills were getting bigger all the time and, as they did, the turbulence was getting wilder. The cloud was at about 2,000ft, so now the cloud was touching the tops of the mountains and it had started to rain.

I could see in front that there were two very big mountains to go between at about 6,000ft. Looking further ahead I could see blue on the other side, should I go for it? I looked at my GPS and I had a wind of 25-30mph as it tunnelled through the valleys.

I looked behind and it was still ok for me to turn back if I needed to.

So I carried on, the trees at both sides of me were now dropping down near vertical drops to the river below and cloud completely covered the mountain tops at both sides. The wind was blowing a hooley still! As I flew around the very sharp peak of a mountain, the wind came over the top of one side of the mountain and hit me hard, it whipped my visor up nearly snapping it off, it tried to rip the map boards out of the trike, my helmet hit the nose pole again and the Quik just dropped out of the sky and my bum left the seat. I looked at the VSI and it had shot down to 1,500ftper min straight out of the sky.

I powered on but it didn't make any difference I was still going down.

If I didn't stop I was almost certainly going to hit the trees.

Then the valley opened to a flat area which was good because it allowed the wind to disperse and so I wasn't going down anymore or going to hit the trees!

Pheeew!!! That nearly filled my pants I can tell you.

I was now in a very big valley with a flat plane and the weather was brighter, EXCELLENT – I might just get to Bangkok after all.

The river headed slightly north before going into the mountains again so I continued north still following the river until it started to go back into the mountains. At this point the wind started blowing a good 25-30mph again. The cloud and rain started closing in, as did the mountains like a wall on both sides of trees. However this valley wasn't as wide as the other I had just come through...

160

Should I or shouldn't I carry on?

I decided to go and have a look.

I went into this gorge like valley - I was getting seriously battered about with gusts of wind hitting me from behind and lifting the back of the trike up and dropping me again this time but this time I was suddenly doing 100mph pointing at the ground.

No,No,No!

I wasn't having that, and in front there was now a wall of monsoon rain.

So with trees at both sides, a wall of rain in front and cloud down to the ground I had to make a life or death decision and turn back or die.

It wasn't the ideal position I wanted to be in really.

"*DEAL with it and get out of there Dave I said to myself*"

As the valley was so thin I had to go fairly close to the trees at one side and make a 45 degree turn in order to avoid hitting the trees at the other side.

But I got round with no big drama, still getting bounced all over.

So now I had to fight my way back through the valley with a ground speed of 48mph, and that mountain down draught to deal with again?

I got bounced all over the place going back through to get back to Dawei,

BUT I WAS READY FOR IT THIS TIME

The cloud base was now getting lower also.

But I got back out eventually and headed back.

As I called back to Dawei to land, the Tower said

"*G-CDVO cleared to land wind calm*"

I thought where's he looking at for the wind??

It was still a 90 degree to the runway, 25mph cross wind I'll tell you.

When I got back in I said "that's it now I can only go over those mountains if the weather is clear enough" and a lot less wind then I might get there without frightening myself to death.

I taxied back in to the area that I had parked in, tied the Quik up and had a word with a member of staff in the control tower who managed to get the car from the hotel sent to pick me up. So I went back to the Pale Elkari Hotel. I had a different room from last night as well, it had a bathroom and there were no big bugs running around trying to frighten me to death.

Day 59 - June 26th

I had a good evening the previous night sat in the hotel restaurant as I was invited to join a group of guys sat having a beer or two after work.

They had recognised me from the local newspaper, and wanted to meet me!.

I had a couple with them before other people starting recognising me and coming over to see me, I was the talk of the town now and a Hero!.

I even signed autographs ☺ and had photos taken with the locals

Anyway I got up this morning and went to the reception to try to get a lift up to the Airport.

The young lad on reception rang for the car that had picked me last night and within minutes it was there with a driver to take me up to the Airport. The weather looked ok at the moment as well - maybe I would get through to Bangkok today!.

When I got to the Airport I could see that the odd black cloud passing by and disappearing into the mountains where I wanted to go. I kept watching and watching.

As it got to lunch time, the weather started brightening up so I thought right let's get loaded up ready to go then.

After about 10 minutes getting the covers off and packing them away, a big black rain shower cloud came over and gave us some rain although it did disperse.

I was looking at the mountains; the visibility seemed to be worse than yesterday.

The guy from the Tower came down with the weather report for me.

Bangkok 6,000ft broken cloud, 10k visibility, wind 10knts, that's fine I said but what about the 162 miles in-between??

Dawei visibility 1-2k in the mountains,

Exactly I'm not going in that I'll give it a bit longer.

He then said "afternoon late evening blue sky here"

Ok so I would wait a while longer then.

All these rain clouds then started coming over with a fairly strong wind and within five minutes we had torrential rain, so I just sat around my Quik watching the crap weather coming and going with a Security Guard who had been guarding my Quik all day. When it got to 3pm local time I said it's not looking good for today - if it doesn't clear up enough in the next 30 minutes I certainly won't get there today either.

30 minutes passed then 40mins.

Then the controller came from the Tower to see me on his motorbike – he was smiling. I said to him:

"I don't like the look of the weather in the hills so I'm not going today now"

There had been a young lad at the Airport helping me out with the Quik and as soon as I said that he got the trike cover out whilst I removed all the toys (GPS, radio etc. etc.).

As we tied it down, the biggest rain storm hit the runway and we grabbed the bags and hid under cover. The wind was blowing like hell and the rain flooded the apron within minutes.

I WAS SO GLAD I DIDN'T TAKE OFF!! TALK ABOUT THE RIGHT DECISION MAKING :-)

The controller gave the Hotel Pale Elkari a call to see if I could stop another night, and it wasn't a problem.

Not long after that while I was waiting for lift to the Hotel, a pickup truck came into the airport full of Police,

They went to a guy called Tah who I'd met who works for PETRONAS. They all looked at me and came over... Oh! Heck what have done now??

Tah said *"Dave this is the Chief of the Police for the Dawei area and he wants to talk to you"*

Ok? Through translation he said

"Hello, Dave we are so pleased to have you stop at our town, we are very proud of you, you are a hero. If there is anything you want just ask! Is the hotel ok for you? Are you happy there?"

We want to help you as much as we possibly can with your stay here in Dawei"

Unbelievable! Myanmar has got to be the friendliest country in the world and have the nicest people.. Ever!

'No sir everything is fine, but thank you for asking'

He asked a few more questions about my Quik and the trip and had a good look around it before leaving.

By now literally hundreds of people had come to look at me – they were just standing at a fence shouting and waving at me at the airport.

I was now truly the talk of the town - a star almost!

The hotel car arrived I got my bag into it and went off through my crowds of fans back to the hotel.

Some of My Fans at the Airport

Day 60, June 27th

Sat in the hotel at 4.30am, my back was absolutely killing me now due to having been sat in my wheelchair too long and hanging around airports in the rain. I sat there looking out of the window wondering if the Quik would be ok today, there was a huge monsoon rain storm going on and an amazing light show that you would never see back in England.

I was hoping and wondering if the weather would be going to clear???...

At 8.30am the rain still had not stopped.

By 10.30am it was still raining like hell, but at least the wind had eased a bit.

At 12.45pm it was raining like hell again with thunder and lightning.

Maybe today just might not happen – once again!

Oooh at 2pm a glimmer of sunshine, Yet at 2.15pm there was rain again.

At 3.30pm I could see the sun now and by 3.35pm I could no longer see the sun and it had started to rain once again!

I only had 162miles to do –on just 45 litres,

I had looked at flying down the coast to another couple of airports and then head direct to Phuket, but I only had 45 litres of fuel left.

You're all going to say"*well just get filled up again then*"

At this point I need to explain that in Myanmar they only have Avgas at certain airports and because I had to land at different airports than planned due to the weather, they didn't have any.

At this point you will probably all say "*why don't you just go to the petrol station then*".

Dawei has got just one petrol station and it only sells low grade fuel. By low grade I should explain that it is about 88 octane, it has water in it and they only use it in the motorbikes. Other than that, you have to order petrol from Thailand that comes in by boat by the barrel. The fuel I have in already is only 92 octane any way and I don't want to put crap fuel in just to go down the coast.

So I needed to get to Bangkok where they have got Avgas where I would be able to top up with 145litres which should take me to Phuket where they also have Avgas.

This was the main reason that I needed to get to Bangkok. On top of this I now didn't have enough fuel to turn back and try again.

The next time I went to have ago at going to Bangkok, I had to get there.

For now it was a case of staying at the Pale ElKari for another night.

I went to the restaurant only to be met by more people interested in me and my flight to Oz. So I sat all night having photos taken and talking to everybody about my flight.

Now I felt I had been here too long and it was time to get away!

Day 61, June 28th

I was up at the crack of dawn 5.00am – was the weather is going to be good today?? It was still raining but I had a good feeling - AGAIN!

I got a lift to the Airport where there was another mass of visitors who had come to meet me and take photos. It was still raining but not that hard and it was due to brighten up later so I sat under the wing of the Quik just staring at the mountains saying "brighten up please"

Around midday it started brightening up but there was still a lot of cloud in the mountains. However by 1pm it really brightened up so I started getting ready to go. But because it was warming up now the cloud in the mountains changed within 10 minutes and it was full of cumulous nimbus building and starting to tower. So it looked dodgy again!!

A man came over shortly afterwards with a few others that I had not met before. He introduced himself.

"Hello, I'm from PETRONAS I'm the radio operator but also I have been the meteorologist for the last 16 years here and I can tell you sir that today you will not go through the mountains. This weather here is really bad it's the rainy season you know"

I smiled at him and said 'thank you sir that is very kind of you, and I am very pleased to meet you'

The CB's were building to flat tops in the mountains now, and I could see rain also coming down, and some of the hills were just disappearing now.

So now I knew I wouldn't be going to Bangkok again, so I just sat and talked to everybody slowly packing the Quik back up for the night. By this time it was after 3.30pm so past my departure time to get to Bangkok safely before dark anyway.

I spoke to one of the guards that had been sat looking after my Quik - oh sorry did I forget to mention that? I was parked next to PETRONAS Oil's fuel slipper tank of Jet A1 and they had a 24 hour a day armed guard looking after it, so because I'm at one side my Quik was being guarded 24 hours too ☺

The guard rang the hotel to ask them to send their car to pick me up – however it was busy this time. I spotted some guys with a taxi looking at the Quik over the fence so I got the guards to ask if they would take me to the hotel.

They were all big smiles and I made my way over to it going out of the security gates of the Airport.

When I say taxi, it wasn't like a taxi in the UK. It was a Vauxhall viva HA Deluxe pickup from the early 60's with a hooped hood over the back and a wooden bench down either side of the back. I wasn't complaining – this is what all the taxis are like in Dawei.

I managed to climb into the front seat and my chair was thrown in the back with another four or so people who had come up to the airport to see me. We set off to the Pale Elkari Hotel again, with the dash board smoking and rattling away.

As I we got to the hotel, I suddenly became really unwell. In fact I thought I was going to throw up!!! It must have been a dodgy banana or something that I had eaten earlier. I thought I know how to get rid of that feeling I'll go to the bar and have something drink. However I only managed 2 drinks of the Myanmar beer before feeling really ill, that was it - I needed to go to my room.

"Sorry everybody in the restaurant that wanted to talk but I feel too bad." I said and went to lie down.

About 15 minutes later there was a knock on the door, *"Sir, your friend to see you"*

'Go away I'm ill'

Knock, knock *"Sir your friend here"*

'Go away, leave me alone"

Then he got a key and let himself in, along with this other guy. So I said without getting too angry...

"Will you both just go away I'm fine, leave me alone, I'll come back later"

'But sir'

"GO AWAY PLEASE NOW"

After a few minutes, they went. I know they meant well and it was much appreciated but I felt like I was dying and just needed to be on my own. Did they leave it at that?? NO! Knock, Knock *"sir a present.."*

"Go away please"

Then the door was unlocked again by staff who brought a plate of food in.

"I said leave me alone and take that away I didn't order it and don't want it thank you'

'A present from your friend's sir'

"WILL YOU JUST GO AWAY BEFORE I GET ANNOYED PLEASE AND STOP LETTING YOURSELF IN THIS ROOM "

Finally they stopped bothering me and there was peace and quiet. The air-conditioning machine was buzzing away and dripping on my feet. I was not stopping here now – I felt like I was cooking and sweating like hell.

I was just hoping that I didn't come down too ill to be able to fly??

Cloud in the mountains

Another view looking at the mountains, complete cloud cover.

THAILAND, MALAYSIA

Day 62, June 29th – Dawei, Burma to Bangkok, Thailand

I woke up at a reasonable time, I must have just fallen asleep the previous night at around 8pm and slept all the way through until 5am.

I couldn't hear any rain so I jumped out of bed shot straight to the toilet and deposited the nasty bits from last night!

Then I grabbed my wheelchair and jumped across into it and then threw my legs in (well you get what I mean!). I went straight outside looking at the sky, it looked flyable!

Let's get going then.

I still felt ill but if it's time to go, I'm not missing it for anything.

The driver from the hotel turned up and took me to the airport for 7.30am. I hadn't been able to get a lift sooner.

I looked at the mountains - there was still cloud covering them and I could not see the tops of them at all!

Well, that was a dash up the road for nothing all that way and the weather was still crap.

However it seemed to be getting clearer from the north, so if I sat here if might just clear (fingers crossed!). An hour later at 8.30am a Myanmar passenger jet flew in from Yangon.

Then there was a group of people coming towards me on motorcycles – they were the pilots and the cabin crew from a Myanmar airways jet coming to say hello.

"Hello, Captain, we are very pleased and privileged to meet you. Would you mind having a photo with us all?"

'Not at all, Captain. Can I ask if the weather is clear coming down from Yangon?'

"Yes, Captain, clear all the way, 6,000ft cloud base also"

Fantastic!

After a couple of pictures the captain turned to me and took the gold wings off his shirt.

"For you, Captain, you are a very brave man."

What a privilege that felt like, little old me from Dewsbury getting that!!.

They disappeared back to their jet and left.

The sky was now clearing for me.

That's it, I'm off.

I started loading up ready to depart although I could still see cloud in the mountains. So I thought I would just give it a bit longer before I left so that the cloud could get burnt off.

It looked clearer now in the mountains so I decided to go for it. I got into the Quik and got pushed out on to the apron to start up.

I sat there going through my checks, making sure everything was fastened in, or strapped down. First I had to make sure my wheelchair wheels were on tight, that the chair and the wiring from the cameras was not dangling everywhere, that the PLB was within reach, the GPS in place, on mains power and working, that the transponder was working, then the electric trim - got to make sure that works ok, that the fuel caps were closed, both map boards strapped in place, helmet OK and fastened.

Then I did the normal wing movement in all directions, a quick look around to make sure the trim pins are still there, and numerous other checks.

While I was doing these checks, the man from Immigration came over and said "*Are you going now'?*"

Yes, I am.

"Can I have your passport to stamp then?"

He took that away and was back within 5 minutes with it all stamped ready to go.

It made a change not having to go through the entire airport looking for them to get my passport stamped.

That's it. I gave Tower a call.

"G-CDVO – Request start-up."

"G-VO approved, report when taxing to runway 16 and line up."

I flicked the magneto switch to ON, and it just went floppy.

There are two magneto switches, but you start up with one on!

I looked down and the magneto switch had just fallen to pieces.

"You're kidding me!"

Helmet off to look at the problem and the switch had crumbled into little pieces.

Right, quick thinking needed here.

I know, just pull the switch off and throw it away.

A guard came over wondering what was wrong, I shouted has anybody got a knife I can borrow they looked at bemused so I pointed at the switch and the guard pulled a knife about 12-inch long and just cut off the switch. I taped the wires apart – with the wires apart the engine starts and with the wires together, the engine stops.

I put my helmet back on and the engine started up fine, I taxied out, lined up and got cleared to take-off straight away.

I then headed towards the dreaded mountains that had been hampering my flight through Myanmar all week.

There was still low cloud in them at about 2,500ft and no way of going over the 8,000ft ones, so I headed back up the river valley, dodging around the clouds.

The wind was only about 10mph now.

As I got further into the mountains, the cloud started going black again and the wind picked up.

Holding on now, I was thinking, I hope I don't get thrown around again like last time. My heart was beating away like a little generator, and my grip got tighter on the bar.

I tightened my seat belt and squeezed my bum cheeks together so I wasn't going anywhere.

Bounce, bounce, bounce, off I went, up and down all over the sky I was, heading my way through the valleys thinking all the time I have to make it now I don't have enough fuel to get back to Dawei.

I got to the part in the valley where I had to turn back last time, and I could see through now. The cloud was clearing ahead. So I carried on.

I lost radio contact with Dawei and I couldn't reach Bangkok Control either.

I was really nervous now.

I was flying at 4,500ft with a 7,000ft mountain on my right hand side, and the cloud base was now about 4,700ft.

I looked at the map and saw that if I could just get to the Myanmar border, the mountains would start to drop a bit.

I looked at the GPS – a Pilot 111 - I was only eight miles away from the border.

I might just get there this time. *Anyway, I have to get there.*

I haven't got enough fuel to return to Dawei and try again.

Then it was seven miles to go, then six miles, then five miles to go to the border and it was getting brighter.

I could now see the tops of the mountains and it was sunny.

I tried and tried to contact Bangkok, but couldn't get a response.

I went over the border and carried on, the mountains started to drop away.

I was going to make it to Bangkok finally, after 20 days stuck in Myanmar.

Now, because the mountains were dropping off, winds were picking up and blowing straight in from them. I had a tail wind to take me to Bangkok, albeit a very rough wind.

Finally I came out of the mountains and it levelled out to a flat area 60 miles across, all flat terrain.

I managed to make radio contact with Bangkok Approach who said:

"G-CDVO - confirm inbound, Bangkok".

I confirmed this and the lady controller vectored me in.

"G-CDVO - turn left heading 060 degrees at 1,500ft and maintain."

Then she said: *"G-CDVO - turn right heading 090 climb to 2,500ft and report."*

I replied: *"G-CDVO at 2,500ft on 090 heading"*

"G-CDVO you have traffic at 1,500ft at your 9 o'clock. It will pass under you"

"G-VO will keep a good look out."

A little later she said: *"G-CDVO - descend to 1,000ft and turn 120 heading and change to Tower Frequency on 118.10".*

A quick change of frequency and they said:

"G-CDVO - cleared to land on runway 34 Right. Report Finals".

'G-VO – Finals!"

I landed and there was a Follow-Me car which I followed through the huge airport to where I was parked up on the apron in the middle of nowhere. I was met by MJET Ground Handling, a charter service. MJET are a private jet company that look after and maintain Cessna Citations and also do ground handling. After a few minutes of talking nicely to them I managed to get my Quik into their wonderful pristine hangar for the night.

I taxied over to the hangar and pulled up just outside. I jumped out of the Quik into my chair, got my gear together then I was thrown in to their luxury bus (with leather seats) and taken to their very nice posh Arrivals lounge, where I was fed and watered while they sourced a hotel for me.

They said that I should just ask if there was anything they could help with.

A guy from Immigration came to see me and stamped my passport, then went on to explain that my Thai permit had now expired so I would not be able to leave Bangkok until it had been updated.

With everything sorted out, MJET offered to take me to my hotel and got a driver to come around to the front of the Airport building for me where the driver threw me back into their luxury bus and drove me to the hotel. I had something to eat in the hotel and was planned to go in Bangkok city for a night out after!

Day 63, June 30th

In the end, I decided to stay in the hotel and listen to a nice young lady singing away with a chap playing a grand piano in the restaurant bar.

I would not be going anywhere for a day or so until my permits to fly out of Thailand were updated with the Thailand and Malaysian authorities. So I planned to get everything sorted that day and go round town.

I spoke to MJET at Don Mueang Airport. They told me that my Quik was fine in their huge hangar, out of the way of the storms that had come through overnight, although my Quik looked a little lost inside it all on its own!

I checked my emails, to see what was going on and worked my way through about 160 posts. For some reason it seemed that everybody had been busy sending me them to me that day.

Now I was here in Bangkok I needed to get physical cash, so I had been going to ATMs every 10 minutes or so to draw out as much as I possibly could.

The cash machines here in Thailand only allow you to withdraw 5,000 Bahts at any one time (about £100). I put my card in three times then people started looking at me, they must think have thought that I was robbing the machine so then I would move onto another machine.

Once I had enough Bahts, I would need to change them to US dollars although I didn't think this would be a problem.

I went back to the Hotel to find out about the local area and where everything was in the city. With that done, I decided to go and have a look around and so I got a taxi from outside the hotel and told him to take me to a nice lively place.

I was dropped off at a place called Patpong, a street that has a market through the night, selling everything from t-shirts to fake Rolex watches.

I had a quick look around, then called in to a restaurant for a beer and ended up speaking to a young couple from Sydney. We talked for a while over a beer or two, while the rain stopped.

It didn't take long before it stopped raining!

I then decided to go and have a look around the market. However, there was a very tall kerb to get up first.

I grabbed of a couple of strangers that were walking past.

"Excuse me, do you speak English?"

"Only little"

"OK, I need a lift up this huge kerb on to the pavement, please!"

They lifted me up and off I went through the market looking at all the Rolex watches and really fancy shirts.

It started raining again.

I thought I would go into one of the busy bars at the side of the market. They looked lively with lots of fancy neon lights and loud music.

They also looked very busy, by now it was almost 10pm.

"Ooohhh, this one has got lots of very pretty ladies guarding the doors"

"Hello, sir, you want to come in?"

"OK, I will, but I need a lift up your three steps inside"

With that, a couple of men on their way in to the bar lifted me in. It was full of bench seats so I couldn't get anywhere to sit.

"I'll just sit here at the bar I said, it's fine. A bottle of Corona beer please, with no lemon!"

What a nice place it was, there were lots of ladies walking about, and it must have been really warm because they were all wearing bikinis.

In the middle of the circular bar, there was a stage where all the ladies could let off a bit of steam and have a good old dance around. The music was good and the bar got busier with what seemed to be a party of men; they must have been part of a stag party or something.

I sat listening to the music and had couple of beers. It was a friendly place - all the ladies smiled and wanted to talk to me.

Some kind ladies even offered to show me how good they were at dancing.

"Hello, I show you dance? Very special dance, just for you."

Oooh, she must have been a bit embarrassed as she didn't want to show everybody on the stage behind the bar.

I didn't blame her for that.

She said, *"I show you special dance, in special room?"*

She must have been chuffed to bits with her new dance because she really wanted to show me.

I'm really sorry, number 120, I have to go but I really wish you well in your dancing career and here's a bit of something for your dance lessons.

I gave her 200 Bahts (about £4) which she was more than happy with.

Dance lessons must be cheap here.

That was it. The rain had stopped and I thought I would go for a wander around a bit further see if I could find a night club or something.

It started raining again! So I thought, right, I'll go to the nearest pub.

Once again, there was now a big kerb in front of me. I looked around and I could see a bar. The two door men said: "You come in, we lift you in?"

OK, no problem, so in I went.

I decided that they must really love dancing out here in Bangkok. I always thought it was karaoke that was the rage. It must have been run by the same pub group as the last bar, because once again there was a nice stage for the dancers to let steam off in the middle. They were all very good, I have to say, not knowing the first thing about dancing! It was also very warm in this bar as once again the ladies were just wearing bikinis. They were friendly again and just wanted to show their dancing skills to me. In fact, a couple of them wanted to show me their skills at muscle relaxation as well.

I had a couple of beers here while they were all practicing their dancing skills on the stage, and introducing themselves to me.

After a couple of drinks I decided to go and find something to eat.

I got lifted out of the bar. It had stopped raining now. A quick wander around and I noticed all the men walking around with what looked like their daughters holding hands with them??

Any way I found a small pub-like bar and went in. There was no kerb which made it easier for me. The bar advertised food but as it happened they didn't have any left, so I just had a beer.

Another friendly woman came over to talk to me.

After a couple of minutes I could feel people looking at me in the bar. I looked at this woman and she was very pretty, but as I was talking I looked at the lady serving behind the bar and nodded my head, smiling and thinking something wasn't right.

I pointed to the lady next to me, she smiled and nodded.

Yes! It was not a woman talking, or a man.

It was one of those in-between.

That was it, with the beer straight down my neck, off I went like a shot.

At that point, I decided to return to my hotel – it had to be safer. I was full up with beer now anyway and it was getting late.

I got a taxi back, smiling and thinking about how lucky I was with the he/she that had just spoken to me, and nothing else.

(You really couldn't tell at all).

Day 64, July 1st

I woke up with a bit of a headache but nothing too bad. I went for breakfast then back up to the room to check emails. I had now got my Thailand Permit through would be continuing my journey tomorrow, July 2nd, to Surat Thani near Phuket.

Excellent!

What I needed to do today then was to get some more money out of the ATM and change it into dollars. That was my mission.

I drew out as much as I could with my card allowance and then got a taxi.

"Take me to a bank, please, where I can get dollars."

"OK, no problem"

So we set off and after 20 minutes I am starting to get irritated.

Where is the bank then? It can't be this far.

He mumbled something and the next thing we were at a bank, which was closed.

Well, where's another one then?

Mumble, mumble, no more banks.

That was it.

"You're telling me that there is only one bank in Bangkok and it's closed? I think you're taking the mickey out of me! You aren't getting paid until I get dollars, dead simple, and the more you try to charge me, the less I'm going to pay you. We had better get to a bank quick, don't you think?"

He said the only place I would get money was at the Airport, and then he started taking me there. I needed dollars, so I said OK. He knew I wasn't happy.

I got to the Airport where I had to explain to a security guard at the door that I was just changing money not going on a flight I went in to change my Bahts accumulated from ATMs over the last few days and even got a reasonable exchange rate.

Once that was done I went back to the hotel and looked at the route for the day ahead when I would be flying to a place called Surhat Thani.

Later I spoke to the lady behind the bar in the hotel and I asked her to recommend somewhere good to go that was nearby. She suggested a local place that had live bands on and was fairly busy, so I got a taxi to take me there.

We pulled up and it was just one American diner, with about three people in it.

"This is no good, take me somewhere with music and clubs".

He babbled something I didn't understand but I said OK.

It was now raining very hard, we seemed to be driving for miles now, I said are you going to find somewhere or are we just going to drive around all night.

We pulled up at this market and a pizza shop and I opened the door.

Music!

Good-oh! Let me out here this will do.

I went up this street full of bars and they even had some live shows to choose from. Excellent!

Maybe "Grease" or "The Phantom" - Thai style?

I would just nip into one of the bars first.

A guy came over who said he was from Denmark.

"Hello, mate, you have chosen the best place to come in Bangkok".

This was better than Patpong any day.

I had a couple of beers, talking to different people and just watching everybody. Then I went to the bar next door, a theme bar called Cowboys, where all the staff were dressed as cowboys (OK, all cowgirls), and they practiced their line-dancing on stage. Once again, it was very warm in here because they started to take their cowboy clothes off.

I had never seen line-dancing from a pole before - it must be the new way!

I had a jolly good night, met many new friends, and returned to my hotel for the early departure to Surat Thani the next day.

Day 65, July 2nd

I was up at 5.30am, ready to go to the airport, with just five hours to fly to my destination of Surhat Thani. Before going, I checked my emails.

What!

Great stuff! I had an email saying that my Thai permit would start the following day, July 3rd, rather than today.

So I sent a quick email to MJET to let them know I wouldn't be coming out to the Airport, and went back to bed.

I got up about 10am and went to Reception to let them know that I would be there another night, before going back to the room to catch up on sleep. I had decided to stay in the hotel that evening, so that I could get away early the following day. At 7pm, I went down to the hotel bar to watch their local singer on the piano and have a beer.

"Sorry, sir, I cannot serve you beer".

"Why? It's Saturday night and only 7pm".

Sorry sir, it's illegal to sell after 6pm

"Are you winding me up like that taxi driver did yesterday?"

I was upset.

"No, sir, it's voting time and they don't sell alcohol, so everybody who votes is sober."

"But I'm not voting".

"Sorry, sir".

What a good night this is turning out to be!

"OK, I want room service, food, but I want to wash it down with a beer".

"Let me make a phone call, sir".

OK, no problem.

So I ordered a burger and 4 bottles of Corona which I had in my room watching 'Die Hard One' and 'Die Hard Two' tapping away on my pc.

Day 66, July 3rd - Bangkok to Surhat Thani, Thailand

I was up and ready to go at 4.30am.

I took a taxi from reception to the Airport and went to the private jet lounge,

I got to MJET's private jet HQ. There was nobody there.

After a couple of phone calls the staff arrived they had all gone to vote which was why they were late. Before you knew it, it it was 8.30am!

After a short wait in the office at MJET, the staff said there was a small problem with my Thai clearance, but they would sort it out for me. Then they filed my flight plan with the Tower.

I was taken out to the apron where my Quik had been removed from the hangar and was waiting.

The fuel truck turned up with Avgas.

I filled up with about 97 litres and the kind staff paid for it for me.

We had a few pictures taken and then I was ready to get in and go. I quickly climb into my Quik packed the wheelchair away and prepared to depart.

I said my goodbyes and was granted engine start-up and taxi to holding point E (Echo)

"G-CDVO cleared for take-off, after take-off turn right".

The airport was really quiet this morning, so there was not too much pressure leaving the airport.

I took off and the route took me straight away over the built-up area,

"G-CDVO - turn right heading 120".

This routing took me straight over the outskirts of Bangkok, which looks amazing from a flexi - a really special moment!

The towering city in the background to my left was quite incredible.

I was vectored to the coast and over the newly-built airpark of Best Ocean, which looked really nice and out past miles of rice paddy fields along the coast.

My intended route to Surhat Thani took me directly over the bay and out to sea, but ATC wanted me to stick by the coast all the way South. I was happy with that.

The scenery was nice and flat as I headed south to start with, then the odd small mountain popped up and with that, the cloud built and went dark over the tops of them looking a bit on the wet side. The further south I went, the more the cloud was building inland, as were the mountains. On the route there were only two alternate airfields I could go into if the weather deteriorated.

Rice paddy fields Bangkok

The first two hours were lovely clear blue skies with the odd cloud. Four hours into my flight I could see in the distance big CB's (CuNims) building and dying off.

I wasn't too worried by this as I still had one more airfield to divert to if it looked too bad.

Five hours into the flight, the weather still looked OK, but I was now well past my last alternate airfield.

The mountains got taller and the cloud got thicker, it became really dark and the cloud base was now about 2,000ft. I looked back to make a judgment about my alternate airfield but the weather had closed in behind me, there was complete blackness.

So no turning back, I had to carry on! I was looking all the time for somewhere to land if I needed to go down, but there was only the beach and beach roads (which had posts running alongside).

The cloud base dropped again. I was down to 1,000ft and at that point, it started!

First the pitter-patter of rain on my windscreen, then the base bar gave me a good shake about.

I looked inland and it was really black!

The cloud pushed me down to 500ft and the rain increased.

I am now seriously looking for somewhere to land, but there was nothing but trees below. The beach was my only option, but I knew if I landed there I would either roll the Quik or just sink, and with no houses around, it would be really dangerous

Trees as far as the eye could see

The rain got harder and the wind started really rattling me about. I could hear all sorts of creaking and groaning coming from the trike and a lot of interference over the radio.

I hope that's not what I think it is! Thunder!

I had heard it before and it was definitely thunder.

Bang, Bang, Bang, and then I was thrown all over. It just came from nowhere!

I was clinging on to the base bar, fighting with it to try to keep level. It was not easy, I'll tell you.

"Shit! What was that?"

I could hear thunder rumbling away over the top of the headsets, and then flashes of lighting started appearing on my right in the mountains. That sounded really close to me. The rain started falling then it got harder and harder.

"I need to get away from here as fast as I can!"

Crash, bang, flash, a huge storm on my right and it seemed to be coming towards me fast.

Getting blacker all the time I looked back and it was now just a wall of blackness and rain.

I couldn't pull speed on to get away fast, because the wind was now too violent, bouncing me from left to right and pulling the bar out of my hands. The bar was ripped out of my hands and hit the front strut. I grabbed back hold of it, fighting with the weather pulling me around the rain really coming down now.

The rain was that hard I could not see out of my visor, so up that came. I was soaked to the skin, the rain was coming inside my helmet and running down my neck as well as hitting from the side. Everything in the trike was wet now, water was getting in my ASI and it just stopped working. It was stuck at 70mph, not moving at all.

"This is bad now; I really don't want to be here."

I was really scared.

There was lightning flashing all around me now.

I kept thinking I am the tallest thing around, I hope I don't get struck. I thought if I go down a bit lower I might be OK!

Don't ask me why I thought of that. If I was at 200ft I would still be the highest point over the top of the trees anyway!

Duhhh!

Suddenly whilst being bounced around at 500ft, there was an almighty bang and crash at the same time.

I crapped 'em.

I felt the bang go through the whole aircraft, and through me.

My heart was beating away like a good one!

The flash of lighting was so bright! You know when somebody turns a light on your face, and turns it off and you can't see for a few seconds afterwards - well that's what it was like.

When I could see again, the SkyDat had gone off, all the engine information, revs, cylinder temperatures, oil temp, oil pressure.

The transponder had gone off, and so had the GPS.

The electric trim had popped its fuse out.

Had I just been struck by lightning? I couldn't have been or I wouldn't be here typing away.

But it must been very close.

There I was, getting thrown all over the sky like a cork out at sea, with no Skydat, no transponder, no GPS, ASI - airspeed indicator - not working, wet through in torrential rain. Even my feet were wet inside!

I was at 500ft with nowhere to land at all.

I had to carry on!

The only thing that I had that was working now was the radio, which was because it has its own battery.

Eventually I could see bright light ahead – I was hoping this was not the same light I saw when I was in hospital dying back in 1993 – and I made a wish.

"I hope it clears so I can find this airfield."

Yes! It was clearing. Finally, I came through it.

I really didn't think the Quik would have survived all that, but it did!

And so did I!

Amazingly, now there was blue sky. That was the weather in this part of the world, it all changes so quickly.

I knew that I had less than an hour to go, and I kept an eye on my stopwatch and worked out where I was on the map. I gave Surhat Thani a call and they came back to me, so the water and lightening hadn't damaged my headset and radio.

I could see the airport in the distance, standing out amongst the trees, and was cleared straight in to land, without any joining.

I went in with no trim or Flydat and with the ASI still stuck.

I taxied into the parking area and sat there dripping, looking at my dead Quik.

Nobody was around for a few minutes, apart from a security guard, and then a woman came from the Tower.

"Hello" I said.

Before I even got out of the Quik she said, *"How much aircraft weigh?"*

"Why?"

"Landing fees and parking, pay now, cash."

That was a pleasant welcome.

"Hello, Welcome to Surhat Thani, and enjoy your stay".

The miserable woman.

I got out in to my sodden wheelchair and explained to the guard that I needed a hotel for the night. He said, no problem and that he would take me to one when I was ready.

So sat in my wet wheelchair feeling like a shrivelled up prune from all the water

I tied the Quik down and climbed into his pickup truck. He threw the chair in the back and off we went.

I would sort out the electrics on the Quik the following day!

It was a nice hotel. I went to the bar as I needed a drink after that flight.

The women said: *"Sorry, sir, no alcohol today, sir, its voting day."*

Fantastic!

No beer after that flight. I know I'll go to my room and raid the mini bar!

I was absolutely knackered.

Day 67, July 4th - Surhat Thani to Phuket, Thailand

I got up fairly early, even though this flight was only going to be a short one at around two and a half hours.

I paid my dues to the hotel and went for a bit of breakfast, I went over to get some toast and jam but when I looked in the bowl that contained the jam, I found ants feasting on it.

Suddenly I was less enthusiastic about breakfast and left it. The Security Guard collected me at 8.30am and I went see if the dashboard was salvageable. I stuck my head under the dash to discover that it had only blown the fuses, so everything was back working again after digging out some spares that I had brought with me and replacing them.

The ASI or Air Speed Indicator was still not working, it remained stuck, but at only 25mph now. I thought it might clear and start working as the flight continued.

My altimeter had now filled up with water and was not working either (great stuff!) so no altimeter or ASI now, but I would be fine without them.

I went over to the Tower to file my flight plan, and a young lad came down and had a look at it. He smiled and said *"No problem, Captain, just give me 20 minutes to get it activated".*

I quickly dashed back to the Quik and climbed in, just as a guy passed with a luggage tractor. He stopped and gave me a hand to get the wheelchair packed up quicker.

I gave ATC a call and they said*: "G-CDVO - advise when ready, clear for taxi, line up and clear for take-off".*

That was it, I was off. The ASI started to move as I took off but I couldn't rely on it, because it said I was doing about 40mph, which I knew to be wrong.

I headed direct to Phuket.

Nothing but palm trees below me as far as the eye could see, so if the engine stopped and I was to go down now, it was going to hurt.

There were two small ridges of low mountains that ran all the way to the coast from about half way out of Surhat Thani. I followed their line, taking in all the awesome scenery. It wasn't too bumpy and I even managed to let go of the bar and take some photographs.

Trees, trees, trees everywhere.

As I reached the coast, the most amazing scenery appeared all along the coast line, the rocks protruding from the sea were also covered in trees. I got some more pictures. In fact it looked like the scenery from the James Bond Film 'The Man with the Golden Gun". As I got closer to Phuket I had to go over a small hill on an island then I could see the runway in-between two big rocks and the ending right at the water's edge.

"G-CDVO - join right base for 27".

I went over a couple of low mountains, and ATC said *"Report finals 27 - G-CDVO."*

I came in over one bay to the runway which stretches through most of the island.

I only needed a few hundred feet to land in, so I flew down the runway until I was near one of the turn-offs to a taxiway and then landed. At Phuket, the control tower is set into the hillside; I flew past that, looking in as I went past. They must have thought I was mad.

I taxied in to a parking spot, and followed in by a Thai Airways 747 Jumbo Jet!

What a feeling, again, to be number one to land to a 747!

I sat in the Quik waiting for MJET to come, but nothing happened.

I got my phone out and rang MJET''s Bangkok office to see where they were.

"Sorry, sir, we'll be right with you."

At that, the MJET staff arrived. I tied my Quik down and was fast-tracked through the Airport Terminal Building to their office.

They booked me into a hotel and I was taken there by their luxury mini bus.

This was a very nice place with a swimming pool, called the Airport Resort Hotel.

I sorted out my route for the next day's flying while sat in the sun which made a change as I hadn't seen the sun for weeks now.

Later after lunch I asked the lady behind the reception desk to get me a taxi.

"No need, sir, where do want to go? We have own transport to take you".

"OK, take me to the nearest bar and restaurant then, please."

We drove down to the beach area. At first it didn't look that busy, but the driver said that it would be. It was at least a 45min drive to the busy area of Phuket town. It was now after 9.30pm and I was needed to be up early the next day. So I had asked him to take me to a good place close by.

I was taken to a saloon bar with live music. As it was the 4th July there were some Americans having a party, so I was having a bit of a laugh with them and I had a few beers to help them celebrate the 4th of July before having something to eat. Then after a short push back up the road, I was back at the hotel for 1am.

Day 68, July 5th - Phuket, Thailand to Pinang, Malaysia

I was awake bright and early with the sun shining through the window. I had a` look outside and there was a beautiful day in front of me.

The staff from www.mjet.com picked me up at 8.30am, and I went straight through the Airport like a film star, through Passport Control and into the MJET office. I had a drink in the office then it was straight out to my Quik.

Within 5 minutes the re-fuelling truck was there and I was filled up with just short of a 100lts of Avgas. I asked MJET to file my flight plan for me, and started to climb into my Quik. Sweat was just dripping from me now, at 38℃ (100℉).

The Operations Manager from MJET came to let me know I was cleared to go.

I gave ATC a call and they said, *"G-CDVO - you are not cleared by the CAA yet to leave this airport."*

OK! So I would wait a bit longer then.

After a few minutes they said, *"CDVO you are now cleared to leave. Start up approved, report when ready to taxi".*

I started the engine and just as I did, the Thai Airways 747 that had followed me the previous evening, taxied passed me.

"Shit, I hope I don't get blown away".

The pilot waved at me and went past with reduced power which was very kind

I was still here.

He taxied out to the end of the runway and took off just before passing me at a distance of about 100ft. What a sight it was as the undercarriage went up straight in front of me.

It looked like a tight take-off from the airport, that's for sure. I was cleared to taxi out.

"G-CDVO - Taxi Alpha to holding Golf".

They told me to taxi all the way up to the same start point as the 747 which I found quite amusing. But I did as I was told and took off in front of the control tower and gave them a wave.

"G-CDVO - after take-off, turn left, and follow the coast. Have a nice flight and good luck on your journey".

It was a beautiful sunny day and as I turned left, I could see for miles down the island. I set the hand throttle and at 1,000ft the camera was out, with me snapping away like David Bailey.

Blue sky, blue sea, what a day, this was what the whole flight should have been like instead of dodging death all the time.

Hotels set in their own coves looked really nice, and beach huts in the edge of the palm trees. As I went out to the sea and headed towards the mainland of Malaysia, there was the odd island on its own which was very photogenic.

One Island in particular that stood out had four small rocks protruding from the sea with a very pale blue sea in the middle. It looked an ideal diving and snorkelling area.

In fact there was a big boat moored there doing just that!

Awesome!

As I got further south, I watched the visibility start to get bad and clouds appeared. Soon I was looking at the sea down at my left hand side to judge where I was going.

The day had started out so well.

I should have known really, I can't have too much of a good thing on this adventure.

I flew over an island called Langkawi, but as I approached it I just could not see it, or go over the top, because of cloud. I had to go around it at 500ft until I got back on my heading to Pinang.

Closer to Pinang, the visibility was still bad, but I could make out the island itself.

"G-CDVO - report when north of the island, not above 1,000ft".

"G-CDVO – reporting now, north of the island at 1,000ft".

I followed the coastline around, and the city was awesome, tower blocks poking up into the sky. There were no beaches, just the city straight to the water's edge.

"G-CDVO - report 8 mile finals for 27".

That made me smile – eight mile finals in a flexi!

I continued down from the islands, with Pinang on the right , and the other part of Pinang on my left at 1,000ft, over the top of a very long road bridge, and then over an industrial estate and to what I would call finals, all the way down to Runway 27.

That was just fantastic flying over the city, so low and so close.

I even managed to get some pictures.

After touchdown I taxied into a GA parking area. They were building a new terminal so the GA parking was actually closed, but I had special permission to land and park there.

A young lad came over on a scooter just to look at what had just landed.

By the time I had finished talking to him he had the boss down with him and a pickup truck to take me to the terminal. But first I had to tie my Quik down so with the help of a builder from the construction site on the Airport we pushed it on to a grassy area, tied it down and covered it up. I was then taken to the Terminal Building and to Passport Control to sort out immigration into Malaysia and get my passport stamped.

That was easy enough! I asked if there were any hotels close by and the guys had a discussion before coming up with a name of one for me. I then wandered out of the airport to a taxi rank where they asked the driver to take me to the hotel.

It was a nice hotel, but there was no restaurant. Never mind, there was always a taxi to take me to one.

I ended up in a really nice pub called O'Reilly's a short ride away. All this way and I end up in an English pub!

Fantastic. I got speaking to a couple of English guys working there and had a few beers with them. They had heard about me and my trip and couldn't believe it.

Day 69, July 6th - Pinang to Kuala Lumpur

I woke up this morning feeling absolutely knackered. I really wanted to stop in bed; I did not want to fly.

I ached everywhere, and felt like somebody had just beaten me up.

And I hadn't had a lot to drink either.

However, I had to fly or my Permit would expire.

I forced myself out of my pit and went down to get a taxi.

The weather was very hazy, border-line illegal for VFR – Visual Flight Rules.

I was dropped off at Departures, went in but couldn't carry my bags. I was aching too much, and onto a trolley they went.

"OK, let's go and find Flight Operations then!"

A quick push around, looking but not really looking, it must have appeared quite funny, a chap in a wheelchair pushing a trolley around the airport, with four gold stripes on his shoulders.

I stumbled across Flight Operations quite by accident, when the guy I had met the previous day came through the door.

I paid my landing fees and parking charges.

The man in charge got this big book out with all the charges in it, and says:

"How much does your aircraft weigh?"

I had seen in his book that the minimum charge was for 500kg's

"It weighs 409kg, sir," I said, and smiled.

He looked.

"We don't have that weight here, and the parking at the GA (General Aviation) area is closed for building work."

"Obviously you can't charge me for parking because I shouldn't be there, and because it's a weight that you don't have, I think that I should be exempt from paying".

I put on my puppy eyes, and smiled.

He said: *"OK, sir no charge for this, but you will have to pay navigation charges at the tower".*

OK, no problem, thank you very much, you are very kind.

I was taken out to the Quik where I removed the covers and a guy from the Tower came down.

"I have my flight plan for you".

He looked at it, and said, *"We want you to go a different route and with these certain reporting points"*.

No problem, I said.

"But captain, you cannot go yet anyway. Visibility is only 4km and for VFR it has to be 5km".

"I'll get in my Quik ready, if that's OK, and will you file my flight plan for me?"

No problem, he said.

"Would it be possible to do a Special VFR then, just in case it doesn't clear enough?"

He said: *"Unfortunately, sir, Special VFR can only be used in controlled air space and you will be going out of it, so no, you can't, sorry"*.

No problem, I thought, I'll get in and wait. I might get to feel better anyway.

He worked out the navigation charges for me and gave me the bill.

It was 8 Ringgits (£1.67), which I thought was very reasonable.

I got in to the Quik and sat there, falling asleep.

After half an hour I looked at the clock and thought, I'll give ground frequency a call to see if it's legal yet.

I put the headset on, turned the radio on, and as if by magic, they said, *"G-CDVO are you on frequency? The weather is 5km, you can go"*.

That was amusing.

I said, *"OK, give me a minute"*.

He said, *"Start up approved, report when ready to go"*.

That was it! So helmet and life jacket on, engine started, and a quick call to ground control, *"G-CDVO - ready for taxi"*.

"OK - G-VO. Taxi to holding point Hotel".

I followed the yellow lines to holding point Hotel.

"G-CDVO - change to Tower frequency, and have a nice time in Australia, bye, bye".

I changed to the Tower frequency and was cleared to take off.

As soon as I was in the air I turned right and went straight out to sea. The visibility was terrible; I don't think it was 5km like they said but at least I could see. I headed down the coast towards my first reporting point.

I was still feeling very tired and a bit sick, but I would survive.

It was absolutely flat calm, no turbulence at all. I didn't even touch the bar, and sat there looking at the trees right up to the water's edge.

I had had an email from a guy called Chris Webb telling me that his wife had started her life here in the palm forests between Phuket and KL, and I was wondering where about that might have been.

Visibility started to improve as time went by, and it was still flat calm.

In fact it was almost boring! All I could do was look at trees without having to fight with the bar or concentrate on a horizon over the sea.

As I got closer to Kuala Lumpur it started clouding over, and even looked stormy, just what I didn't want. After a smooth flight, a storm to finish it off was just great.

I talked to the Tower frequency and was told to hold off and orbit while three aircraft came in.

There I am at a thousand ft, circling over a housing estate to the east of the runway, and a storm is heading towards me.

I'm in my T-shirt, no jacket and it started raining and rumbling.

I'm saying to myself, *"Come on, come on, hurry up and land, so I can get in!"*

Then I got the call, *"G-CDVO, cleared to land, report finals"*.

That was it, wing-over and get it in.

I reported finals as I turned right over the threshold and landed right at the side of the exit to the taxiway.

I was instructed to taxi to the Systematic Hangar where I was met by a group of people waving their arms like mad. I was told to taxi straight into the hangar, out of the way and just as I did, the heavens opened and a thunder storm came through the airport banging and flashing with torrential rain. I had been very lucky.

I had a few pictures taken and got out of the Quik.

Then I had a drink of coffee in the office, meeting everybody there and talking to them. I was very welcomed, I have to say, they were an extremely friendly bunch of people.

One of the guys I had been in contact with by email met me there he came and picked me up and we went off into KL. However first we had to go and swap cars at a petrol station which was a bit odd so we did that then he drove me around until we found a hotel for the night. His name was Rohaizi Md Hussin. Thanks for that. The hotel was small and cheap but would do.

I went for a wander about to find something to eat and came across a huge shopping centre with bars and clubs, I had something to eat then it was back to the hotel for the night.

Day 70, July 7th - Static, Kuala Lumpur

Awoke this morning, tried going on the internet but it wasn't working.

I went down to Reception and said that I needed the internet.

"Sorry sir, I'll reset the router for you".

She did and I went back to the room, but it was still not working.

Back down to Reception, *"It's still not working, I need internet"*.

"Sorry sir, it's working".

"No, it's not".

After about four attempts at trying to get the internet working, failing each time I said to them *"It's no good, I have to have internet and if you can't supply me with it I will have to find another hotel"*.

She continued to say that was working.

I'm still feeling ill from the day before which didn't make things any better. I packed my bags and went to settle up.

"Can you ring me a taxi please?"

"Where are you going?"

"I'm going to another hotel that can supply me with internet as you cannot"

"But which hotel?"

"I don't know, just get me a taxi!".

She went on and on, saying *"Which hotel?"*

I was slowly getting madder.

"Look, can you just get me a taxi please, away from here?"

When I said that another woman came over and said, *"What is problem?"*

"I need a taxi to a hotel that can supply internet, and you cannot!".

Then she said, *"Why don't you move to this side of the hotel, where the internet works?"*

"Prove it and I might stop".

I got the laptop out and sure enough the internet worked.

"You can move to a downstairs room over here if you want".

Which is exactly what I did? I moved hotels over to the other side of the road, and then I had internet access. I had just discovered that I would be here in Kuala Lumpur for a few days waiting for the Indonesian permit to come through.

Great stuff!

So I might as well go out for a few beers then. So once the room was sorted, I went off to the local pub for the night.

Day 71, July 8th - Kuala Lumpur Still

There was not a lot to say about this day really. I was really fed up because I could be there for a few days, waiting for my permit to enter Indonesia.

I had been sending emails everywhere trying to get things sorted out but nobody was responding.

While I was awaiting them to get back in touch I went for a look around the local area.

There was a huge shopping centre next to my hotel called the Sunway Pyramid, with elephants and tigers at the entrance (plastic ones!). I went for a look around, and after half an hour, I thought, that's it, I'd had enough so it was time to go. I then spent another 25 minutes trying to get back to where I went in.

I couldn't believe it, I was laughing to myself.

I had flown over 10,000 miles in my Quik and then I had got lost in a shopping centre!

Eventually I got out and went back to the hotel to check my emails.

There were about 80 to delete but none from the people I wanted to hear from.

Right, I'm off clubbing tonight!

About 100metres away from my hotel was a pub. I called in there, and got talking to some of the staff, and a young lady at the bar. She had a laptop, so I showed everybody my website and what I was doing in Kuala Lumpur. The pub just happened to have a night club at the side of it.

Meanwhile, the roads were totally grid-locked, jammed up because of a political demonstration, so the police had put up road blocks. The young lady was waiting for her boyfriend to turn up, and once he arrived we went into the night club.

It was R&B night, but it was good, and I stopped there until silly o'clock, then went back to the hotel and started talking on Skype to everybody.

Like you do with a skinful of beer!

Then bed.

Day 72, July 9th

I woke up quite late, as you would expect, at around 10am with room service knocking on the door.

"Go away, I'm fine, leave me alone."

I got up anyway and went out to Reception because the internet wasn't working.

The woman on the desk said, "*You have to pay for another night.*"

I said, "*I have paid for it, check the credit card.*"

She did and still she said, *"You pay."*

"The internet has gone off again" I said.

"Get the internet working and I'll pay, but as I have said before, if the internet doesn't work I will have to find a hotel that it does work in".

"I have reset it twice this morning".

Well, reset it again then please.

She huffed and puffed and walked around the counter, plugged the router in *that wasn't plugged in.*

I said, *"I'll just check, shall I?"*

I went back to my room and hey presto, it worked. Isn't it amazing with technology that you have to plug these things in to make them work?

I paid her for another two days, went out for some food and then got ready to go out for another night at the pub next door.

It was extremely quiet in the pub, even though they were having the demonstration that day. Everybody had been warned to stay near where they live and not to venture further due to road blocks.

It stayed like that all night and I only saw about eight people go into the night club.

I was drowning my sorrows, on my own, 9,000 miles away from home. I wished someone would get in touch with me about my permit to Indonesia.

More beer, and back to a local café next to the hotel for some chicken things and naan bread.

There were also a lot of these Shish pipe things around! I'd never tried one before, so I was tempted, but not tonight!

Back to my hotel room which was the size of a shoe box! It had one single bed with just enough room to get my chair at the side and a shower room with a toilet that I had to crawl to because of steps to it.

So into bed and Skype everybody again!

Day 73, July 10th - Kuala Lumpur Still

It was 8.30am and as there was no sign of the permission yet, I decided to go to see the twin PETRONAS towers today, just to say that I'd been there.

I did a quick search on Google maps to see how far they were from the hotel and to find out whether I needed to call England for some more money to pay for a taxi to get to them! No I should be ok; the towers are only 20 minutes away.

I went to the taxi rank in the shopping centre next door. *"Taxi to twin towers, please".*

"27 Ringgits" (£5.61)

No problem! You had to buy a taxi token from a kiosk so that the driver wouldn't ask for any cash. I jumped in and watched them struggle with the wheelchair, scratching their heads for a minute, then smiled *"If you give me it here, I'll show you".* Wheels off, in the boot it went and off we go, destination the twin towers.

As we got closer, we disappeared into tunnels that stretched for miles and just popped up in the middle of Kuala Lumpur and around the corner from the towers.

It started raining very hard, so hard that you could not see the road lines. Cars were all over the place and it made a pleasant change to be travelling in the rain without being wet. I was a bit worried because the taxi driver seemed to like jumping on the brake pedal and swerving around. Yet he got me there in one piece, no big drama.

I have to say they are quite large, the towers, covered in stainless steel and glass, and must have cost a fortune to build..

PETRONAS twin towers Kuala Lumpur.

In between the towers was a shopping mall. I was determined not to get lost in this one, so I had a good look at the map beforehand.

I spent an hour wandering around taking photos, then got bored and went to a bar just underneath the towers and sat there with a beer, watching a fountain, and thinking of what I had done over the previous two months.

From the winery in Italy with my Quik tied to the tractor, to being in the presidential suite in Abu Dhabi airport, to armed guards in Pakistan to just trying to get over the English Channel on the first couple of days.

How lucky I had been to see it all.

I had another beer, and then went back to the hotel to check emails. Off to the local pub for a while, then back to the hotel to Skype everybody

Day 74, July 11th

I got up late, but my mission was to find some spares for the Quik,

I had now named my small hotel room 'Cell 109' because of the size. I decided to search the local area first, starting with the shopping mall where surely there must be a hardware or car accessory shop.

A good look at the map in the doorway revealed a hardware store so I went to find it. I found some oil which said high- performance semi-synthetic on it. It was the most expensive and it looked OK so I picked it up. Then I found a switch that would do for the magneto switch that failed in Myanmar. I thought it unlikely that I would find an oil filter for a Rotax somehow. It would be like going to B&Q and seeing if you can get one, answer is no.

I found some sticky Velcro to replace that which held the side skirt up, which had failed, ruined by a spillage of fuel.

Right, with that sorted, I knew what I would be doing the next day.

What should I do now? I decided to take that lot back to Cell 109 and check emails. There was still nothing about a permit, just another 50 or so to delete.

"Time for food and a beer!"

I went to a local Pizza place for something to eat and then onto the local pub. Later back to the hotel to Skype everybody.

It was starting to get very lonely out here and I was feeling it more because I was just sat around waiting. I couldn't venture too far as it was a taxi ride everywhere which just eats away at the funds. I need all the money I can to get me to Oz.

Maybe I would feel better once I saw the Quik again the following day. And with that it was *"Night-night, world."*

Day 75, July 12th

I was still stuck in Kuala Lumpur, but I had to have something to do! So I was off to the airport to change the oil and do some repairs to the Quik.

I contacted Rohaizi to see if he would be able to take me or to find out how and where to go in a taxi. He soon responded. *"I'll pick you up at 3pm and we'll go over."*

205

Our first job on arriving at the Airport was to get security passes so that we could get airside which didn't seem too fussy. When I got to the hangar I could see the Quik just wanting me fly it. But not yet!

With help from one or two people in the hangar, I changed the oil and fitted a new switch to the bare magneto wires I had been using since Myanmar. I also managed to replace the Velcro on the side of the skirt because, some places I had been, they had managed to spill fuel all down it which completely wrecks the Velcro.

With those three things done, I cleaned out the front of the pod and removed the rubbish that had accumulated over the past couple of months.

I managed to retrieve six plastic bottles, a dead tuna sandwich that had been in there since Qatar, and a pile of papier-mâché from weather reports that I had been given - the rain having changed their shape somewhat.

Les, my girlfriend, will call me disgusting.

As I was doing this, I started feeling a bit ill, not because of the tuna sandwich but just generally crap.

A couple of other guys in the hangar gave the Quik a wash down, so that it was ready for the next leg to Indonesia, whenever that would be.

Repair day in KL

Once I had finished messing with the Quik I was led back into the 4x4 and taken back to Cell 109.

I checked emails again, but nothing as far as a permit goes.

To get rid of this crap feeling, I had decided to go clubbing that night, and see if it makes me feel any better.

I wandered back from the nightclub about 3.30am feeling really bad – I decided that it must be the beer so I would sleep it off.

I got lifted up the step into the hotel, then off to bed.

I hoped that the permit would come shortly!

Days 76 to 78, July 13th to 15th

Not too much to say. It was like Ground Hog Day. I had been getting up, going to the local shopping centre, trying out the different pubs and night clubs.

I suppose you could call it a bit of a bender!

Places I have been to?

Republic, a pub and night club just next door to the hotel.

Then I would go down to Bubba Shrimps, a restaurant which also had a bar. Next door was a place called Borneo Forest, that's good, I ended up there until about 3am one night watching a live band?

Just around the corner was the Ministry of Sound night club.

I had been having plenty of refreshments over the past few days.

On the fifteenth, though, I must have eaten something bad as I was in Cell 109 all day throwing up, with a very high fever and just feeling downright Ill.

That didn't help either.

I just wished this permit for Indonesia would hurry up.

I would be glad to get back home and see all the pale European faces for a change and to have to put a long-sleeved top on, never mind a coat. I haven't had a coat on since Malta, except for the odd flying day when I got very wet.

I had been away for two and a half months and I was really missing home and the normal things like a good old English curry or kebab from the local take-away on a Friday night.

Day 79, July 16th

Today I forced myself out of bed, still sweating and then threw up again. Right, I needed to give my head a shake and stop being so miserable.

"Get your arse in gear and sort it out!"

After an hour or so of talking to the big white telephone in the bathroom, I ventured out into warm and humid Kuala Lumpur, and headed towards the shopping centre on the route that had been well trodden over the previous week or so.

As I reached the Republic Bar, I could hear loud noise coming from it (which would be normal, as it is a club)... but at 4pm?

I found a custom car show just outside, cars with body kits on and the most amazing paint jobs done to them.

That cheered me up, as I had been a car painter many moons ago.

There were all sorts of sooped up Protons and Suzuki Swifts, which made me smile but they did look good.

The stereo sound systems they had in them were out of this world, so loud that some were louder than the club itself.

The famous drifter cars were here too.

After looking around, I sat at a table and had a bottle of Tiger beer to see if it would settle my stomach and sat people-watching for a while.

Crowds were gathering and then they all seemed to cluster around four cars in particular. They started revving them really high with their noisy big exhaust pipes until they back-fired, but not only did they back-fire, these cars had flame throwers straight out of the exhaust, they were having a flame-off!

You would never have seen anything like it! These cars were outside a pub next to the benches with people walking about and there were flames coming out of the cars about 20ft into the air, with people fighting to get away from the heat.

The flame from one car melted a street light!

If you did that in England you'd get hung - health and safety and all that!

But I was enjoying it and the Tiger beer seemed to be sorting my guts out a bit (not much but a bit).

I went and got a Whopper from Burger King and had a wander around the cars for a closer look. Around 9.30pm about 50 motor-bikes turned up to join the party. I was sat at the Republic Bar surrounded by custom cars with flame-throwers out of the back when the bikers started burn-outs and donuts in the same area with people all around.

Around 11pm, the drifter car started doing donuts in the middle of the crowd to compete with the bikers. Don't forget this was all on the paved area at the side of tables of a pub, not even in a car park or road.

By now it was 1am and I am feeling a fair bit better. I haven't been sick in almost seven hours.

Happy days!

I thought I had better not risk going into the night club and anyway they were queuing a mile long. So, I decided to go back to Cell 109.

Day 80, July 17th

Kuala Lumpur. I had a really good day today. I got up early and went out for a wander after checking my emails.

The forecast had said it would be cloudy, but when I looked up, there was one lonesome cloud up there. I hoped that the next time I go flying and they say it's cloudy, that I would get the one on its own again.

It was so warm here! Those who know me, know that I like the sun, but it's too warm to sit out in it, honest! I have sat in the shade the whole time with a big Air con unit blowing at me.

Anyway, there was still no permit to fly, so I was off to try out another restaurant called Thai Thai's where I chicken noodles. It was OK.

Then I went to the Rain Forest bar. It was so dark in there, that all you could see were silhouettes and eye-balls. I must have stuck out like a sore thumb! I had a few drinks there before going around the corner to the Borneo Rain Forest Night Club to watch a live band and do some thinking and people-watching.

I had a really nice relaxed evening, doing a lot of thinking about what I was going do over the next few days to get things progressing if possible.

And then I had a slow push back up the hill to the hotel and went back to Cell 109.

I know this sounds really boring.

But it was! Honest! Ground Hog Day!

Yes, Kuala Lumpur is a nice place but all I wanted to do now was to get going. It was taking its toll on my body also.

If I sit around for too long I get very stiff and weird things start happening.

I won't go into detail - it's a wheelchair thing.

We paras and tetras know.

All my aches and pains are there and they really hurt. I'm in pain 24hours a day.

I had been thinking how my own bed would feel when I get there, and having somebody at the side of me again.

After that, you start really thinking on how much everybody means to you and stuff, a bit sad, I know, but you do. So I decided I have to go to bed now.

It was 4.30am.

Let's see what tomorrow brings.

Day 81, July 18th - ANNOUNCEMENT

As I had now been away from home for the best part of three months and was still stuck at Kuala Lumpur, I'd had a long, hard think and a lengthy chat with Lesley my girlfriend back in UK. We were both in agreement; enough is enough, so the next day I would be searching out the necessary person or people to sort this situation.

I was going to go and find a barber that could cut my hair!

I now looked like the mad professor from 'Back to the Future'!

Now you didn't think for one moment I was packing up this trip, did you?

Shame on you! Shame!

I would stay here until the Permit showed up allowing me to carry on - trust me!

Today I took one of the tablets that I have for Malaria. Well, it knocked me for six and I had bad side effects with it! My eyes went blurry, my heart started beating like a F1 car, I had pains all over my body and physically could not move far.

So I didn't move. I couldn't believe how bad I felt. It was like being hit by a bus or something.

I came around about 8pm and thought I'd better try to get up and get some food in me First I checked emails - still nothing!

I should point out that it was not White Rose Aviation who was sorting the permit out for Indonesia.

I forced myself out of bed and made my way to the shopping mall and searched out a Burger King. At least I knew what it would look like.

I must have looked a right sight going down the road – I had to go on the road as the kerbs were too high to try get up. I was pushing like a 95 year old, sorry to all you 95 year olds, respect.

Legs in spasm, trying to throw me out of the wheelchair uncontrollably!.

There were cars swerving all around me.

And I hadn't even had a beer!

I didn't know what I would be like on the way back with beer.

I sat in the queue at Burger King, people looking at me and prodding each other *"Look at him, poor lad".*

"Whopper burger please and a coke."

It had to be carried to the table.

I couldn't put it on my knees because there would have been nothing left of it! I sat there kicking away, trying to do the River Dance underneath the table, sweating and swearing at my legs!

But they would not stop. It was getting very tiring.

There was nothing else for it - I had to see whether beer would stop it!

So I set off to the pub, hair everywhere, sweating all the while doing the River Dance in the chair. The only thing I wasn't doing was dribbling!

I had a few at the nearest pub before accepting defeat and retreating very slowly back to the hotel.

I hoped I would feel better the next day.

I had to have a haircut, and chase up my Permit.

Day 82, July 19th

I got out of bed after a night like the exorcist, legs bouncing up and down uncontrollably all night, trying to throw me out of bed.

I was still feeling the side effects of the malaria drugs.

I was absolutely knackered now, I was on a mission to have my hair cut and get some laundry done. I thought I'd better do this at some point.

I needed some done before I went off again on my travels.

I filled my carrier bag and off I went down the road to where I had seen a small laundry and gave her the bag.

It came to a grand total of 6 Ringgits (about £1.60).

That was well worth it.

And it got better than that. There was a barbers next door. I stuck my head through the door and a man looked at me, smiling.

"You cut my hair?"

I took off the baseball cap I had been wearing, so as not to frighten any kids!

He looked and nodded.

I said, *"I want a number 2 cut, please".*

He looked puzzled, so it had to be done

"Brrrrrrrrrrr, Brrrrrrrrrrr" - You know clippers?

"Ah machine?"

"Yes, that's it, machine."

I went in and he had a good go at my hair for me.

I thought he'd done a splendid job of it and our conversation really grew,

He was from Bombay and I was from London

(We all know I'm from Dewsbury in Yorkshire, 200miles away from London)

I was telling him that I was flying to Australia, flapping my arms up and down and saying, *"Flying, you know?"*

Then the cut-throat razor came out. I didn't think my miming was that bad!

I thought it best to leave it as, he came from Bombay and I was a tourist from London.

He took a lovely sliver of skin and hair from my neck and around the ears - or at least it felt like he did! He had made a really nice job of it.

I paid him and left, and then all I did was go back to the hotel and check mail and get my laundry at 7pm, before going for something to eat.

Day 83, July 20th

I got up today and checked my email, and I finally had the response I was waiting for, that my Permit might be ready for tomorrow the 21st.

Hurray!

I shall be good boy today, and within ten minutes it was confirmed.

I can go!

I packed my bags and emailed Rohaizi to see if I could do any paper work prior to going tomorrow!

He got straight back in touch and said he would pick me up at 1pm.

Rohaizi collected me as promised and we also picked up one of the air traffic controllers at the airport at Kuala Lumpur and where I was parked at WMSA.

We pulled up at the ATC Centre and went upstairs to the main control room.

I met the Head of Operations and sat down with them to get my DCGA Permit updated for leaving Malaysian airspace the next day/

Once that was sorted out we went into the Flight Planning Office and sorted out the best route so I wouldn't need to get permission to enter Singapore's airspace.

I filed the plan ready for the next morning.

We had a look around at the main ATC room and I met the people that I would be talking to in the morning. They showed us all the screens with the transponder blips on them, which was quite interesting. It was also nice to place a face to ATC for a change.

I was dropped back at the hotel, but I was getting a bit hungry now so I went into the Mall and to Burger King. Afterwards I thought I had better get some money for the rest of the night.

Out of the blue, this chap said, *"What you still doing here? You should be well on your way now".*

I looked at him and thought, I can't remember talking to you over the last week.

He smiled and said *"I have been following your blog since Egypt"* - he was English, by the way.

"I think you're very brave and mad."

His name was Capt Phil White

It turned out he was an Airline Pilot who knew all the places I had been with the bad weather. He told me that even in Airliners they divert or get thrown around, so who know could imagine what it would be like for me in the Quik?

I got some more money for the night.

He asked what I was doing later.

"Just going to the pub then back to the hotel, I suppose".

He asked if he could meet up and have a couple of beers.

"Why not?"

That was it, he found me later and we started talking and drinking. We must have flown nearly half way around the world with all my stories and by the sound of it many times around the world from him. I had a really nice night talking to somebody who actually knew how bad the weather got in the areas I had been. It was funny because he just kept shaking his head at me.

Thanks for a good night with all my tales to tell, and all his.

And also I must thank Rohaizi for helping get the paperwork sorted out that day.

After a quick talk on Skype, I was off to bed.

I couldn't wait for the day ahead.

INDONESIA – ISLAND HOPPING TO A CRASH

Day 84, July 21st - Kuala Lumpur, Malaysia to Palembang, Indonesia

I was collected by Rohaizi and went straight to airport security so that he could get his pass and I could get cleared to go through to my Quik.

When we got there I loaded the Quik up and waited for Mr Zaini to come with a bit of extra fuel that hadn't been put in yet.

Once that was done we pulled the Quik out. I checked the route and that my map board was in order and then got in ready to go.

I packed the chair away and gave ATC a call.

"G-CDVO, request engine start and taxi to Apron 3 for CIQ please".

"G-CDVO, Engine start approved advice when ready for taxi".

I made my way down to Apron 3, where I met with Rohaizi and to go and see Immigration. But before I had chance to get out they came out to see me and have a look at the Quik.

That was good, because I thought I might have had to mess about and get back out of the Quik to go inside and see them.

After a small mistake was sorted out on my passport, I was given the go-ahead to depart. Ground Control gave me clearance to taxi straightaway, down to Runway 15.

I changed to the Tower frequency.

"G-CDVO, Good Morning, David."

"G-CDVO, ' morning, holding at Hotel".

"G-VO, Line up Runway 15 and cleared for takeoff, turn right after takeoff to 1,000ft and report Port Klang".

I took off, turned right as instructed and basically headed out over the city to the coast where Port Klang was.

Then I headed south following the coastline with a 10mph headwind, and had a quick look at the GPS which was indicating 9 hours to Palembang.

This was going to be a long day then.

I worked it out that the sun was going down about 7.30pm so I had plenty of time, even with a headwind.

The only thing that crossed my mind was the 60% chance of thunderstorms that had been forecast!

It was a nice, sunny day at 1,000ft. About 20 minutes into the journey there were lots of small dark clouds with showers, but nothing too scary to worry about.

An hour along the Malaysian coast it was time cross over to the Island of Sumatra, the northern most island of Indonesia, and follow that coastline all the way down to Palembang.

After I had been in radio contact with an airport called Mallaka I made the cross-over, not far really over the water, but far enough at 1,000ft.

A couple of big CBs were brewing in Sumatra, so I decided to stay out to sea for a while, as my route into Palembang would be along the coast.

Still only at 1,000ft and out at sea, I diverted slightly to say hello to an oil rig and flew around it, waving. They must have thought, *what is he doing, the Prat?*

As I headed further south I could see some seriously big cloud formations over land,

"Mmmm, I wonder where they are going then?"

I hoped I wouldn't come across them, especially as I hadn't flown for two weeks. They made me nervous, just looking at them.

Further south these big formations were getting bigger and starting to come on to my track.

I looked at the chart, and could see where they were, right on the tip of coastline that stuck out. However the CBs were not only at this tip of land, they were right out to sea towards Singapore.

I wouldn't be able to get past them.

I looked right and there was another formation of rain and cloud brewing, which was also very dark, but there was a gap in between them over land.

Would I be able to make through?

It certainly looked a safer option than the coastal route.

I took a picture of this one because, as the top of it was building and it came towards me, the shape of a claw appeared from it!

"Right turn! I'm off inland".

In I went and because I was only at 1,000ft it was pretty bouncy with 36 degree heat thermals over the trees, and there were a lot of trees.

The storms did just what I didn't want. They wanted to be together!

They both wanted to put me in the middle and give me the claw.

Not a chance, I was off!

Bar in to the chest to 60 mph - don't forget the ASI is still stuck – and I was doing about 90mph. I took my camera off the base bar just before I got a good soaking, but I looked left where I was supposed to have gone.

It was just rain down to the ground in a wall, so I was glad I made this re-route.

Then it cleared up to nice blue sky all the way to Palembang.

I was looking at miles and miles of trees and winding rivers. It reminded me of some old films I have with the views and the boats on it. I could see a couple of rainbows.

I called Palembang Tower, and the response was, *"G-CDVO - report airport in sight".*

"G-CDVO - Airport in sight".

"G-VO - Report finals, clear to land".

As I was approaching finals I couldn't see the other end of the runway. There was a huge downpour heading my way.

I landed and went to the South Apron where I was met by the Indonesian Air Force. I switched my engine off just in time.

And it rained, oh, and it rained. I had spotted a hangar on my way so I said *"I'm going to take it round there out of the way"*

"I need to get out of this rain", I said.

I started the engine and taxied around a corner to the hangar which had a Pegasus GT-450 microlight in it!

I asked whose it was and was told it belonged to someone they knew.

As it turned out, the Indonesian Air Force were putting me up for the night in the camp. That was a turn-up for the books. After I got my bags out and covered the Quik, I was taken to the Air Force guest house with the troops in a military vehicle. When I got there I asked if there was anywhere close by where I could get something to eat but they said no don't worry we will bring you food and drink. So I said Ok I'll have a KFC and a couple of tins of beer then.

They just laughed and said *"there is no beer here we are all Muslims but we will get you a KFC and coke"*

They were all very friendly and couldn't do enough for me.

So my thanks for that to the Indonesian Air Force.

I sat and tapped away on my computer for the night, completely bored, and sorted out my route for the next day's flying.

Day 85, July 22nd - Palembang to Jakarta

I got up early and a guy called Pam Pang came around to the residence. He told how much I owed for staying there and for the food, so I paid him and then said I needed to get some money for the Avgas.

He said *"when do you want to go?"*

I said, *"Now really"* so he made a radio call and a truck arrived.

I was fed into the front seat and we went to the airport ATM with everybody looking at me given my military escort!

Then we went to the Control Tower to file the flight plan for my trip to Jakarta.

It only took a few minutes to do then we were off again, I didn't even need to get out of the truck to file the flight plan as they came down from the Tower to me. We drove around the outskirts of the runway to the Quik and met up with the waiting TV crews and newspaper media.

I had a few interviews while the troops re-fuelled my Quik for me.

It was soon time to go, but there was a horrible dark storm right above the runway, so I couldn't go just yet. This gave time for more photos with the Indonesian Air Force.

It cleared up and I got a weather report from one of the military which indicated 10k visibility, so it should have been be clear once I got into the air.

I thanked everybody for running me around and looking after me for the night.

I pulled the Quik out and pushed it onto a parking area narrowly missing a big hole on the grass that could have caused damage. Then I got in the Quik ready with help from the military.

I gave the Tower a call. They came straight back and cleared me to taxi to Runway 29 and I was cleared for take-off. It was clear, beautiful blue skies with some very wet flooded fields as far as the eye could see. What a fantastic view.

At 1,000ft you see much more. I looked at all the houses built on stilts to cope with the floods, and there were lots of small villages that didn't even have roads. They were all linked by waterways, so everybody had a boat, and this went on for miles and miles.

As time went on the heat was picking up and building the dreaded storms again.

Only an hour into the flight, I was being bounced all over, holding on to the bar for dear life again, and dodging the huge CB clouds starting to cover the countryside.

I was spending a lot of the time now with the bar in to my chest, just trying to either keep level or go down, with all the lift I was getting. It got to the point that I could not carry on overland because the storms were building too big and too dangerous to fly near.

I decided to see what it was like over the coast so I took a short cut out to sea.

As I approached, the coast looked clear but before I could get there I had between two big rain storms. They started closing in at either side of me and getting lower.

I'd had to fly this trip now on a day by day basis, and you must think that I'm just using the same words over and over, but it was true that every flight was done 'by the seat of my pants' in one way, shape or form! There had been numerous instances where two storms were trying to close in on me. I assumed this must be the way that CB's build or something – either that or I'd just had a lot of bad luck!

I took my camera off the base bar before it got wet, and as I did the rain started. Both storms had now come together so I had fly underneath the towering CB's above.

When you don't have gloves on ... the rain hurts!

I was now at 800ft, trying my best not to get pulled up into the clouds, keeping low and trying to ready for some bouncing around to start.

I was very wet but I got through it to the coast.

The transformation was amazing, beautiful pale blue sea with very small scattered clouds at 1,500ft and no turbulence.

That was it then, I was going this way. I spoke to ATC who sent me to a reporting point out at sea before giving me a direct route to Jakarta.

I flew over a few container ships and the odd Island, so I could even get my camera out to snap away. Looking back the cloud was covering the sky completely, with all sorts of colours in it. I was very glad that I had come this way even though I was back out to sea again.

This was now stunning flying - I had never seen such pale blue sea before.

Forty miles from Jakarta there was a group of small islands huddled together. The view was fantastic and at 1,000ft you could see people on the beaches of the deserted islands.

The Airfield I was heading for was just at the far side of Jakarta city, a place called Cibubur. I looked at the map, wondering where ATC was going to send me.

"G-CDVO, Report 20 miles off coast".

"G-CDVO, will report 20 miles off coast".

"G-CDVO - Report 5 miles off coast".

And so on.

I looked at the coast line and it was nothing, but Jakarta city now.

S###t, am I going the right way? What do I do?

"Jakarta, G-CDVO, reporting 5 miles to the coast".

"G-CDVO, continue on current heading at 1,000ft"

I was now heading directly towards the city. I hoped that he knew what type of aircraft I was... He was taking me straight over the top of the city at 1,000ft!

"G-CDVO, report overhead WIHH".

"G-CDVO will report overhead WIHH"

WIHH is Jakarta international airport and he was taking me right over the top of it at 1,000ft I could not believe it.

I looked to my right and over the city was the blackest storm you have ever seen heading south towards me. Picture this, one flexwing at 1,000ft flying straight across Jakarta City. There was nowhere to go if anything happened - skyscrapers on my right with a huge storm over them, and on my left the other side of the city.

So I got there and reported

"G-CDVO overhead WIHH".

I flew straight across the middle of the main airport looking down at a jet taking off. I was getting thrown all over the sky now as well.

It just didn't seem real it was like something you would do on a computer game rather than in reality.

I was convinced I was doing something wrong, but I wasn't..

Once I had reported overhead Jakarta Airport, ATC said, *"report Cibubur airfield in sight".*

The storm was just about on me now.

"G-CDVO - Cibubur airport in sight".

"G-CDVO, change to Cibubur on 119.30, goodbye".

As soon as he said that, it started raining very hard.

I gave Cibubur a call

"G-CDVO – Cibubur".

"G-CDVO, Runway 09, clear to land".

I bent the wing over like a good one because now I was getting seriously wet and the visor was up so I could see.

In fact, I couldn't see a thing now even with the visor up. Finals were just over the main motorway into Jakarta City and in-between trees, the airfield was 900 metres long with trees all around.

In I went, head out of the side of the trike because I could not see through the screen for the rain.

I flew in between the trees, landed and taxied back into be welcomed by a guy called Bagas, the Airfield Manage, who had been in touch with me.

But not only him, there were a few TV crews filming me.

I pulled straight into a' hangar and the rain really came down.

It looks like I had got in to land just in time.

I got out of the Quik with TV crews filming me really close up which was quite annoying my legs were kicking and dancing in spasm.

Once out I did a couple of Interviews and then I was taken up to the club house where I met a few other people in wheelchairs who had come to see me.

I told everybody about my flight for an hour or so, and then I asked Bagas where I would be stopping for the night.

He had arranged for me to stop in a room in a scout camp which was very kind of him but I needed to get internet access and there wasn't any there.

So after a discussion I was taken to a hotel in Jakarta for the night on the mad really busy roads.

Day 86, July 23rd - Cibubur (Jakarta) to Semarang

Today the lady who had sorted out my Indonesian permit out in the British Embassy in Jakarta picked me up from the hotel. We went to Cibubur airfield where I watched the "Cibubur aero model show", which looked very impressive with the different types of remote controlled aircraft they had showing.

I had a chat with Bagas and a few others, and asked for my flight plan to be processed for me. After about 30 minutes he came out with the flight plan,

I said, "*Are you sure it is right?*"

His friend showed me the reporting points along the way, and the different frequencies I needed for my next leg of the trip.

It was really warm now, and there were a few people coming to their model show. I got another 20 litres of fuel courtesy of Bagas (thank you), and got into the Quik, ready to go.

There were cameras everywhere, taking shots of me. I was ready to go and so the area was cleared for me to start the engine.

I taxied out and lined up.

It was really hot now, with trees all around the runway and very little wind.

With all the weight on board the Quik would take some getting off the ground so I decided not to get a full load of fuel.

In addition, a grass runway was going to slow the take-off down quite a lot.

I took off, made a right turn then came around and gave the airfield a fly-by before heading off to Semarang. I headed straight across the west of Jakarta city ATC kept me down at 1,000ft until I was clear of the city and just before it turned into the countryside.

It was very bumpy as the heat was building up.

About 30 miles out of Jakarta there was a ridge of low mountains - 2,000ft - so I flew to the right of them, heading towards the coast. On my right was a mountain or volcano. I couldn't really see because it was really hazy now. I was getting bounced all over the sky with wind coming down from the mountain on my right and from the ridge on my left. It was horrible.

Eventually I could see the coast.

"*I hope it calms down a bit.*"

It was still very windy, but it was OK. I finally got to the coast where it did calm down, and actually became a nice pleasant flight.

When I got to twenty miles away from Semarang, Approach kept asking my position and altitude and not understanding my accent

"G-CDVO - what is your altitude?"

"G-CDVO – my altitude is 1,000ft on 1010".

"G-CDVO - confirm 4,000ft".

"G-CDVO – Negative, one thousand ft."

"G-VO – confirm 4,000ft".

"G-CDVO is at one thousand ft, one, zero, zero, zero ft."

An airliner pilot told him: *"G-CDVO is at one thousand ft."*

"CDVO - maintain 1,000ft, report airfield in sight".

That was hard work. It must be my posh Yorkshire accent that he couldn't understand.

I reported airfield in sight and was cleared to land at Semarang. Once down I was instructed to park at Bay 23 on the Apron, facing the Terminal, which I did.

Straight in front now I could see the sky getting darker. There was nobody around apart from a guy who was sorting out another aircraft to my side, so I called him over, I said that I needed to get my aircraft out of the way for the night and before that storm in front let go.

I also asked: *"Do you have a ground handling agent?"*

He said *"No, we don't".*

While this was going on the storm was getting closer and meanwhile a group of Fire Fighters came over to have a look and take pictures with me and the Quik. After a few calls were made from one of the Fire Crew to the Airport Manager agreed for me to park the Quik up near the Fire Station. And with that the Fire Crew pushed the Quik, with me still in it, over to the Fire Station.

Just as I put the brake on, it started to rain, monsoon-style, extremely heavy.

I sat there getting a good soaking, trying to cover the instruments up on the dashboard. The fire fighters brought out some umbrellas, but it wasn't stopping it so with help from a couple of the fire crew I got out of the Quik in double-fast time, to get out of the rain.

I had a good laugh and a joke with them in the station and we even had a beer. It stopped raining so I got all my things out and covered up the Quik and then went to Operations to sort out the paperwork and find a Hotel for the night.

After a few calls were made to different hotels and a trip to a desk in the Terminal the hotel was sorted. I had got a hotel that was just 10 minutes away from the airport and a member of hotel staff even came to pick me up.

It was a small room sat on its own away from the main building with just one step into it. So after I had dropped my bags into it I sorted out my route for the next day's flight then made my way to the restaurant where I had chicken something or other and fries (not really sure what it was) and a couple of Bingtang beers before retreating to my room to type up a bit and catch up with my blog..

Day 87,- July 24th - Semarang to Surabaya

I was taken to the airport at 7.30am, so I could get my flight plan sorted, and get re-fuelled. This was to be another relatively short trip, at just 175 miles, all over land for a change!

However, as I have found out, trips over land in this part of the world are likely to result in a rough ride with winds rolling off the mountains, thermals off the trees and possible rain.

I got to Semarang where I met two Fire Fighters and the Airport Manager who then took me to the Quik, and organised the re-fuelling..

After ten minutes a fuel bowser with a trailer of Avgas turned up and 100 litres was put in my Quik. This wasn't airport fuel; apparently it was from the Army and I paid the man who had managed to sort it out with the military for me.

Once that was done I went over to the flight operations room and filed the flight plan - with a bit of luck I would be at Surabaya for lunch time.

The Fire Crew kept saying to me: *"Surabaya is a very big and busy airport, you know. You will have to be careful, have you got clearance to fly in?"*

"Yes I have got clearance to fly in don't worry."

The wind started to pick up as I got loaded up, I climbed into the Quik in the shelter of the trees at the Fire Station and then I was pushed out onto the apron.

"G-CDVO, ready for engine start and taxi".

"G-CDVO, approved, taxi when ready"

As I warmed up the engine, a local jet taxied out past me and took off – this just left me at the airport.

I said goodbye to the Fire Crews and thanked them for all their help and then I gave the Tower a call telling them I was taxiing out.

Then I got, *"G-CDVO - line up and cleared for take-off, wind 12knts, climb to 1,000ft and maintain".*

I took off and headed east. The visibility was terrible, in fact I think it was border-line illegal. There were trees everywhere so it was really bouncy. I also had a head wind of around 10-15mph. It might not be far but it wasn't going to be a short ride by any means. On my right hand side, somewhere in the mist and murk, there were mountains and already I could feel the winds blowing down from them and hitting me at the side, up and down, left and right,

I was fully exercising the movement of the base bar, so I tightened my seat belt ready for the big ones.

After an hour the ground started to rise up with small hills producing wild rotor, kicking me around. I was trying to maintain 1,000ft, which wasn't easy. The revs on the Quik at some point were at 3,600rpm to maintain level flight and with the aircraft also full of fuel it would usually be at around 4,000rpm with all this weight.

If I climbed higher to get out of the turbulence I could see even less, so I stuck out the turbulence at 1,000ft.

As I got to within 40 miles of Surabaya, with trees still everywhere as I skirted around small villages, I finally got Surabaya approach on the radio. They told me to continue on the same heading however this heading would eventually take me straight over the city of Surabaya.

Before changing to the Tower frequency I was cleared to land from 8 miles finals. So there I am going straight over the city at 1,000ft on 8 mile finals and I can't even see the runway in front of me.

The runway finally came into view *"G-CDVO reporting finals now"*

227

"G-CDVO wind 15knts, cleared to land"

I flew down the very long runway before landing about 50 ft away from a taxiway, then I followed the yellow lines and changed over to the Ground frequency and was sent to Bay 26, way out in the open, with nothing around to shelter me from the wind. I sat there for a while, waiting for the handling agent to arrive.

Shortly afterwards, a small passenger airliner came and parked next to me. Another handling agent was dealing with that aircraft and I called them over to see if they were my agent. They told me that they weren't but they did give me an in-flight meal.

I asked if there was any where that I could park out of the wind. A few phone calls were made and the Airport just said no, you have to park it there where it is.

My Handling Agent finally turned up and I got out of the Quik.

I fastened my aircraft down as best I could with some concrete blocks that were brought for me. I jumped into the agent's car and was taken to a hotel for the night although on the way I had to call at an ATM as I was running out of money again.

Day 88, July 25th - Surabaya to Bali

After a night in the bar laughing my head off at a couple of singers doing karaoke and thinking they were absolutely fantastic, I was collected at 7.30am to return to the Airport. Another guy from the same Agents was waiting for me as I came into the reception area,

it was quite funny because a young lad came over to me and asked my if it was me that was doing the York to Sydney flight as he had seen me on TV. I said yes and had a photo taken with him and his girlfriend.

I went into the Airport through a side entrance and straight to the Quik. This made a change from having to go here, there and everywhere searching for the right office to go to and the right piece of paper to fill in.

I got the Quik ready while asking the Agent at Global Handling about my flight plan. *"Don't worry, it is in hand"*. When they say things like that, you just know it not sorted at all.

After 10 minutes the chap that I had been dealing with the previous day, turned up with my helmet and headset, and produced a flight plan already filled in and approved. Was that it, then? Could I go?

"Yes, sir, Captain!"

That was it. I packed up and got ready to go in super-quick time. So a big thanks to Global Ground Handling for sorting that out for me. I didn't even have to bother requesting engine start, I just had to give them a call when I was ready.

I gave Ground control a call, in what was a really busy airport now. There were jets coming and going every two minutes. I got the oil up to temperature, above 50°C, and gave the ground frequency a call.

"G-CDVO – ready to taxi".

"G-CDVO - taxi to holding point November 1".

It was a very long way down to the end of the 14,000ft runway and I didn't really need all that. I called back to the ground frequency.

"G-CDVO - requesting an intersection take off from November 3".

"G-VO - erm - just a minute.......G-VO - intersection November 3 take off approved, taxi to November 3 and hold".

That saved a lot of tyre wear and fuel!

By now there were jets coming in and going out all around, it was hard getting a word in on the radio. I taxied out and waited at November 3 holding point while two jets came in, then I was changed over to the Tower frequency for takeoff.

"G-CDVO – line-up and advice when ready for take-off".

"G-CDVO lining up and ready for take-off"

I lined up, the wind now at 15mph, and was cleared to go. The route I was cleared for took me straight out over the sea for what would be at least an hour, but as soon as I got to the coast the visibility was really bad, so I started to follow the coast line slightly. ATC came back to me and sent me back on the heading out to sea.

It started clearing up a bit but not much, but I could see where I was going so I didn't mind. About an hour in to the flight the route took me back into the coast. The murk was clearing to reveal the coast line with a volcano way out in the distance. It was a truly awesome sight, and then further down there was another volcano just by the coast edge. It was not active but it still looked awesome from where I was sitting. I carried on around the coastline, taking in all the views until I had to cross over to the island of Bali. With the wind blowing between both islands it was now quite rough as it funnelled through the Straits.

Volcano on my way to Bali

I followed the coast of Bali having to suffer wonderful views of the mountains (!) and headed towards Bali airport at the south of the island.

As I got close, Bali approach changed me over to Tower for landing, but it was quite funny.

"G-CDVO - report runway in sight".

I reported runway in sight. It sticks out into the sea a good few hundred metres. Still with a head wind, I was cleared to land 6 miles out. Then Tower came back to me. *"G-CDVO - how long to landing?"*

"G-CDVO - ETA touch down about 8 minutes".

"G-CDVO - can you do a left orbit then please? We have a 747 coming in."

230

"G-CDVO - orbiting to my left, no problem".

As I orbited over the Bali beaches the 747 went past me and landed.

I was cleared to land again, and flew in without incident. As I taxied, in the ground frequency sent me right to the far end of the apron to park up among the helicopters,

After a bit of paperwork, a trike pilot from Oz came to meet me. Her name was Kathy Little from York in Australia, one of the many Face-bookers following the flight.

We went to stay at the same hotel, and were there the following night as well (day off). We went out for a meal and had a few beers in Bali.

That accounts for Day 89, July 26 as well.

Day 89, July 26th - Day in Bali

I'd had a nice time the previous evening with Kathy and Made in Bali and so I had a lay-in this morning. I got up at a mind blowing 9am!! What a lazy git!

Then I did a bit of tapping away on the PC for a while.

Later we went out to the market area of Bali - I went one way and Kathy and Made went the other. I came across the beach so I had a bit of a wander down the front and found a nice spot in between some trees where I could get onto the beach.

There was a guy selling Bintang beer from a fridge, so that was it *"yes please beer"*

I sat there watching the waves rolling over and over with the odd surfer. It was just nice to sit and do absolutely nothing for a change. The only thing that I was concerned about was the wind blowing over the trees and was my Quik OK at the airport?

However, after a couple of beers I wasn't too concerned! ☺

Then a load of people started harassing, me trying to sell me things

"NO, I DON'T WANT IT, GO AWAY"

"NO I DON'T WAN'T A SUERONG"

After a while and a bit of haggling with a couple of women, I came to a deal and had my nails cut and done and my ears cleaned and plucked.

All a bit strange but there you go.

I watched the sun go down on the beach talking to a group of Ozzy's that were there for a few days. Then I hunted down a taxi to take me back to the hotel.

I dropped some things off and I went out with Made for the night to sample some different bars and clubs.

And I have to say Bali is now on my list of places to come back to on holiday.

Day 90, July 27 - Bali to Bima

Kathy and Made took me to the airport at 7.30am and after a few calls, we were met by the handling agent.

I sorted the paperwork out with them before going out to the Quik.

When I got out to the Quik it was quite windy, they said 12 knots but it was more like17 knots, but any way I said *"Where's my fuel?"*

"If give the man some money he will go to get if for you"

What you haven't even gone for it yet, you do realise I have a 5 hour flight to do don't you?

By now it was 10am. So I got all my stuff loaded up ready as the wind picked up even more.

The guy finally turned up with the fuel and it was filled up.

I said *"What about my flight plan?"*

"It's here sir", so I had a look at it and said

"That route is no good to me you are taking me straight over the top of the islands and mountains.

As you know I'm not an airliner and it says VFR I'm filing it for.

There will be cloud cover over them so I have to follow the coast line."

So after a couple of calls to ATC they agreed to let me fly the coast line.

I asked the handling agents to pull the Quik around into wind where I could get into it without it blowing over as the wind was now at about 17 knots.

I was cleared for engine start and taxied to November 6 holding point right at the end of the runway and set off, because the wind was that strong. I just let the brake off and I was off on my way following the yellow lines November 6.

"G-CDVO holding November 6"

'G-CDVO HOLD DO NOT MOVE"

What have I done now I was thinking? I was sat where they told me to go and was holding on to the wing for life here in the cross winded.

But there were two aircraft on finals, so I was sat there for a good 15 minutes.

Then a third came.

"G-CDVO I can go in between this one"

"G-CDVO ARE YOU READY FOR TAKE OFF"

"G-CDVO YES"

'G-CDVO LINE UP CLEARED FOR TALE OFF"

That was it I taxied straight out and took off.

Bar all over the place I got to 500ft at the blink of an eye and turned right so the other jet could land.

Then I set of direct to Bima following the coast line.

There was a 25mph wind straight on the nose - fantastic I thought....this is going to be a long trip.

I'll trim off and get going.

NO YOU WON'T THE ELECTRIC TRIM IS STUCK ON AGAIN.

So to get a ground speed above 38mph, I had to override the trimmer and it takes some strength to do. I pulled the bar in and to get a 48mph ground speed.

This was going to about 5 hours flying.

Blowing a gale and getting bounced all over the sky, I crossed from Bali to the first island of Nusa Penida where I encountered some wild rotor coming as this island was full of mountains.

Nonetheless, the view was very spectacular along this coast line, there were plenty of clouds covering the tops of the peaks, so it would have been impossible to follow the route that ATC had suggested.

Truly stunning scenery started appearing as I continued down the coast going past the islands of Sumbawa and Dompo, tugging on the base bar all the time, fighting with the wind.

After four hours of it I was absolutely knackered and I was feeling tired from the night before which didn't help.

Mountains all the way down now AWESOME!

I was now only about 40 minutes away from Bima and there were still mountains everywhere. For some reason, I just had a feeling that this place was going to be in the middle of them!

Twenty minutes from Bima I had to climb up to 4,000ft where the ground speed dropped to a very respectable 25mph (if you were on a bicycle).

I was really getting bounced all over now. I could see where I needed to go; it was at the other side of the mountain in front of me. So I just went for it, 4,000ft just skimming the tops of the trees on tops. I was really getting nervous again and then as I flew over the other side of the peak it revealed a very flat area with a big lake and what looked like rice paddy fields all around.

I slowly eased the power off now, my arms were aching all over – I'd had enough and I stopped pulling the bar in.

I descended all the way down to join downwind for runway 13 at Bima. It was still very windy probably a good 20 mph now.

I was cleared to land – it was only a small airport compared with some that I had been in to recently.

I was met by a group of people some from the Indonesian Air Force together with some from the Airport itself.

I got out into the wheelchair and a car turned up with about 10 small plastic cans full of fuel for me. I was refuelled straight away and then I packed the Quik up.

I grabbed my bags before being bundled into a car and taken to a hotel 20 kilometres away down some dirt tracks.

I had some rice and things brought for my evening meal and a drink but there was nothing else to do around the area so I had to stop in the hotel. I was the only guest in there.

In the early hours of the morning there was a crash and bang coming from the roof that woke me up and really made me jump.

Then the noise got louder and it sounded like it was trying to get in to the bathroom through the ceiling. It sounded huge like a dog or something equally as big. Whatever it was it was clawing away trying to get in. I was crapping myself. It did eventually go away but I just couldn't sleep after that.

Day 91, July 28th - Bima to Kupang

A knock on the door at 6am saying, *"Are you ready, sir?"*

Erm yes - I was still in bed.

I got up really quickly and waited for the lad to come back and lift my wheelchair down the steps of the room I was in.

I thought I should get off early and beat the thermals.

After a quick rice and noodle breakfast with warm orange juice, we were off to the Airport. As we pulled on to the Apron a Security Guard was just taking his camp bed away. He had been sleeping at the side of my Quik all night (what a star).

You wouldn't get that in Dewsbury!

I loaded up and asked about my flight plan.

They said *"Just a minute,"* and pointed to a guy who was coming across with the flight plan for me to fill in. This was just another example of the very fast and efficient service by the smaller airports. Thank you everybody at Bima for all your help.

With that filed I asked for my bill so I could pay my dues. The lad who had taken me to the hotel gave me a bill for a hire car, I said *"who's the hire car for?"*, *"you sir I have had it for 3 days for you"* oh you have, have you well that's all well and good but I didn't ask you to hire one did I?? He said no so I refused to pay for it, they will try anything on for more money.

Then I got in to the Quik. And it was still nice early to get going.

I took off on Runway 31 and flew through a gap in the mountains and around the north of the island, and it was absolutely flat calm, no wind at all.

I started to track down the coast line of the other islands.

What a stunning morning it was, blue skies, only a 10 mph headwind, no turbulence.

The views were amazing with mountains coming all the way to the edge of the sea and looking like something from Jurassic Park

Some of them even resembled the feet of dinosaurs!

This was one of the best flights of the whole trip so far in terms of the scenery.

There were volcanoes sticking up through the clouds with what looked bits of smoke coming from them, in contrast a stunning very pale blue sea and beautiful beaches that could only be reached by boat.

I was so lucky to be here, after nearly 3 months away from home.

I was flying at 1,000ft and it looked awesome.

After four hours of coastline flying it was time to cross the sea past the island of Sumba to Kupang in West Timor. This leg started out OK. With just a 10mph headwind and lots of cloud building, the cloud base came down to 1,000ft, and I dropped to 900ft out at sea.

It cleared up nicely, but then the base bar started shaking and pulling me around with turbulence - I couldn't understand where it was coming from.

I climbed up to 2,000ft but it wasn't going away.

In fact, it was getting worse.

I tuned to Kupang's frequency and I was sure I heard winds gusting to 17 knots mentioned. I looked down at the GPS. My ground speed was now deteriorating in a head wind of 30 mph.

Oh, great stuff, and after such a lovely flight so far as well.

"G-CDVO - report 10miles out."

"G-CDVO - will report 10 miles out".

"G-CDVO - be advised the wind is very bad and gusty here."

Great! Just what I did not want to hear!

Still, I had to carry on, there was nowhere else to go.

I reported 10 miles out. The lady at ATC said, report airfield in sight.

By now I'm getting seriously bounced around.

The high winds I landed in Kupang

I didn't know the best way of holding on.

I reported airfield in sight and she said, *"G-CDVO - continue and report finals, wind 20knts gusting 35knts".*

And then everything went very quiet.

"G-CDVO - finals to land."

I was trying my best to keep the trike under control, but not only was it a strong gusty wind, but it was also a cross wind.

I'm at 500 feet over the threshold and battling with the bar, trying to get down.

At 300 feet the wing was going from left to right, power-on, power-off, bar in, bar left, bar right.

At 100 feet I was just about there, when there was a fierce gust of wind and by now really fighting with bar, I touched down - Phew!! I had got it down!

Then a really strong gust lifted me off the tarmac again, so I fought with it and landed again.

The wind got hold of one side of the wing to try to turn me over, but I managed to save it, by jamming my arm in to the corner of the 'A' frame. In doing so, I was blown off the runway into the grass, just missing a landing light. This was no problem, but there was a big hole covered with grass.

I went over it and it ripped my front wheel off and trapping my feet in the pod.

The wind remained really violent, trying to tip me over.

"G-CDVO – are you OK? Somebody will be with you shortly."

"G-CDVO – I am fine."

A pick-up van full of Airport workers came racing along to help me.

They grabbed hold of the wing. To stop the wind rolling me over in to a ball

I got my feet out from underneath the damaged trike. I was giving instructions about how to get my chair off the Quik so that I could get into it and save the aircraft from destruction with the wind. There must have been about 20 people holding on to the Quik to stop it from getting wrecked.

We dragged it away from the hole and decided the best thing was to de-rig it.

So there I am with a really strong wind, trying to explain to 20 people – foreigners - how to de-rig a Quik.

But we did it! We got the wing off onto the ground flat, then I had a look at the damage scratched my head and decided to pack the wing up all together.

A small pickup truck came over and we put the wing and trike in the back and got it out of the way of everything for the time being.

By the time we got sorted out it was around 6pm. Someone found me a hotel for a few days and with the time difference from where I was in Timor to the UK, P.M Aviation were just opening their doors and it was a Friday.

So I ordered a new front fork to be sent out to me and within the hour they were boxed up and ready to be sent out. So a really big thank you to P.M for doing that at a drop of a hat for me.

So now I would have to just sit here in Kupang West Timor and wait for the parts to arrive here. And I was just one stop from Australia.

I had two bruised feet, a bruise on my left leg, a hurt left wrist and a cut finger

But I'm fine. This was just another setback in my attempt to fly to Oz.

Just after the nose wheel came off

Days 92 to 94, July 29th to 31st - Static in Kupang

At this point I had to apologise for the delay in getting the blog up to date. Firstly my computer crashed, and combining that with the very poor internet at the hotel meant that the blog wasn't updated for a few days and I spent some time messing around trying to get it all sorted out..

I got up on Friday morning with a couple of good bruises on my feet where they had been trapped under the pedals in my trike, and my wrist was really painful. I think I have done some damage somewhere in it but I'm not going to the hospital as they will only tell me the same, that it's damaged or broken, and charge me for going to ask them.

I rang up P&M Aviation to give them the address to send the parts to at the airport. It was 8.30am UK time and Roger Pattrick had already got the parts ready to go. What a super fast service from them. Thanks, Roger.

I spent the next couple of days sat around the hotel recovering and drinking Bintang beer.

On the Friday night I went to a place called Teddies Bar down at the front near the beach, had a Bintang, and then heard music across the road at the sea front.

I went across only to discover that there were around 60 sailing boats that had come in from "Sail Indonesia" and there was a big party going on.

I basically gate-crashed the party and I ended up sat at a table with two Americans and a Canadian who were sailing around the world.

I had a really good night with them dancing and talking about our different ways of travelling.

On the Saturday I went down to the sea front again and the boats were still there, so there was another party on the Saturday night. By now everybody knew me and what I was doing in Kupang. People were coming up to me and asking about my trip and how long I had been away.

I was telling them that it's been a long time now, three months and the trip was only supposed to take two months.

I ended up sitting at a table with two Australians who were delivering a boat from England to Bangkok for somebody, and a Canadian couple sailing around the world who had been away for four and a half years.

That made my three months seem a bit tame.

After the party I just went back to the hotel.

On Sunday I got up with my wrist still throbbing and a lump on the side of it getting bigger. I really have done something to it as the pain doesn't seem to be going away. Bruises are still there; in fact I found a new one on my side this morning.

My aircraft parts were due to arrive from P&M on Tuesday or Wednesday, so hopefully I would be away for the weekend.

The British Embassy was closed over the weekend so I hoped to be able to put the permissions to fly in for the following week as it would take seven days to get them sorted out.

I went down to the bar again on Sunday as there were still some of the sail boats around. This time I was talking to a guy from England who was sailing the world with a crew from Poland and an engineer from Switzerland.

I had a few Bintangs with them.

Days 95 to 97, August 1st to 3rd - Still Static in Kupang

I was now into the fourth month away on what was supposed to be a two month trip.

I am getting tired and really need to get going as my money was running out.

I had put the permissions in to the British Embassy to leave on Monday the 8th August as it would take a week to get them.

I had a tracking number for DHL so I could see where my parts were. On Monday they were in Jakarta, so I hoped they would be with me by Tuesday or Wednesday

I hadn't bothered going up to the Airport over the last few days as I know that the Quik was being looked after.

Once all that was sorted out, I went down to Teddies Bar and met the Swiss guy from the night before, we had a really good laugh joking around and singing Karaoke. I forgot to mention, but this guy had a false leg and used a walking stick, so you can just imagine the sight, one English guy in a wheelchair and a Swiss guy with a false leg wondering around full of Bintang beer, and neither of us understanding a word of Indonesian.

We had a good night and it cheered me up as he had been here in Kupang waiting for paperwork to get sorted also so he could continue sailing (somebody else with paperwork issues!)

I was sat there at the bar just looking over it, as I was so low down, and he was sat at the side of me with his leg on the bar, SO FUNNY.

Then the microphone came out and I just couldn't help myself.

Karaoke!

I tried singing "In the shadows" by Rasmus, but decided, actually, I was quite bad at it due to the alcohol.

On Tuesday I did much the same. I checked the internet when it worked for more than 10 seconds to see if my parts were any closer. They were not.

Then I went to Teddies Bar again, except this time I was talking to a local who spoke English and an Australian guy.

Somehow I ended up in a car going to a party at a local's house around 5km away.

There I was fed and watered for the night, and I talked about my flight and all the good parts and the really scary parts.

Before long - maybe 3-4am - and full to the top of beer and food, I decided it was time to go back to the hotel. I shared a taxi with the Australian as our hotels were close together.

On Wednesday I checked the internet again. After more than an hour messing with my laptop, it just said "can't find operating system" and then froze.

My parts had now left Jakarta! Maybe I would get them later today or tomorrow?

I spent the night down at Teddies, singing Sweet Caroline like a good old bad English singer does, drowning my sorrows.

My wrist was still the same.

I have damaged it somewhere, as the pain is just the same and I have a lump on the side now like an egg...

Should I go to the hospital? Probably.

But if I were to do that, I just knew they would stick a plaster cast on it which would make it impossible for me to fly and so that would be the end of the trip.

It looks like, with pain, I would get to Australia.

The Bintang takes the pain away.

I have a broken bone already in my other hand, so it can't be that bad and let's face it, a lot worse happened in 1993.

I am just going to struggle on until the parts arrive to fix the Quik.

When I broke my leg in the Lake District parachuting – before I took up microlighting - I drove home 3hours before going to hospital to have it operated on.

Day 98, August 4th

I got up and the computer crashed again. I was getting really fed up of it now.

When my last laptop started doing this to me, I took outside, poured ½ litre of petrol on it and set fire to it - it didn't cause me any more problems after that! I finally got the piece of dog dump going, and DHL still had the same tracking message!

I got on to my mate Yoza at the airport to do some searching, and the parts were there!

They told me I had to pay some duty on the parts before I could have them.

I jumped into a car that the hotel provided - or should I say I got thrown in by the young lads from the hotel - and went straight to the cargo depot.

DHL wanted 1,655,000.00 rupiahs, claiming it was import duty (£120).

I said to them, *"But this is my own personal aircraft and the parts are stopping airside and going back to England so not stopping in Kupang"*.

"But it's customs," they kept saying.

I said

"You wouldn't charge somebody for bringing a suitcase into the country then charge them import duty would you? No! So how can you charge me then?"

After two hours of arguing with DHL in Jakarta over the phone they still would not have it. I had to pay the one million six hundred and fifty five thousand rupiah.

Now I had my parts.

I said to Yoza, *"Can I go and make a start then?"*

He was a handling agent here at Kupang and really good.

"Of course you can, Dave".

We went out to the Quik and within seconds there was an army of people there. I said I needed the trike lifting up so that I could remove the pod to get at the front end.

Two tyres were lifted out of a truck, they put them under my Quik, and I started to take the pod off.

Struggling a bit with the probably broken bone in my wrist, I was helped out with the aircraft engineers from www.susiair.com.

We removed the front end of the trike, put the pod to one side with the electrics just left dangling, and we replaced the broken forks in record time.

I think there were six people helping me at one time, maybe more.

What nice lads they were.

We got the new forks done and the pod back on before it started getting dark.

I would be back to the airport the following day to see what, if anything, had been missed.

I took a taxi back to the hotel and checked emails for the permissions, but the computer was kaput once again.

Nothing more to do than go out and eat and drink.

I have to say I was getting a bit fed up eating noodles and sea food. I was hoping that Ozzy food would be as good as people said.

Day 99, August 5th

I got up and thought I had better have a good look and check over the work that we had done on the Quik yesterday. I took a taxi to the Airport which was mad busy with passengers, but being a "Pilot", I would just get rushed through the gates with Security. It was quite funny really as everybody would look at you as if you had done something wrong and had been arrested.

I got to the Quik and checked it out. I had to relocate the wiring for the transponder and GPS, change a few bolts around that had been put in the wrong places and do a couple of adjustments. But otherwise, it looked OK.

My permissions were for Monday August 8 so I didn't need to put the wing back on the trike just yet – the wing had not been damaged in the accident. It was fairly breezy and I didn't want the aircraft rigged and getting blown around.

I had a good chat with Yoza from Koka Pura Handling Agents who had been getting me through Security and generally helping me. Then it was time to go.

I went back to the hotel and thought I'd get the blog up to date.

The computer crashed again. I spent a while messing around with that again, before going down to the front and having a few beers with people I had met.

Tomorrow will be 100 days since I set off.

Day 100, August 6th

One hundred days since I set off and I wasn't not even in Australia.

Only one more hop and I would be there.

Today I didn't have anything to do as the permission to fly out was for Monday.

I went down to the restaurant next to the hotel, then down to Teddies Bar where I was meeting a guy who had some Australian Dollars that I could buy from him.

When 6pm came I met him, did the deal with a good exchange rate and then I went over the road to another bar where I met all the pilots from www.susiair.com and had a few beers.

I met an Australian guy called Jon and his wife, talked beer talk for a while and had a good laugh, then we went across to Teddies Bar where we spent all night singing Karaoke and making fools of ourselves.

Nobody knew me so it was OK.

I even looked at singing in Indonesian, but I decided I would just stick to singing in English – I was having trouble doing that late on as the Bintang took over my mouth.

After that Jon's wife drove us to a roadside chicken shop where we had what I can only describe as Barbequed chicken. It was stuck on a Barbeque style stove thing and just burnt until black - I think it was to kill all the bacteria, but it did taste nice at the time.

By now it was about 3.30am, and we went back to the hotel.

Day 101, August 7th

At 6am I was woken up by the hotel staff banging and clattering around – I was not impressed. Then I got a knock on the door.

"You want laundry doing?"

This was just what I didn't want after a night on the Bintang until 3.30am.

Then I got another knock on the door and a couple stood there.

"Hello, you don't know us, but we heard you're going to Darwin tomorrow."

"Yes, I am" I said...

"We are travelling around the world and wondered if you had a spare seat, we could have and work for you"

"I'm flying a microlight to Darwin; I think it might be a tight squeeze for all three of us in it, don't you think?"

"Ooooh! We thought you were sailing to Darwin" they said, and they left.

It was now 9am.

I was going up to the Airport for 10am to get the Quik rigged. This should be interesting as it was pretty windy now. But I needed to get it done that day as my permission to fly was for the next day.

I got a lift up there at 9.30am from my new friend Jon who kindly offered. I went to the Quik with Yoza and got the wing out, and I checked the profiles of the battens while he was ringing around to get the boys together.

Only one batten was deformed, but I think it had been stood on in the de-rigging process a week ago.

With the wind blowing a good 15-20mph now, I said to Yoza that we need at least four people to keep control of the wing so it doesn't blow away while we put it up. I put all the battens in and got the wing tensioned before getting it up on to the nose ready to attach the trike.

With one guy at either side of the wing, holding on, and one at the front holding it down, we got the trike in-between the A frame and bolted it to the wing.

Trust me; it was *not* easy, trying to explain how to do it with the foreign language.

After two hours of struggling we got it rigged and tied it down to the ground so it didn't blow away.

I fitted the rear fuel tank, and then a couple of the lads went to the petrol station for 100 litres of top quality fuel – *err, Not! But it was all they had.*

While I was connecting the fuel pipes, one of the jubilee hose clips broke, so we had to go searching the Airport and various tool boxes to find one.

An hour later we found one (phew!).

Then we fuelled up the Quik ready for departure.

I wanted to test-fly it to make sure everything was OK, but I would have had to have another permission just to fly, and then do a flight plan which would take days.

So the test flight was going to be the following day over the Timor Sea. This was known in the 1930's as the 'white knuckle route'.

For 513 miles.

Really, an eight-hour test flight.

In England a test flight would only take 15-20 minutes.

I got everything ready on the Quik for the following day and then I had Customs and Immigration come in and inspect the aircraft. They don't work on Sundays so I had to have them come in especially for me.

We got all the necessary paperwork stamped and taken care of. I did the flight plan and Yoza took that to the Tower to get it processed for the next day.

That was it, all ready, now just my hotel to sort out and pack the huge suitcase that I carry.

I just had something to eat at the restaurant and I sat there relaxing into the night, ready for an early departure.

And worrying thinking is the Quik going to be OK.

AUSTRALIA – A BLEAK AND LONELY OUTBACK JOURNEY

Day 102, August 8th - Kupang to Darwin

I was up at 4am as I was to be the first aircraft of the day to take off at Kupang. There was a knock on my door and I came over all sick with the thought of this leg so a quick dash back to toilet before I went out to the taxi.

It was deadly silent in the hotel as I went through - it was quite eerie. I got thrown in the taxi and we set off for to the airport. As we pulled up and it was dead, there was just one guy waiting for me at the door. We made our way out to the Quik in the dark and untied it by torch light. I loaded my bags on board and I jumped in. still dark the guy helped me put the chair on the Quik, he could see better and I was ready for the off

The sun comes up at 6am which was the time that I would be leaving for Darwin. I was just sat there, waiting in the dark for the sun to show and the Airport Tower to start operating now.

I was a bit nervous as this was my test flight of the Quik from when it was rebuilt.

Before long, it was 6am and the Tower became active.

"G-CDVO Kupang"

"Kupang, G-CDVO good morning sir"

"G-VO permission to start engine for flight plan to Darwin."

"Approved. Just let me know when you're ready to go G-CDVO"

I started the engine and the revs were a bit high.

It must have been from the bump.

But I would cope with it, I was not stopping now I will be fine.

I got up to temperature (50℃), gave them a call to go, and was cleared to taxi out and take off. I set towards the runway with the high revs pushing me along slightly faster than i should have been, but the break slowed me down very well.

I sat there on the runway doing all my checks looking at the pins and bolts to make sure everything looked as it should.

Then gunned it, full throttle and off I went.

253

It came off the ground as it should do and I let go of the bar, it was flying straight with no turns.

Once off the ground I had to turn right which took me over a mountain, with nothing but trees everywhere and up to 3,000ft.

What a nice feeling that was – *not!*

I was looking around for somewhere to go if anything happened but it felt fine so I just carried on and climbed over the mountain at 4,000ft.

Instantly I had a 25mph headwind!

I thought I would let it go for a while, as it could have been the mountain causing it. Then I headed straight out to sea, direct to Darwin.

After an hour at 4,000ft with a 25mph head wind I had to drop down to go underneath some low clouds, that brought me down to about 900ft.

The head wind dropped to a respectable 20mph, and the GPS said 10hours to Darwin.

I thought that's fine if it stays at that, but another 30 minutes or so went by and it still said 10hours to Darwin.

I had now been in the air for one hour and 30 minutes.

It was looking like it would take 11hours 30 minutes to get to Darwin.

I pulled the bar in to see if it would make a big difference, I was only at 1,000ft underneath cloud now.

Then, completely out of the blue, the engine gave a quick cough.

I crapped myself, thinking I was going in to sea. Keep going don't stop now.

I was two hours into the flight and I seemed to be using more fuel than usual for some reason.

I did a calculation and it was now obvious that I would not make it to Darwin direct as I only had an endurance of 11 hours.

That's it, decision made, I would be going to the alternative airfield on the flight plan Truscott *(a former WWII desert field where RMH and MHB went on the blind flight to Oz in 2007).*

As I turned towards Truscott the estimated time of arrival time said 3hours 45mins from where I was. There seemed to be more low cloud in t his direction, but I had no choice.

I was now heading to Truscott at 1,000ft, with a crosswind. Darwin probably wouldn't be happy with me but if was to risk trying to get to Darwin and the winds didn't change I would all most certainly have to ditch in the sea.

My heart sank, as actually getting to Australia was to be one of the most important flights of the whole trip.

I had heard so much about this stretch of water being very dangerous with high winds and had not been looking forward to it.

I was now 200 miles out, in the middle of the open sea at 900ft and I had lost radio contact with everybody so I was now truly on my own. I was listening to every beat of the engine hoping it didn't stop.

The transponder didn't seem to be sending out as many signal blips - was anybody watching me? Did they know I had changed my route to Truscott? If the worse happened and I did ditch would they come looking for me in the right place. It was all going through my mind.

And then the time had come to do the in-flight refuelling I hoped I had connected all the pipes up correctly! I opened up the fuel tap and plugged in the power pump and switched it on, nothing for a few seconds on then it burst in to life and started filling my tank back up.

Also up in Darwin were all the media awaiting my arrival. Another hour went by listening to the engine

Fifty miles out and the coastline of Australia came into view - what a relief that was. It put a big smile on my face, I was just about there now not long left to go.

Keep going little engine and do me proud I don't want to swim the last few miles.

The closer I got to the Australian coast line, the sea just turned a really beautiful pale blue, and there was the odd small island scattered around with lovely sandy beaches.

For some mad reason I was looking down at the sea to see if I could see any sharks swimming around. I don't know why with the engine doing what it did - crazy fool!

I flew over a small island call Troughton and it looked to have an airfield on it so I headed close to that to have a look.

Then I was over mainland Australia - I had made it! More than 12,000 miles and I was finally here, I couldn't believe it. All the planning had finally paid off.

Truscott came in to sight but there didn't seem to be anybody there it was just a nice tarmac runway in the middle of nowhere.

There were trees all around it and no road to it, no other aircraft on the ground and nobody walking around.

This was going to be a very lonely night but at least I'm alive and more importantly I AM IN AUSTRALIA.

I radioed Truscott on 128.00, but got no response so I joined downwind for Runway 30, giving calls but nothing, no reply.

This airport really did look deserted.

I landed anyway, taxied back onto to the apron and to my surprise I was met by a group of helicopter engineers and pilots.

"*Where you come from, mate?*" they said.

"*Kupang.*"

'*You're f##ing crazy man*" they said, smiling. "*How can we help you?*"

I said "*I need to contact Darwin and tell them what happened and why I have come here.*"

"*No problem mate, are you stopping or going?*"

"*I won't make it in daylight hours now so I am stopping here for the night.*" I jumped out of the Quik while they were all shaking their heads saying "*mad F##ker*".

We went into the office where we found the necessary numbers.

I rang SAR to cancel the flight plan, so that they didn't go looking for me, and then I rang Customs and Quarantine.

They all seemed fine that I had gone in to Truscott for safety, and we sorted somewhere for me to stop the night. This turned out to be in a complex of very nice converted containers, and they had a canteen that served real food. While I had sorted that out my Quik had been put in their hangar out of the way.

No more rice and noodles for me tonight! It was real food chicken and chips with baked beans. I had a few low alcohol beers with the lads at their bar as that's all they are allowed to drink and then went to my room for the night.

So much for me having a big welcoming committee on landing. Never mind Darwin tomorrow with the TV crews waiting for me.

It was funny as the guys there warned me not have my door open during the night as there was a crocodile in the compound wandering about and two of Australia's deadliest snakes around.

The coast of Australia

Day 103 - August 9th - Truscott to Darwin

Having being up most of the night with some bugs running around in the room trying to eat me, I got up.

It was 5am, still dark, but there was lighting so I had a wander down to the hangar, the place was really busy with all the guys at CHC Helicopters. They were getting two of their Pumas ready for departure to fly out to the oil rigs.

I loaded up my Quik and then went for a bit of breakfast, real sausage and beans and even bacon; I hadn't seen any of that for weeks.

I went into the office where I filled in a flight plan and then Captain Ed Manning faxed it off for me.

That was it, time to go - destination Darwin, 324 miles.

I took off at 8.30am and headed up the coast for a while. The wind was just about zero for the first 30 minutes or so and flat calm so I was taking in the amazing scenery, really pale blue seas and a really stunning coastline lined with trees.

I decided to go straight across the bay from Truscott direct to Darwin to get there quicker, even though it was 300miles over the water.

About half-way across I encountered a huge cloud bank and had to descend to 500 ft to get underneath it. That lasted about 30 minutes before I could climb back up to a respectable 1,000ft.

I had been flying over the water at 1,000ft because the horizon was better when all you could see was blue; at 1,000ft you can see the ripples of the sea so it breaks it up.

I was also looking out for sharks to photograph, but I didn't see any.

About 85 miles off Darwin a strange thought entered my head; what would happen if I had an engine failure and went in?

All the time I had spent over water over the last three months and I had just really started thinking about it over the last two days. How mad!

But I soon got that out of my mind, and gave Darwin a call on the radio.

"G-CDVO, Darwin"

'G-CDVO - Continue your approach and report 5 miles away."

259

Still out at sea, *"G-CDVO 5 miles away."*

"G-VO report left base for Runway 16."

I continued but just over land, slightly before left base, it was as rough as hell with turbulence. I went down the Bay of Darwin and reported left base.

"G-CDVO, change to Tower", which I did, and then *"G-CDVO cleared to land Runway 16."*

As I came over the land again and over the edge of Darwin I was getting thrown all over. The wind had also picked up to about 17mph.

Was this just for me?

I battled it all the way down to the ground and landed long so I didn't have far to taxi. Where I thought I was taxiing to wasn't where ATC had wanted me to go and they had me taxi right to the end of the runway and down to a General Aviation section that I hadn't seen on the airport map. There was a marshal waiting for me at a parking spot.

I taxied up and turned the engine off.

I said hello and within a minute there was a TV crew there.

"Hello, Dave, we're from ABC, we missed your landing - could you just go back up and land again for us, please?"

I thought about it for a fraction of a second before saying *"No."*

"Oh, OK then" she said.

That's the trouble with people that don't fly, and more to the point, don't fly flexwings, they just don't know how hard it is.

Customs and Quarantine came to see me.

I explained what had happened the previous day with the wind and they were fine. There were a couple of forms to fill in and I had my passport stamped. Then we had a quick chat about my trip and then they left.

With a TV camera up my nose I got out of the trike and then had an interview with them. It was a really busy day and I had only just landed.

Then a good friend of mine, Mick Gothard, who now lives in Darwin, turned up on the apron. We packed the trike up and tied it down, threw all my things in the back of his pick-up and we were escorted off the airport.

I had a few people to telephone once I got back to his house, but first stop was to call in a beer shop. It was a drive-through beer shop. Somebody came out, asked what you wanted and then brought it out for you.

How lazy.

We went back to Mick's house, opened a beer and I made phone calls to the different newspapers and did some telephone interviews.

After that I relaxed celebrating me getting to Darwin, the phone didn't stop ringing - it was mad!

Darwin from above

Days 104 to 106, August 10th to 12th - Static in Darwin

Over the previous 3 days I had been going out with my mate Mick who had been showing me the sights of Darwin.

On the Wednesday, August 10th, we literally just went out for a bit of a drive, having a look around. What a nice place Darwin is.

Then we went out drinking. We had a beer on the front overlooking the beach before going back to Mick's house. Then we went out and met his friends down at the marina, where there were lots of places to eat whilst watching the sun go down.

While I was there I had a Kangaroo burger and chips washed down with an Australian beer. More beer was consumed while we were all talking and getting slightly inebriated. We stopped at the marina until it closed, before returning to Mick's house for the night.

Day 105, August 11th

We went out to get an Australian sim card so I that could ring around in Oz, then I changed all the American dollars I had left and then strangely enough we went for another beer to a lovely place right on the beach front.

I wanted to go and find a microlight airfield that I had heard about so Mick made a quick phone call and we found out where it was, a place called Noonamar. It was only about 30k down the Stuart Highway, so we headed off down the highway by car.

I was looking at the road trains that they have over here, some up to seven lengths long, but I only saw one towing four trailers although it was still quite a sight!

We found the flying school but nobody was there, so we had a chat with a guy working on an old Cessna 172 in a workshop.

I ended up being invited to a fly-in on Saturday night if I was interested? Yes, why not? I said.I found out where it was on the maps. And it was on my route anyway so I said I would see them there on Saturday.

I said to Mick, "*It looks like I'm stopping here until Saturday now then, mate.*"

"*No problem, Dave,*" he said.

We went for another beer at a place called Humpty Doo, just outside town. What an amazing transformation difference there compared with the townies - everybody had big long beards.

We went back into Darwin to find me a hotel for the night - I thought I would have a night on my own in town and not be too much of a burden on Mick. That took at bit of doing as everywhere was full. But I finally found a nice apartment for the night then went in to town trying out the different bars and clubs. The amazing thing was everywhere I went; somebody recognised me and came to talk to me about my flight. I had a really good night, with all the people in the different bars.

Darwin is one of my top places to come back to.

I went back to the apartment about 3am.

Everybody drives a 4x4 and has long beards here.

Day 106, August 12th

We were up at the crack of dawn and on our way for 7.30am, our destination being the jumping crocodiles at Kakadu. We got on the boat for 9am and went down the river with a woman called Wendy who was feeding the crocs with a rod with some pork on the end. The crocs jumped up out of the water to get the pork.

It was quite an amazing sight really. You wouldn't want fall into that water. The biggest croc was seven metres long! And there were hundreds of them along this river. The trip lasted for an hour. After that we just headed back to Mick's house and chilled out for the afternoon. I had organised to fly out of Darwin International on the Saturday morning.

Then we just stayed in all night, talking and drinking.

There was to be a party the following night at an old WW11 airfield call Coomalie Creek. It was not disused but had Mosquito bombers based there in the war - should be interesting.

Day 107, August 13th - Darwin to Coomalie Creek

was up at 7am as we were meeting a guy at the airport at 9.15am who would be giving me my customs clearance and letting me in to the airport. First I had to get some WAC charts (aviation charts) for the trip

We were lucky enough to get the charts from a Flight Training School just around the corner from the Airport. Then off to the Airport to meet the Customs guy at the gates and after a few minutes waiting we went through the gates to the Quik and started to get ready.

There was no wind (great stuff).

I climbed in and Mick gave me a hand to put the chair away quicker.

And as soon we did that the wind picked up, I couldn't believe it!

But I have had bad weather all the way from England, so what's another day?

I gave Ground Control a call but no response, so a guy in an operations car gave Ground a call - they couldn't hear me.

He gave them a call for me on their radio apparently the hangars around the Airport shelter the radio waves; I taxied out until I could see the Tower on Zulu 1 taxiway. They could now hear me, so I was given clearance to taxi out to Zulu 1 holding-point for Runway 11, the big runway at Darwin.

"G-CDVO, line up Runway 11."

I taxied out and lined up, and I looked down all 15,250ft of it, waiting for the go ahead.

"G-CDVO Cleared for take-off"

I climbed to 1,000ft, heading out to the Elizabeth Bridge reporting point.

It was very windy and rough now but it was ok.

I thought I would have a little detour on my way to the fly-in at Coomalie Creek as it was only about a 30 minute flight to it. I decided to follow the other highway out of Darwin to the Kakadu National park and over the Humpty Doo motel instead of following the Stuart Highway and then returning on track to Coomalie Creek.

The scenery out here was completely different to any where I had been. You can certainly see why they call it the bush because that's all there is – bushes!

As I returned on track and got closer to Coomalie Creek the wind was now really blowing. I flew across the runway to have a look at the wind sock, and as usual it was now a 90 degree crosswind. I joined down-wind getting thrown all over, and called 'Finals' still getting bounced about.

Just as I touched down a huge thermal took me off again but I got the Quik back down, and taxied in, which wasn't easy with the wind rolling over the trees surrounding the airfield. I parked up, a couple of guys that had flown in came over to say hello who instantly recognised me and gave me a hand to push the Quik into wind. I then got out and tied the Quik down for the night and made my way over the runway to say hello to everybody who was there.

There weren't that many people there when I landed, but as the day went on more people started arriving.

I got talking to a really nice chap called Reg who gave me a beer or two as we watched the aircraft flying in. In came a Yak 52, a Harvard, an old Tiger Moth, a few Cessna 172s, a Robinson R44 helicopter, and a Piper Aztec twin.

It was getting fairly busy as time went on.

Then a Para-trike flew in just as it was becoming dark.

We had beer and food while a band in the background was playing old Irish folk music and other folky type music. Then there was an old Antonov biplane that had just been brought over from Russia there, the owners fired that up doing some ground runs up and down the runway before taking off and flying a couple of circuits. It sounded awesome with its huge radial engine. I sat and watched the sun go down then, talked with lots of people who had flown in until late, then a bonfire was lit, fireworks were set off and we all sat around the bonfire with three guys playing two guitars and an accordion until the early hours.

As it was so late when we finished talking I just went over to my Quik and got into that for a couple of hours sleep instead of going to the tent

There was no telephone signal or any contact to the outside world it was wonderful.

What a nice night it was, and thanks to everybody who invited me.

Day 108, August 14th - Coomalie Creek to Mataranka

I was awake at 5.30am and started to get loaded up, ready to go.

I had only had two hours sleep but I felt OK.

I had been going to go to a place called Tindal but everybody there told me not to bother as there would be absolutely nobody there and it would be closed. Instead they told me about a place called Mataranka in the middle of nowhere with its own private airstrip so that was my new destination. About a four hour flight.

Reg turned up and we pushed the Quik back a bit so I could turn around and taxi straight out. Then I just sat there for a short while waiting for the sun to come up.

Once it did, I started the engine, and it was nice not have to radio anybody and ask permission. As there was no active control tower where I was I didn't need to file any flight plans either – *fantastic!*

I said my farewells to everybody and taxied out on the old runway, where there were even paint markings of some old Mosquito's still on the ground from the war.

The trees all around this airport had obviously hidden it from the Japanese when it was back in the war.

I took off and headed south down the Stuart Highway.

The air was flat calm and smooth for the first two hours, just literally following the highway, then it started getting bumpy and then bumpier and bumpier. It became so rough that I was trying out different altitudes to find some clean air so it wasn't as bad.

At 500ft you had to have more power just to keep airborne or you sunk to the ground. At 1,300ft or above the thermals wanted to take you to the moon.

At 4,000ft I was getting thrown all over, holding on for life.

It just seemed to get worse the higher I went.

I found that 800ft to 1,000ft was the best altitude, although there was a head wind – but this was normal for me.

I really do know why the Australians call the outback the bush, because all you can see is bushes.

As far as the eye could see were bushes and trees - it was a very nice scenic flight. It must have been really boring for everybody on the roads as they were just so straight with hardly any bends anywhere.

After about three hours I came across where Matarana should be, but all I could see was trees. I saw a small opening in the trees and headed for that, over-flew it and saw that there was a small dirt strip in the middle of what looked like a campsite.

Mataranka Homestead

That must be it from what I had been told although it looked like it had a very dodgy approach.

I had to come in very low to get in, weaving in between trees to get to the landing strip before touchdown, and then stand on the brakes without locking them up in the rough dirt ground in order to stop before the trees at the other end.

I turned around and taxied back to somewhere that looked OK for me to park, out of the wind. People were coming out and looking at me I just hoped that I was where I was supposed to be and not in somebody's back garden!

Then I got the chair out and jumped in had a wander around to find some life.

followed a sign that said Kiosk/ Reception and came across a nice restaurant and camping area with a bar. It can't be a back garden so I must be at the right place. I went in to the kiosk and explained that I had flown in and needed a room for the night.

"No problem, sir."

got a Motel room for the night. I also asked if they kept fuel.

267

"Yes, sir, we can sort that out for you later, no problem." He was a really polite man

I found the room, took my bags there, and then had a look around before going back to reception to sort out the fuel. The man on the desk asked me how much fuel I needed.

"About 80 litres" I said.

"OK,' he said, *'What you need to do is get into your aircraft and taxi through the campsite and onto the road then follow that until you see our pump at the front".*

I got into the Quik, just pushing my chair to one side as I would be returning back to it, and taxied through the back of the campsite along dirt tracks and past the motel until I came out onto the road. Then I went down the road to the fuel pump in the parking area for the homestead.

Everybody in the cars watched me as I taxied past them, smiling.

I pulled up at the pump and was refuelled with unleaded 95 petrol, whilst people were taking photos of me, then taxied back the same way and parked up for the night.

Later I went to the bar and met a few people who had seen me on TV.

As the evening went on a female singer came over and asked about my trip and then advertised it over the microphone to see if it would raise any money for the air ambulance. By the end of the night, $185 dollars had been raised, so thank you to all who donated.

I headed back to my motel room and just as I turned a corner an animal jumped out of the undergrowth at me and ran off, but not without a bit of a kick from it first. It was a kangaroo.

I jumped out of my skin a bit, but it was funny.

Then I went to bed, ready for my flight to Renner springs which was a Road house on the Barkley Highway some 200 miles away.

It's quite amazing this country you just don't realise how big it is, from Darwin to Sydney is about 1,800miles. It's like going from the North of Scotland to Cyprus again.

Day 109, August 15th - Mataranka to Renner Springs

I was up at the crack of dawn and made my way to the Quik. It was still dark and there was nobody around, it was nice and quiet. I loaded up the aircraft and climbed in, put the chair on the trike, did my final checks and then started up the engine.

About 30 seconds later people appeared from nowhere and started to wave at me and take photographs.

After getting my oil up to temperature, I made my way out to an area that looked like it was smooth enough to take off from; I was looking at the trees all the way around it hoping I would make it out. I held the brake on, applied full power, then let the brake off and I was off hurtling along the narrow gravel track and got airborne with plenty of room before the trees that surround the airfield.

I did a quick circuit of the campsite, waving at everybody, before heading off down the Barkley highway towards Renner Springs.

It was lovely and smooth for the first two hours, and then it started to get windy and bumpy again. I tried the different heights out again, 500ft still wanted to put you on the ground with sink and anything above 1,300ft just wanted to take you to the moon so 800ft it was, still getting bounced around,

Sydney was getting closer all the time.

After three hours of following the Highway and buzzing the cars and caravans, I came across a bush fire.

The smoke was black and covering the road in front, and the whole sky.

I had to go around it just north of the road to get out of the way. You could see where the fire had started, it looked like the side of the road at a parking area and then the wind had just taken it further.

After passing the fire and getting bounced around even more from its flames, I could see Renner Springs coming into view on the highway, a roadhouse on the highway with no landing strip. I had rung them up and they said no problem, come and stop, just and on the Highway.

over flew the roadhouse and the Highway, looking at it closely, then did a low pass to see what road signs there were, and how high they were. After a couple of passes I knew where I needed to touch down to avoid them.

I orbited until the road was clear then made my finals approach, only about 200 metres from the entrance to the roadhouse.

Just as I was about to touch down a camper van pulled straight out in front of me from the station. I powered on and went around again.

I had another go and the same thing happened, just about to touchdown and a car pulled straight in front. I could have sworn they did it on purpose.

But they weren't going to do it again.

I decided to carry on to Barkley Homestead, another 250miles away.

The thermals got bigger and the wind got stronger, and I got thrown around a lot more.

It wasn't nice at all!

Some of the thermals were lifting me out of the seat, as they had done in Saudi Arabia.

After seven hours of been bounced all over the sky like a cork out at sea, Barkley Homestead came into view. It had only a small runway but I could see it from miles away, in among the trees, a white, chalky-looking runway.

There was nothing for miles except trees and there in the middle was Barkley and its white runway.

I called long finals, which they were, all the way from Renner Springs.

After I landed, I taxied along a track and met a herd of cows and a bull looking me. The bull wasn't moving, in fact it didn't look that happy that I was there so I gave a quick blip on the power and it soon moved out of the way for me to pass. I carried on until I came across somewhere that looked safe to park up. I got out and went in search of some life.

I found reception in the petrol station and booked a Motel room for the night, then asked about fuel for the Quik.

Rob was one of two brothers who came out and said he had Avgas if I wanted it.

"Yes, please," I said.

After I sorted out my room we went and filled the Quik up – by pure luck, I had parked right next to the pump.

Then Rob said, "I was going to pay for your room, but I will pay for your Avgas instead."

Thank you very much, Rob.

I covered the Quik up and went to the restaurant for a beer and something to eat.

I was absolutely knackered after that flight.7 hour flying. It must have looked funny though. My arms were aching that much I was just sat with them still waving around like I was still flying sat at the bar. I could not move my wrist.

Because of the wrist I decided not to fly tomorrow and to stop here at Barkley homestead to get some rest.

I had something to eat, but not much as I didn't have the energy to eat.

And then Just a couple of beers and I went back to the motel room.

Day 110, August 16th - Static - Barkley Homestead

I got up at 10am with my wrist as stiff as a piece of wood. I launched myself into my chair and had a really slow push to the Quik.

I checked it over and topped up the oil, then went searching for somewhere to do a bit of laundry.

After doing that I just went back to bed. I was so tired now - the trip was really taking its toll on me. I know I had said York to Sydney but the way I was feeling then, I could just pack it in any time now as I had made it to Australia.

Around 6pm I went and had something to eat and drink before going back to the room for an early start the following day.

My wrist was really playing up now and didn't seem to be getting any better. I was hoping it would be better the following day.

I think this was the first day when I physically would not have been able to fly in any way, shape or form.

Day 111, August 17th, Barkley Homestead to Mount Isa

was up at 5.30am in the dark. My wrist seemed OK!

We would have to see as the day went on. This was a big flight of 423 miles, so I would be in the driving seat a long while.

Sunrise was at 7am and I loaded up and managed to get away just after 7.15am.

After I took off I gave the Homestead a quick buzz then headed off down the Barkley Highway for a while. I saw that a 4x4 had just pulled out onto the highway in the same direction as me.

I dropped down to a nice 100ft out over the bush, so I kept the 500ft rule and followed alongside him for a few miles waving.

Then I set a direct route to Mount Isa. It was a lovely flight for the first two hours then the wind picked up and I was faced with a 25mph head-wind right on the nose, and that was at 1,000ft.

The Barkley high way

The scenery was still very green with trees and flat as far as the eye could see. The wind was very gusty so if I relaxed for even one minute it caught me out and reminded me who was boss, giving me a good shake about.

And as the day went on the thermals continued to grow bigger again - they gave my wrist a good physio session, that's for sure.

Five hours into the flight the wind started to turn around a bit, it wasn't a head wind but more of a cross wind, but it still wasn't letting up.

If anything, I thought it was getting stronger.

As I came closer to Mount Isa the ground became slightly rocky, and I could see small mountain-type rocks poking up here and there. With the wind swirling around them, it was causing havoc with the base bar.

At Mount Isa the frequency they use is called CTAF, and basically all you do is blind call to let other traffic know your whereabouts and to which airfield, similar to Safetycom in the UK.

I tuned in to it and listened. I could hear a couple of aircraft going into Mount Isa and I heard which runway they were using, so it was easy enough to fit myself in. There were small mountains surrounding the airfield, causing some quite bad turbulence.

I joined right-base to land, facing a full 90 degree cross-wind blowing at about 20mph.

I was getting used these now but also getting sick of them.

I landed safely and taxied in to an area with the hangars. I saw one hangar with a couple of chaps working on a King Air, so I went there and asked where would be the best place to park up for the night out of this wind. One of them said *"Have you just flown in, in this wind, in that thing?"*

Holding on the bar getting yanked around I smiled and said *"yes why?"* and he said *"it's a bit windy for us in them things"* pointing at the king air.

One of the other men, Rob Bisiani, said, *"We'll pull the King Air out and you can put it in this hangar."*

Just the job, they pulled it out, I taxied in and then they pushed the King Air back in. He then asked, *"Have you got a hotel?"*

"No, not yet. Do you know a good one?"

He said, *"You can stop with me and Gary at my house"*

Bonus!

I got out and got my things ready then just sat around talking for a while before we jumped in his pick up went for lunch – as we were out he showed me his house – then we back to the hangar.

I asked if there was any fuel around I could buy and they just happened to have a drum full of Avgas that they didn't have a need for so donated it to my Quik.

We refuelled the Quik - thanks again, Rob - I pumped up the tyres, and gave the engine a quick oil check.

Later in the day we went to Rob's house, freshened up and went out to a local restaurant bar.

A big thank you to Rob and Gary for everything at Mount Isa.

Day 112, August 18th - Mount Isa to Barcaldine

After a nice night with Rob and Gary we were at the airport for 6.50am. There was a bit of a breeze (12-15mph) but it wasn't too bad.

This was a flight of around 470 miles so it was to be another long time in the driving seat.

We pulled out the King Air and then got my Quik out; I loaded up straight away and climbed in. it was really cold in fact there was a bit of frost on the ground After putting the chair on the Quik I started up and sat there for a good ten minutes, waiting for the oil to get up to temperature.

I taxied out and lined up. The breeze was still about 12-15mph and it seemed a bit rough even on the ground. I applied full power and took off.

Then the fun started.

As soon as I reached 200ft I had a 40mph head-wind, gusting God knows what.

Left, right, up and down, then the trike got a gust and I was going sideways with it whipping the visor open.

It was as rough as hell. It seemed to be just rolling over all the small mountains that surround Mount Isa and the mine, and in the process giving me it all.

The only thing I could do, without it slamming me into the rocks, was climb, and in the process of climbing the wind got worse and worse, the wind speed still at 40mph.

I got to 4,000ft and it started to smooth out to a manageable condition, but I now had a 43mph wind straight on my nose.

This was going to be a very long flight if the wind didn't ease up.

It was so cold up there as well; I was shivering, draughts blowing straight down my neck. It was horrible.

I looked at the map and saw that the mountains causing the turbulence disappeared and merged into flat land ahead eventually, but it would still mean spending about four hours up there in the cold.

100 Miles of rippling hills on my way to Barcaldine

Five hours went by and the hills did turn to flatter land. I dropped down a bit, then a bit more until I was at 800ft - the same height that I had flown most of the way through Australia.

It was still as rough as hell, but I only had a 25mph head wind now, so I just sat and rode the sky like a rodeo in a trike, with it trying to throw me out as much as it could. By now I was starting to really hate turbulence

It was nearly eight hours before Barcaldine came into view, with two large runways, and luckily one of them was directly into wind! That's got be a change.

I went in, landed and taxied in to be welcomed by a group of locals. Rob Chandler, the local mayor turned up and had a couple of photos taken then I was taken over to the Avgas pump where I got filled up ready for the next day.

Then a hangar was opened up for me and I taxied my Quik into it, out of the wind for the night. After that Rob Chandler took me for a guided tour of Barcaldine.

We went to see the tree of knowledge in the town centre, the race course, the rodeo, the football cubs, the local attractions. Barcaldine has a population of only 1,600 people and there were at least 6 hotels on the main street with caravan parks scattered around. If anybody was passing through this Outback town, it would seem an ideal place to stop, that's for sure.

I was taken to a motel where I dropped my gear off then Rob invited me across the road to his Bar and restaurant for the night, where I had a steak the size of a house side and some beer.

A real big thank you to everybody in Barcaldine for the fuel, the motel and especially to Rob for sorting everything out for me it was a pleasure to have stopped there.

What a lovely town.

Day 113, August 19th - Barcaldine to Charlieville

I was picked up by a local pilot from the town at about 6.30am and taken to the Airport. It was freezing this morning, just five degrees above zero centigrade.

I got into the Quik inside the hangar before being pushed outside. I was now back to wearing British flying clothes with three t-shirts and two coats on.

And I was still cold; I must be too used to flying in the warm temperatures over the last couple of months.

This was a fairly short flight of only 200 miles (if you can call 200 miles short!). Heading south now alongside of a group of mountains called the dividing range.

Once in the Quik I got the engine started and it took a good 15 minutes before oil temp was up to 50C. I said my farewells to the two guys at the airport and taxied out.

I could feel the cold biting, I was very glad that it wasn't to be a marathon flight that day.

The weather would usually be like this back in England on a really nice crisp frosty morning.

I took off and flew over Rob Chandler's Bar and Hotel where he was doing breakfasts for his hotel guests, and then headed off on a direct route to Charlieville.

I was facing a 30 mph headwind *again!*

It seemed as though I'd had a headwind ever since I took off from England, and it seemed to be getting stronger the closer I got to Sydney. I tried going up and the wind got stronger and rougher so it was back down to 500ft and ride the Rodeo winds again. What I had thought would be a relatively short flight was now going to be another long flight. The first two hours were relatively smooth. I only needed one hand to hold on and steady the bar.

During the other six hours I had to hold on with both hands and even my bum was clinching on to the seat at times.

It is funny how you get to read the land for thermals and wind effect. Just the slightest difference in colour, even contrasting coloured sand can make a difference. There I was at 500ft, dodging light coloured sand to avoid been lifted out of my seat. And looking out over the sandy outback there were some amazing dust devils whipping around.

You could see them once they were developed, but when they were building you couldn't see them at all.

Flying along your wing tip would suddenly get lifted and the dust devil would try to turn you over.

It certainly kept you on your toes.

Every time I did something and thus taking my eye off the ball, such as looking down at the radio, then whoof!! - up 2,000ft a minute and no power at a 45 degree angle.

Not nice!

It was very tiring.

After close to eight hours, absolutely frozen and having been thrown from pillar to post, Charlieville came into site.

At this stage I could feel something wrong with me.

My head felt like it was going to explode and my whole body ached all over and not due to the turbulence. I gave Charlieville a call on the radio but there was no response so I joined down wind and saw that I was going for the right runway

I landed, taxied in and parked up near to the Avgas pumps. I turned the engine off and sat there feeling really crap, shaking, head absolutely banging, feeling sick.

The place seemed dead. Was nobody around?

I put my wheelchair together really slowly and forced myself out of the Quik. Just as I did that a nice man turned up and asked if I needed fuel.

"*Yes please, just fill it up.*"

Then he said "you're *that chap who's flown from the UK aren't you?*" yes I am I replied and on that we had a few photos taken.

After the refuel he gave my Quik a push and we managed to put the nose of the aircraft into a hangar. It wouldn't go all the way in because of the height of the kingpost. I tied it up and grabbed my money bag.

I was still shaking like a dog trying to shit bones and headed to the clubhouse reception to pay for the fuel.

While I was sat in the club reception I got worse and worse. I could not stop shaking. The guy who served me fuel made me a coffee and I had some Panadols.

He asked if I needed hospital, but I said I would be fine. He asked if I was sure as I did look really ill.

So he rang a woman called Jane who was a local tourist guide. She came over, we had a chat and I convinced her that I would be fine; I went out and just about rolled in to her car.

We went off into Charlieville to find a hotel for the night for me.

I did nothing more than go straight to bed, shaking and feeling really bad.

The last time I had felt this bad was in hospital 18 years ago after my motorcycle crash I booked a taxi for next morning

But if I felt just as bad I wouldn't be going anywhere.

Day 114, August 20th- Charlieville to Nyngan

Day 114, August 20th- Charlieville to Nyngan

After having been up most of the night feeling sick, shaking and sweating, I rang reception to ask to stop another night.

"Sorry, sir, that room has been booked for tonight."

"Are there any more rooms I could have?"

"Sorry, sir, the whole town is booked up. There is a big workers group coming in."

That was it. I had to go, no matter how crap I felt.

I couldn't lift my bags up because I was so tired so I left them on the step of the room. I went to reception to settle up and get the taxi that I had booked for 6.30am.

As I got there the taxi was waiting.

I waved and said just one minute and I'll be there.

I paid for the room and as I turned to the taxi, he looked at me and drove off!

I said to the guy on reception, *"Get that prat back now, he's not getting away with not taking me."*

He agreed with me, and called the company. The taxi pulled up, the driver old and miserable. I got in and made him go around the corner to pick my bags up from the steps before taking me to the airport.

There was deadly silence in the taxi. It was like being back in England.

When I got to the airport I had a code to get through a security gate and I made the guy carry my bags and push my Quik out of the hangar before I paid him.

I felt absolutely crap, but said to myself that I would be fine. I was going to just get in the Quik and go to sleep for the day.

There was nobody around so I just took my time sweating away and got loaded up, making sure I hadn't forgotten to do anything.

I sat there for a good ten minutes getting my head together before even starting up.

I was saying to myself, I hope it's smooth today because I really need a break from all this weather.

My wrist was hurting like hell; I was still feeling bad, what a gooooood start to the day and it was freezing cold again.

I gave my head a shake and started the beast up.

There was no wind - at ground level anyway.

I started up and got the oil temp to 50 degrees, taxied out and lined up.

I could feel the cold biting again on my face *(after the repairs to my headsets back in Qatar the Visor on my helmet won't close all the way, so it causes massive draughts)*.

I just thought of *England* and gave it full throttle.

The first two hours were absolutely flat calm. I didn't need to touch the bar even though there was a 30mph headwind, and it wasn't rough. I was cuddled up behind the windscreen trying to keep warm but I just couldn't I was absolutely frozen.

Then it started getting rough again.

For the next five hours I was getting bounced all over, still at 500ft.

I looked at several places to put down from small dirt tracks to tarmac roads just for a break from it all, but as I approached them the wind would try flipping me sideways.

I decided to carry on all the way to Nyngan

My head was going light headed all the time. The views were lovely though and I kept coming across wild kangaroos running around as well as emus and there were sheep everywhere.

About 40 miles away from Nyngan it started to cloud over, so the thermals weren't as bad. As I got even closer to the airport it was just a constant wind - and not gusting! – so perhaps I wouldn't have to fight my way down to on to the runway.

I gave Nyngan a call but it was deadly silence as I would have expected given the wind. So I gave the calls out and joined downwind for Runway 18, but at the last minute as I turned for finals to land the wind changed runways. As there was nobody around so I changed runways as well.

I taxied in and parked up on a grass area behind some trees to shelter from the wind and just sat there getting some energy back.

The place was deserted so I got my chair off the Quik and struggled putting it together and then jumped across into it. In the flight guide I had I found a phone number for the airfield. So I gave it a call.

I said I wanted a taxi to pick me up from the airport and take me to a hotel.

The guy on the phone said, *"There are no taxies in this town."*

Ooooh! *"But don't worry,"* he said, *"I'll come and pick you up"*

Super stuff, I thought, and started to tie the Quik down.

He was called John, a very nice man; I didn't even need to tell him what sort of hotel I wanted he took me to a very nice motel in town that was all on one level. As soon as I got there I asked the receptionist if I could have the room for two nights.

"No problem" she said.

That was it then, I paid for two nights and went straight to bed.

I came-to around four hours later and made my way across the road to a local working men's club where there was a bistro.

I had a bite to eat and a coke then went back to the motel to bed.

Day 115, August 21st - Static Nyngan

There was nothing much to say about this day except that I stayed in bed until lunch time really feeling crap falling asleep on and off sweating and throwing my guts up, I forced myself out of bed and headed out over the road to the club for some lunch. I returned and watched TV all afternoon, falling asleep on and off all day.

Then I rang England to hear friendly voices to cheer me up. That made me feel better, I could have really just thrown in the towel and packed in the whole flight in the way I felt.

now have less than 300 miles to go now to Sydney so I am not giving in now, NOT EVER. No matter how ill i am.

Day 116, August 22nd - Nyngan to Dubbo

got picked up by John at 6am to go to the Airport.

I had said to him, just pick me up on your way to work but as we were on the way to the Airport he told me that he wasn't going to work now.

I said, well you should have rung me and I would have gone in a bit later on.

Just goes to show you what nice people there are in the world.

We got to the Airport and I was heading through the gates when I suddenly had thorns stuck in my hands - it's a wheelchair thing.

So while I was pulling them out of my hands and tyres on the wheelchair John pulled the Quik out of the way of the trees. I got my bags and put them in the Quik while wiping blood off me.

Once loaded up I got in. It was still dark but the sun was edging its way up somewhere!

By the time I was ready to go there was light and I got the engine started, brought the oil temp to 50C and then taxied out.

There was no wind, well at ground level anyway, so I took off and headed south east. The wind was now 25mph at 500ft again, and a headwind, so no change from two days before.

But at least it wasn't as rough.

As the sun came up the first two hours went very smoothly, it got to 9am then the thermals started again, throwing me about.

It seemed to be part of flying now, being kicked about.

I just sat there and went with them. It was only a 90 mile flight - not long at all!

Dubbo came into sight. I made my calls which were basically finals from Nyngan, but said that I would join long finals.

I reported 5 miles out, then 3 miles out and there was another aircraft reporting downwind.

He knew I was on finals.

I reported one-mile final and this dickhead came along and literally cut in front of me by about 50 ft. I moved to the right slightly to avoid his prop wash and he landed right in front of me.

I had to really slow down to land and as I touched down he was still on the runway ahead of me.

What a complete Prat!

He doesn't deserve to be flying with that airmanship.

I taxied past him, shaking my head. He just waved as though he had done nothing wrong.

If I hadn't felt so crap I would have reported him but I couldn't be arsed with the hassle.

I found a piece of grass to park on and then got out and tied the Quik down with the help of a passing pilot, I got talking to him and he turned out to be Scottish, living here, and a flying instructor.

I had already booked a hotel so one of the pilots at the flying school had rung a taxi for me. It turned up - at this rate I would be in the motel by 1pm! I got to the hotel and when I had booked it the lad on the phone hadn't completed the booking so after a bit of confusion with the receptionist, I got a room for the night. I was feeling a bit better now and coming around a bit instead of being so miserable. I had only got 2 more flights to make and I was getting really excited. I had almost got there just another couple of days of flying left.

I went to the motel restaurant and sat there getting my blog up to date – this has been rather neglected over the previous couple of days. Then I made numerous phones calls about my landing in Sydney...

I checked my emails and I had over 500 to make my way through so I spent the night in the restaurant.

Day 117, August 23rd - Dubbo to Wallsair

The taxi turned up at the hotel at 6.30am to take me to the Airport.

felt a bit sick - not because of having been ill, but just because I was getting so close to my goal of getting to Sydney. This was going to be a tough flight as I had to get over a mountain range called the Blue Mountains. I had to get over these to get to Sydney. I did a bit of talking to the local pilots at Dubbo airport and at the other side in Sydney and asked the best way to go to get through them.

285

I was advised to head slightly north where I would be able to pick up a valley that would take me through the range to Newcastle then head south to Sydney.

There seemed to be a stiff breeze and it was also cloudy this morning.

I got to the Airport and managed to get through the security gate to my Quik; I loaded up and got the engine started. Then I sat looking at the mountain range ahead of me. The wind was blowing about 15mph and gusting on the ground and looked a lot stronger in the air the way the clouds were going past me over the Airport.

I taxied out to Runway 11 and lined up. As I looked across to where I was heading; the sky looked pretty wild and full of clouds.

The edge of the Blue Mountains and the Great Dividing Range

I took off and headed slightly north as I had been advised to. There were some lower mountains before the valley that I could head down. Thirty minutes into my flight the wind increased, until I had a 40mph wind straight on the nose. It was really rough and violent the sky looked like a Venetian blind, all ripples running east to west.

About an hour into the flight the cloud changed, the ripples running east to west had a right angle in them and the ripples came from north to south, as they met.

It looked really odd.

The wind started getting really bad and as I tried to get to this valley I was getting thrown all over the sky.

I couldn't climb as the cloud base was only 2,000ft.

I was feeling very uneasy with the turbulence and did not like it. A gust of wind hit me coming from a small mountain and lifted my left wing up. In the process trying to pull the bar out of my hand I got the bar back straight again but it had turned me around 180 degrees.

Then another gust just dropped the left wing and it felt like I was going over inverted.

I had had enough I couldn't cope with it anymore and this late in the trip I wasn't going to kill myself to get to Sydney.

I turned around as slowly as I could trying all the time to keep control of the trike and headed back to Dubbo. On the way back I had a ground speed of over 100mph with the strong wind behind me. It was so rough.

I landed back at Dubbo and parked back up to see if the wind would drop. I didn't bother getting out of the Quik I just sat there watching the sky to see if it would calm down. Maybe if the cloud goes I would be able to get higher and out of the turbulence?

At noon the wind was just the same, if not now stronger on the ground, but the cloud was clearing up.

I rang Rob Hibbard at Airborne Microlights over in Wallsair where I was heading and he said the wind was calm at Wallsair, so that was it. Engine started again and I taxied out, holding on to the wing like a gorilla again as I had been doing on lots of occasions on the flight. Just so I didn't get blown over on the ground.

When I took off the wind was just as strong at 40mph, still a headwind but I could now climb to get out of the rotor from the Blue Mountains.

I climbed up to 3,000ft and it started to calm down a bit.

I continued, heading slightly north towards the valley through the mountains, skipping in, out and around clouds.

As I went past the point where I turned back earlier I got buffeted again. I climbed higher to 4,000ft and just got out of it, then it got a bit smoother although there was still a 40mph headwind and scattered cloud.

After two hours, I had reached the valley that would take me to Newcastle and the wind had started to ease off, until there was just a 10mph headwind. The views were now stunning as I went down the valley to the coast with the Blue Mountains on my right.

Cloud was building again but it was over the mountains and I was well out of the way of it now.

After three hours I could see the sea at Newcastle, my face must have been a picture, big smiles all over! There wasn't far to go now – I was almost at the end of what had been an amazing expedition. I dropped down to 2,000ft and headed around the town of Wallsend to the area where the airfield was. Only a small dirt strip to look out for, then I spotted it the small airfield of Wallsair.

I over-flew it still at 2,000ft. It looked very wet on the runway in fact it looked more like a river than a runway. I watched the wind sock and the winds looked very light, so I dropped down and made my approach along the side of the power lines and dropped in onto finals.

As soon as I touched down I hit a big puddle of water, and then went into a bigger puddle. Water sprayed everywhere as I went through them and slowed me down very quickly.

I pulled up outside a hangar and was met by Rob Hibbard who was from www.Airborne.com.au Microlights. I was so happy now to be so close to Sydney.

We had a good chat for a few minutes with the others that had also turned up to see me land. Then I taxied up against the hangar and was pushed in.

I got out and into my chair the poor Quik covered in mud and water from the landing.

I loaded up my bags into Rob's 4x4. Rob said I would be staying at his house. We had a beer in the hangar, and then we headed off to Rob's house for the night, where I met his wife and girls.

I spent the evening having a few more beers to celebrate my getting to the south coast Thanks Rob and Family.

Day 118, August 24th - Static Wallsair

Day 118, August 24th - Static Wallsair

On August 24th, we went to the Airborne factory and spent most of the day chasing permission that would allow me to fly down the helicopter route, through the Sydney heads of the harbour and then over the Sydney Harbour bridge, to finish off my flying into to Bankstown Airport.

Rob was emailing backwards and forwards to different people in CASA, the Australian CAA.

At about 5.30pm I got a phone call from a guy called Leonard Yates from CASA he said to me

"What would you like to do Dave?"

I said

"I would like fly the helicopter route in my flexwing please I have flown over 12,000 miles to get here and it would be just nice to finish the trip off with that"

He said to me OK I will organise it for you! Finally I had got the answer I was waiting for. It was, YES, I could!

Fantastic!

I had been given permission to fly a microlight down the helicopter route at no higher than 500ft. One of the factors was the famous Australian aviator and adventurer, Dick Smith who had been a big influence behind it.

And the man himself, Leonard Yates, who signed the permission for me do it.

Thank you very much Dick and Leonard.

This would be a dream come true after two years of planning.

Dick was also planning to escort me along the route in his helicopter. FANTASTIC I could hardly wait now. I was so happy.

Now it was back to Rob's to celebrate and get ready for the flight tomorrow. Rob was planning to come along and fly at the side of me for a short time. I didn't have too much beer and we had pizzas delivered.

By 9.30pm I had had the permission emailed to me and a Notam was issued for the day advising everybody what I would be doing.

I spent I don't know how long on the telephone back to England telling them the good news about tomorrow and it was the big day.

Day 119, August 25th – Sydney... The Big Day!

This was the day I had been waiting for and had planned for more than two years. I was going to fly over the Sydney Harbour Bridge and in to Bankstown.

I didn't sleep much and I was up at 6.30am, wide-awake.

We went into the airport for around 9am. The plan was for me to meet up with Dick Smith overhead the Long Reef golf course and reporting point for the Victor 1 VFR route on the coast, just outside Sydney Harbour.

While we were at the airfield getting the Quik ready there was a phone call from 7news - the TV helicopter was just outside Newcastle, heading down to film me.

It got to 10am and my mouth as dry as a bone, I had a quick drink of water and then I was ready for the off. I climbed into the Quik and Rob pushed me back away from the hanger so i could get the engine started and warmed up I was staring at my maps and the route so I knew where I was going – I didn't want to mess it up.

The TV crew then landed and started filming me on the ground.

When I was up to temperature I taxied out, my heart beating faster all the time. Rob took off first in an Airborne XT 912 topless wing, and went overhead to wait for me.

I was filmed taking off and we headed out to the coast flying down the river past Newcastle to a place Knobby's Head and turned south towards Sydney, dropping to 500ft.

The TV helicopter came alongside and filmed me flying down the coast, and I did an interview while I was flying. I was a bit too early for the meeting at Long Reef so I just orbited over the sea for a while getting myself ready for the pinnacle of my flight the Harbour Bridge.

While I was orbiting another helicopter flew alongside of me and started to film me then I was joined by a third helicopter.

I had three helicopters buzzing around me filming now.

At about 12.25pm Dick arrived in *his* helicopter and we headed in to Sydney Harbour, at only 500ft, helicopters everywhere buzzing me and filming.

My route was to fly straight up the middle of the Harbour and go over the southern tower of the Sydney Harbour Bridge, still not above 500ft.

And that's exactly what I did.

My heart was beating away like a little generator and I was smiling like the Joker from Batman - a permanent smile.

All I could think of was how lucky I was to have the privilege to be doing this. It was Awesome.

This time I really wished I had somebody with me to share this moment with, it was truly spectacular.

Unlike almost every other day of my flight, it was beautiful and sunny with very light winds. This I what I had wanted it to be like and this is what I got, no fighting with the bar for a change, so that also made it special.

As I headed into the Harbour I could see the bridge coming up, and the Opera House sitting below it. I did as I was instructed and flew to the southern tower, the Opera House just below me to my left, and I went over the southern tower with only about 150ft below me. I looked straight across at the top of the Bridge and I could see people doing the bridge walk waving at me. It was truly mad - everybody else in the world normally gets to see these things, but today it was my turn.

Once over the Bridge I had to follow the river right up through the centre of Sydney to Rose Hill race-course before turning left and heading direct to Bankstown Airport

Still under 500ft, the view was really special, and the TV crew helicopters were still very close to me, filming away.

was cleared to land straight in to Runway 29 Right, a northern runway where a Follow-Me car was waiting for me.

touched down in Sydney after 4 months of flying and covering over 16,000 miles in all.

I followed the Follow-Me car up the different taxi ways with people coming out and clapping at me as I went passed the different hangars, and it took me to Dick Smith's personal hangar where a host of different people were waiting to meet me.

I pulled up and turned the engine off. TV crews came straight over to me before I had even had the chance to take my helmet off.

Dick Smith came to say hello and we had a good chat and talked together to the media for a good thirty minutes.

I was presented with a beautiful plaque from the Recreational Aviation Australia Inc. in recognition of my flight from the UK to Australia. It is very much appreciated.

They have pledged a cheque for the air ambulance, and are putting up a scholarship for disabled flyers in Australia in my name.

That brought a tear to my eyes.

All this for me just a normal kid from Dewsbury

THANK YOU.EVERYBODY.

My Quik was then put into the hangar for the night and I went over to John Cameron Aviation where they found a hotel for me.

John took me towards it, but on our way he noticed that the tyres on my wheelchair were held together with Duct tape, so he stopped off at a cycle shop and treated my chair to a new pair of tyres.

Thanks John.

Later John and I went around Darling Harbour and into the bars and had some food, so another thanks to John for the night out. www.jcaviation.com.au

But really big thanks to Dick Smith for everything.

I was now really looking forward to a few days around Sydney.

Days 120 to123, August 26th to 29th

I spent the next few days spent travelling around Sydney seeing the sights.

On the Friday, 26th August I got up in the Novotel where I was staying in and did a newspaper interview, then went off around Darling Harbour, generally relaxing after my amazing flight the day before..

I sat at a bar overlooking the Harbour, reflecting on what I had been doing over the last 4 months.

John Cameron from www.jcaviation.com.au came to meet me, and we went around Darling Harbour for the night eating and drinking.

On the Saturday I did much the same really except I went down to the marina to see John working on his yacht. After that I went off looking at the different boats and ships moored in the Harbour.

Later that night John picked me up and took me to an area called Kings Cross for the night, where there were a lot of bars and night clubs, so I had a chance to try the night life in Sydney.

On the Sunday I got up early and went down and jumped onto a ferry that took me up the river and under the Sydney Harbour Bridge and past the Opera House to a place called Manly. I had a look around there, took another ferry down to the Opera House where I did the photograph tourist things, before finding a bar overlooking the bridge and at the side of the Opera House.

It was a nice sunny day and it was nice doing nothing and drinking beer.

Funny thing was, as I sat there people recognised me from the TV. They wanted to shake my hand and congratulate me on my trip.

That was a weird feeling!

Over 12,000 miles away in Sydney, and people knew who I was!

After talking to a few different people about my trip I headed up into the city for a look around, and then found a taxi rank.

After an argument with one taxi driver over the chair, and him parking miles away from the kerb, I got into another taxi.

First thing I said to him was, *"Take me to Darling Harbour and don't take me the long way around. I know where I am."*

So what did he do?

He tried going the long way around.

I said, *"You're taking the mickey out of me and you're not going to get paid what it says on the meter."*

Finally we got there and after him pulling up too far away from the kerb again, I had another argument with him over the cost and paid him what I thought it was worth.

Then I went down and had a look around the Sydney aquarium, at all the fish - that was riveting stuff! There were little fish and there were big fish, there were even some sharks to look at. That was good because I looked at their teeth as they were swimming around and thought how glad I was that I didn't have to ditch in the sea, and come across one of those when it was in a bad mood and hungry.

After a good look around there, I went back up to the hotel with the bits and bats that I had bought, and later went out for some more beer and food.

On the Monday John Cameron picked me up and we went to the Airport to check over my Quik and do a repair to my radio; the aerial cable had pulled out of the BNC connector as I had gone into Bankstown.

I fixed that so it would be ready for my flight out of there and checked the oil and water. I sat around talking before I went over the road and tried out the local pub.

John picked me up and ran me back into Sydney to my hotel.

Day 124, August 30th- Bankstown to Wallsair

had some breakfast and then returned my keys to Reception.

A very big thank you to Dick Smith and John Cameron who very kindly paid for my hotel while I was in Sydney.

was picked up at about 8am by John and we went to Bankstown Airport where I was met by a reporter from Sky news.

To do an interview with me, So as the cloud over Bankstown started bubbling up we did the interview and some filming.

The weather was forecast to rain and get quite windy which was typical as it had been nice and sunny over the last few days, but anyway it was not so bad that it would stop me flying..

We finished the filming and then I said my goodbyes to all the staff at www.jcaviation.com.au/

I started up the Quik, gave Bankstown Ground a call to taxi out and then taxied out to "Juliet 2" holding point.

Then I changed over to the Tower frequency who said " *G-CDVO do you want to take off into wind or crosswind take off"*

So I just said *'G-CDVO will take off cross winded'*

"G-CDVO you are cleared for take-off not above 1,500ft and turn left after takeoff at your discretion"

That was it the final take off of the whole trip, I took off and turned left to head to a reporting point at a place called Brooklyn bridge about 20 miles away.

And it was really nice flying over the outskirts of Sydney. The cloud base was only about 2,000ft and it was looking a bit wet in places, and just a bit windy.

Bankstown didn't even bother me asking where I was every 2 minutes either as I was squawking 3000 on the transponder a code they use for aircraft that are leaving the airport.

At this point, I want to say a big thank you to Dick Smith for escorting me into Bankstown and getting the Media out for me and also to Leonard Yates at CASA for sorting out the flight clearance for me to fly the helicopter route over the Sydney harbour bridge.(just fantastic)

I flew up as far north on the VFR route out of Bankstown as I could before the cloud became too low and wet and then I headed out to the coast and flew up there towards Wallsair at 500ft getting wet.

After about 20 minutes of the low cloud it started brightening up and turned into a nice flight and it was sunny in places.

Up the coast line there were some lovely sandy beaches with secluded coves, and after about 45 minutes of enjoying that – which also allowed me to dry out from the rain - I came to a place called Nobbys head where I turned in land and followed the river around Newcastle town and head to Wallsend and to Wallsair airstrip.

I could see the runway in sight, the wind was about 10mph and slightly cross winded so it would be a nice reasonable landing without having to fight the quik down to the ground.

I came in alongside of the power cables and landed, the ground was a bit harder than last time I flew in, no big puddles to run through. ☺

A camera crew were filming me as I came in, so when i pulled up outside the hanger I did an interview with them before I got out of the trike.

Then Rob Hibbard from www.airborne.com.au/ pushed the Quik into the hangar for the last time, and then I emptied out all the things that I would be taking back to the UK with me.

And so to the end of an amazing four months away... I can't wait to sort out my next trip - I just hope it will be as exciting as this was!.

Dave Sykes.

Date	Airport	Airport	Miles	Hours flown
28/04/2011	Rufforth	Headcorn	215	3hr 50 min
28/04/2011	Headcorn	Headcorn	152	2hr 10 min
29/04/2011	Headcorn	Abbeville	88	1hr 40 min
30/04/2011	Abbeville	Bernay	91	1hr 30 min
30/04/2011	Bernay	Wanafly	193	3hr 00 min
2/05/2011	Wanafly	Fayence	340	5hr 50 min
3/05/2011	Fayence	Ill Gabianno	200	3hr 20 min
4/05/2011	Ill Gabbianno	Scalia	360	5hr 20 min
5/05/2011	Scalia	Oasi demodica	218	3hr 30 min
5/05/2011	Oasi demodica	Malta	55	1hr 15 min
8/05/2011	Malta	Corfu	394	6hr 00 min
9/05/2011	Corfu	Zakinthos	138	3hr 20 min
10/05/2011	Zakinthos	Rhodes	478	7hr 40 min
11/05/2011	Rhodes	Paphos	276	5hr 15 min
12/05/2011	Paphos	Paphos	146	2hr 15 min
14/05/2011	Paphos	Alexandria	311	5hr 10 min
15/05/2011	Alexandria	Cairo	127	1hr 30 min
17/05/2011	Cairo	Luxor	309	5hr 00 min
18/05/2011	Luxor	Jeddah	493	7hr 30 min
19/05/2011	Jeddah	Riyadh	469	7hr 40 min
20/05/2011	Riyadh	Doha	469	5hr 10 min
27/05/2011	Doha	Abu Dhabi	303	5hr 00 min
29/05/2011	Abu Dhabi	Muscat	232	5hr 00 min
30/05/2011	Muscat	Gwadar	280	4hr 00 min
31/05/2011	Gwardar	Karachi	307	5hr 00 min
1/06/2011	Karachi	Ahmadabad	370	5hr 15 min
3/06/2011	Ahmadabad	Raipur	630	8hr 45 min
4/06/2011	Raipur	Jamshedpur	369	5hr 05 min
5/06/2011	Jamshedpur	Calcutta	145	2hr 15 min
5/06/2011	Calcutta	Dhaka	149	2hr 30 min
7/06/2011	Dhaka	Chittagong	143	2hr 35 min
9/06/2011	Chittagong	Kyaukpyu	218	5hr 20 min

10/06/2011	Kyaukpyu	Kyaukpyu	23	0hr 20 min
11/06/2011	Kyaukpyu	Thandwe	86	2hr 35 min
11/06/2011	Thandwe	Thandwe	145	1hr 35 min
11/06/2011	Thandwe	Thandwe	72	1hr 05 min
12/06/2011	Thandwe	Thandwe	142	2hr 00 min
19/06/2011	Thandwe	Thandwe	104	1hr 30 min
19/06/2011	Thandwe	Thandwe	36	0hr 30 min
20/06/2011	Thandwe	Yangon	228	3hr 00 min
24/06/2011	Yangon	Dawei	322	4hr 20 min
24/06/2011	Dawei	Dawei	37	0hr 30 min
25/06/2011	Dawei	Dawei	105	1hr 30 min
29/06/2011	Dawei	Bangkok	175	2hr 35min
3/07/2011	Bangkok	Surat Thani	345	6hr 00 min
4/07/2011	Surat Thani	Phuket	90	2hr 30 min
5/07/2011	Phuket	Penang	239	4hr 00 min
6/07/2011	Penang	Kuala Lumpur	175	3hr 00 min
21/07/2011	Kuala Lumpur	Palembang	509	7hr 45 min
22/07/2011	Palembang	Jakarta	285	4hr 45 min
23/07/2011	Jakarta	Semarang	245	4hr 00 min
24/07/2011	Semarang	Surabaya	169	4hr 00min
25/07/2011	Surabaya	Bali	202	3hr 45 min
27/07/2011	Bali	Bima	243	5hr 00 min
28/07/2011	Bima	Kupang	366	6hr 00 min
3/08/2011	Kupang	Truscott	327	5hr 45 min
9/08/2011	Truscott	Darwin	325	5hr 00 min
13/08/2011	Darwin	Coomalie Creek	92	2hr 10 min
14/08/2011	Coomalie Creek	Mataranka	553	4hr 30 min
15/08/2011	Mataranka	Barkly Homestead	481	7hr 05 min
7/08/2011	Barkly Homestead	Mount Isa	277	7hr 10 min
8/08/2011	Mount Isa	Barcaldine	476	8hr 00 min
9/08/2011	Barcaldine	Charleville	206	4hr 05 min
0/08/2011	Charleville	Nyngan	386	7hr 20 min

22/08/2011	Nyngan	Dubbo	93	2hr 10 min
23/08/2011	Dubbo	Dubbo	178	2hr 00 min
23/08/2011	Dubbo	Wallsair	56	3hr 30 min
25/08/2011	Wallsair	Sydney Bankstown	87	1hr 30 min
30/8/2011	Sydney Bankstown	Wallsair	82	1hr 20 min
	TOTALS		**16,161**	**257hr 40 min**

Awards To Date:

The Royal Automobile Club Highly Prestigious Segrave Trophy 2011 For outstanding Achievement by land sea or air

BMAA (British Microlight Association) Chairman's Trophy 2011

BMAA Steve Hunt Memorial Trophy for outstanding Microlight Achievement

The Royal Aero Club Britannia Trophy for the British aviator accomplishing the most meritorious performance in aviation 2011. Presented at the Royal Air Force club London by His Royal Highness Prince Andrew.

The Air League Highly Prestigious illuminated Scroll for determination, courage and skill on my microlight flight to Australia. To be presented in May by His Royal Highness Prince Philip the Duke of Edinburgh at St James Palace.

Aerobilty's Aviator of the Year 2011 for outstanding Microlight Achievement presented with the Pooleys Sword

FAI - Fédération Aéronautique Internationale the Colibri Diploma 2011 Awarded in October in Turkey.

GAPAN The Masters Medal Awarded to a pilot over the age of 30 for outstanding achievement and endeavour in any field of flying activity 2011-2012 was awarded in London on the 23rd October by Air Marshall CR Spink

Recreational Aviation Australia Inc awarded a plaque in recognition of an amazing feat of aviation. And have named a Disabled Scholarship to be awarded annually after David "Wheely" Sykes.

On the 8th of December 2011 attended a Reception at Buckingham Palace and met Her Majesty the Queen, His Royal Highness Prince Philip the Duke of Edinburgh, The Earl of Wessex and Princess Beatrice.

Runner up for Fund Raiser of the year 2011 at Pride of York Awards